A Guide to Project Management Using Prince2

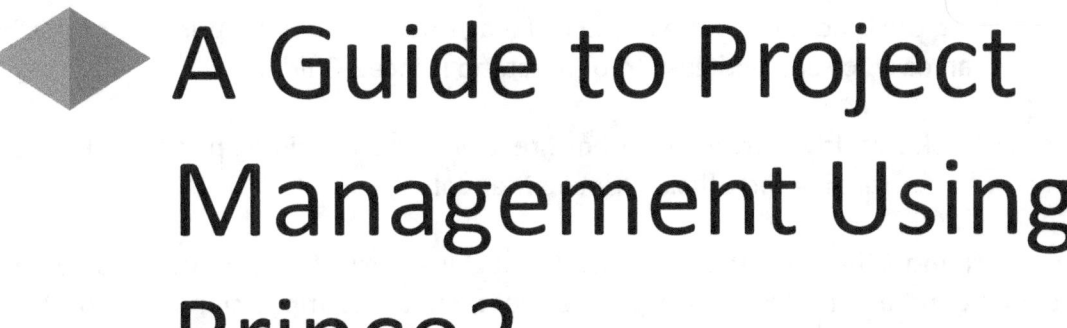

By CJ Pitts

Foreword

Thank you for taking the time to read the Project Management Guide, the purpose of this book is to provide you with an easy to read and easy to understand Prince2 Guide.

The idea for this book was driven from questions I received whilst training people in Project Management and after reading the official Prince2 Manual.

Whilst I agree with most that the official Prince2 Manual is an excellent product, it is perceived as a difficult document and the first time most people see it, their first impression is one of fear.

My intention for this book, is to provide you with an easy and gentle introduction into Prince2 and an aid to passing your foundation and practitioner exam, whilst also being something you can refer to once you have passed the exams to support your Project Management career.

PRINCE2®
2017 UPDATE

Acknowledgements:

Written by: Carl PItts
Reviewers: Omar Al Marzouqi, Phillip Rae

Thank You – to my wife Rachel who has supported me, whilst not always understanding anything I talk about and a special thanks to my friends Omar and Phil who read the countless versions of this and stayed friends with me.

About me
Carl Pitts has been a Program and Project Manager for almost 20 years and is currently an associate trainer in Prince2 and other Project Management Qualifications.

Table of Contents

Prince2

Prince2

The official Prince2 Manual is called "Managing Successful Projects with Prince2" and this is designed primarily for supporting the training to become a certified Prince2 Project Manager and also for those Project Managers who have been in the role but wish to become certified.

The Prince2 Training Guide is aimed to sit somewhere in the middle and supports the official manual,

The Prince2 Guide aims to support you in the following ways:
- Provides explanations of the Prince2 terminology in plain English
- Supports the manual with examples, making it easier to understand
- The diagrams contained are simpler and (hopefully) easier to read and understand

What are Projects?

The Prince2 definition of a Project is

"A Project is a temporary organisation that is created for the purpose of delivering one or more business products according to an agreed business case"

Projects in their essence introduce change or changes, and this in turn ensures that each project is unique in its very nature. No two projects are identical. You may believe this is not the case, you have run identical projects before – however the reality is that if you are running what is believed to be a project and it is a piece of work that is completed over and over again, this is classed as "business as usual" and is not by definition a Prince2 Project.

There are other definitions of a what is a project –

"A project is a unique series of actions designed to accomplish a unique goal within specific time and cost limitations ensuring a valid return on investment"

This definition was used in an organisation I worked for previously and I remember thinking it provided an excellent and simple view of what a project is by highlighting they are unique, have a finite time period to be delivered against and highlights the cost and return on investment.

OK, so let's break this down a bit to explain the definition.

Each project has a definite start and end – which means that a project has a start and an end that is defined, a project must have a defined stop point to enable a closure of the project, and this itself supports the temporary organisation criteria. A project should have a defined closure to ensure that the work stops and allows the measurement of benefits or the return of investment.

The "temporary organisation" is referring to the project team. This is personnel who are involved in the delivery of the project.

The unique reference is a key differentiator, if a project is identical and happens on a regular basis or is a consistent piece of work, by this definition it is not a project but either operations or business as usual (for example the installation of a quarterly software patch or the upgrade of a network switch).

The final piece of this puzzle is the term business case, the business case is a term used to describe the document that contains the information pertaining to the project and its justification. It includes the details on why this project is required, what problem it is resolving or opportunity it is taking advantage of, the costs to deliver and support the project once it is live, the time to deliver the project and the benefits that will be delivered.

What is Prince2

Prince2 is an acronym and stands for Projects In Controlled Environments. It is a generic methodology that can be used on any project. There was a perception that Prince2 is an IT methodology, however this is not correct. Prince2 can be used on any project from a small implementation to the management of a large office move from one end of the country to another.

Prince2 is essentially a repeatable process that can be tailored to fit your organisation or project. It allows separate management layers to be used for different types of projects through the use of tailoring. This management layer is known as the organisation and consists of 4 layers,
1. Corporate or Program Management,
2. The Project Board,
3. The Project Manager (PM),
4. The Team Manager (TM).

The Project Management Team consists of 3 of these layers (Project Board, PM and TM). This is part of the process model within the integrated elements of Prince2 which will be discussed further into the guide.

Prince2 is based upon Principles, Process and Themes

The Principles are:

Continued Business Justification	• A project must make good sense, there needs to be a clear return on the investment and the use of time and resources should be justified
Learn form experience	• Project teams should take lessons from previous projects into accounts, a lessons log is kept updated to ensure continuous improvement
Defined roles & responsibilities	• Everyone involved in a project should know what they are doing, what others and doing and should know who the decision makers and approvers are.
Management by stages	• Difficult tasks are better off broken into manageable chunks, or management stages
Management by exception	• A project running well doesn't't need a lot of intervention from management, • The Project Board is only informed if there is a problem that requires their attention.
Focus on Products	• Everyone should know ahead of time what's expected of the product. • The products requirements determine work activity, not the other way round
Tailor to suit the environment	• Prince2 can be tailored to suit the environment, the project or the organisation

Figure 1 - Prince2 Principles

The Processes are

Starting Up a Project (SU)	• Ensures the prerequisites are in place for initiating a project by answering the Question - Do we have a viable Project
Initiating a Project (IP)	• The purpose of Initiation is to establish a solid foundations for the project enabling the organization to understand the work that needs to be done to deliver the projects products before committing to a significant spend
Directing a Project (DP)	• The purpose of directing a project is to enable the Project Board to be accountable for the projects success by making key decisions and exercising overall control, whilst delegating any day-2-day management of the project to the Project Manager
Controlling a Stage (CS)	• The purpose of controlling a stage is to assign work to be done, monitor the work, deal with issues, report progress to the project board and take corrective action to ensure that the stage remains within tolerance
Managing Stage Boundaries (SB)	• The purpose of the Managing Stage boundary process is to enable the Project Board to be provided with sufficient information by the Project Manager so that it can review the success of the current stage, approve the next stage, review the updated project plan, and confirm continued business justification and acceptance of the risks
Managing Product Delivery	• The purpose of the managing product delivery process is to control the link between the Project Manager and the Team Manager(s), y placing formal requirements on accepting, executing and delivering work packages.
Closing a Project (CP)	• The purpose of the Closing a Project process is to provide a fixed point at which acceptance for the project product is confirmed and to recognize that objectives set out in the original PID have been achieved (or approved changes to the objectives have been achieved)

Figure 2 - Prince2 Processes

The Themes are:

Business Case	• How an idea is developed into a viable investment proposition • How project management maintains its focus on the organisations objectives throughout a project
Organization	• How work is allocated to managers with clear responsibilities • How the roles and responsibilities within a Prince2 project team work together efficiently
Quality	• How the project management team ensure the requirements are delivered
Plans	• How plans are developed using Prince2 techniques • How plans are the focus for communications and control throughout the project
Risk	• How Project management handles uncertainties in its plans and the environment
Change	• How project management assesses and acts upon the need to change, either as a result of changes to requirements or to issues that arise
Progress	• How to decide whether to approve a plan • How to monitor progress, and what to do when things don't go according to plan

Figure 3 - Prince2 Themes

Along with Tailoring, the 7 Principles, 7 Process and 7 Themes form the integrated elements of Prince2

What is a Project Management Method?

Project Management is the management of the planning, monitoring, controlling and delegating of the project. These are all tasks that are carried out by the Project Manager (PM), whose role is to deliver the project within the agreed tolerances or aspects of Project Management, these are Time, Cost, Scope, Quality, Benefits and Risk which together form the "6 aspects of project management".

Prince2 enables an organisation to deliver projects comprehensively and in a manner, that is systematic and integrated. It allows the consistent management of change, management of risk and controls costs. Allowing for an increased confidence in the successful delivery and achievement of the benefits identified.

The six aspects of Project Management

Prince2 projects are delivered based upon the six performance targets or 6 aspects of project management.

These are:

Time	When should it be finished and is it on schedule?
Cost	What is the budget and are we keeping to it?
Quality	Are the projects products fit for purpose?
Scope	What will the project deliver?
Risk	How much risk are we prepared to accept?
Benefits	Why are we doing this?

Figure 4 - Prince2 Aspects

What is not covered in Prince2

Whilst Prince2 is focused on delivering projects, it is also important to remember it does not cover everything, there are areas Prince2 does not cover

These are:
- Specialist aspects
- Detailed techniques
- Leadership capability

An explanation of these is below

Specialist Aspects – Prince2 is a methodology and as such is generic in its form, this means it can be applied (and should be applied) to any project type. For this very reason Prince2 does not give specific information on how to run a specific project.

For example, IT projects will often include very specialist skills and additional process to ensure a successful delivery and Prince2 will form a method of controlling and linking all of these together, but is not concerned with the specific details.

Detailed Techniques – Within project management, there are countless additional techniques and process that can be used during your projects. For example, Mind Maps, Critical Path Analysis, Feasibility Analysis, Marketing Surveys can all be used to support various stages within a project and Prince2 recommends you select those that are suitable for your project, however it does not provide the details on how to use them or implement them.

Leadership Capability – Soft skills and leadership motivation is important, however these are not discussed or included in Prince2. As above with detailed techniques, Prince2 only recommends you choose the best approach or training to suit your environment.

The benefits of using Prince2

So, if Prince2 is only a methodology and doesn't recommend any specific techniques or guidance on how to manage a specific project type, why use it?

In reality, there are many advantages to using Prince2 and this is one of the easier areas to explain.

Prince2 has been in existence for over 30 years and is now in its latest incarnation Prince2 2017. It is constantly learning and is refreshed regularly. This ensures that your Projects are being managed using

"A tried and tested method of Project Management that is reliable, robust and repeatable"

Prince2 also provides a structure for the Project Management Team with detailed roles & responsibilities. This ensures that the members of your project know who is doing what, when it is required, why it is required and exactly what is expected of them. This level of detail is more important for the Project Manager whose role it is to check that the tasks are completed as agreed.

Prince2 is product focused, this means that a Prince2 project is well defined at the start and its stakeholders are all informed as to what the Project is, what is being delivered and why and most importantly what the benefit of doing the project is. This ensures all stakeholders involved in the project have the same information and the same understanding of what the end product is.

A Prince2 project is managed by using a technique called Management by Exception. This provides each of the management levels with a clearly defined and agreed set of tolerances to allow them to manage issues that arise during the lifecycle of the project, however once an issue is forecasted to go outside of the tolerance, it becomes and exception.   This is then managed by escalation to the next higher level of management

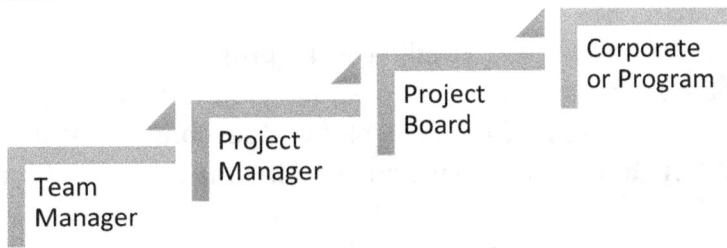

Figure 5 - Project Escalation Path

This escalation method allows both the management by exception but also allows and empowers a lower management layer within the project

Prince2 continues to ensure the Project is viable and achievable, which means that through the creation of the Business Case and the regular Business Case reviews throughout the project lifecycle the continued viability of the project is ensured.

For example; If a business case review at any point of the project confirms that the projects benefits can no longer be achieved, Prince2 would recommend the closure of this project.

What is the role of the Project Manager?

A Project Manager is essential to the success of the Project and this role is key to the continued success of your project by monitoring and ensuring that all of the tasks are on track and all issues or escalations are effectively managed. The Project Manager also ensures that the project produces the required products in accordance with the performance goals (6 aspects) which are Time, Cost, Quality, Scope, Benefits and Risk.

You may already have a good idea about the actual role of the Project Manager and what a Project Manager actually does, but Project Managers often find themselves managing countless tasks to ensure the project actually stays on track. This may feel like the role of the Project Manager; however, this often leads to the actual project not being managed and can lead to scope creep, delays or over spends.

So where do you start? I often find like an old program I used to hate as a child

"Like every good story, the best place to start is the beginning and are we sitting comfortably"

There is a project, which in turn needs a project plan to deliver against, which will ensure the project effectively stays on track and the end product is fit for purpose and the benefits are achieved.

The Project is created from a need that has been identified, one of the first tasks usually completed by the Project Manager is that of the creating a project Plan (which in Prince2 is not a Gant Chart!) The plan is created with the help and support from the specialist's (often subject matter experts involved in the project on either a user or supplier level) and it includes the tasks such as planning workshops, requirements workshops, supplier selection processes, contract negotiations, defining the products to be delivered and any identified dependencies.

It may also include the resources required to deliver the project, if additional resources are required (Specialists that are not available at present for example) and will include the schedule for these tasks or activities. The plan will also include the roles and responsibilities for those involved in the project at this stage (although this can often change during the lifecycle of the project)

The main objective of the Project Manager is to ensure that the project is proceeding according to plan. The Project Manager reviews the completed tasks and products, arranges the approvals (or sign-offs) and confirms that any follow-on or following tasks can start etc.

If your ever asked in a conversation (as most people are at some point) what a Project Manager does, here is a good answer –

"I monitor the project which implements a change into the organisation as to how well it is going according to the plan and I ensure that the benefits are delivered"

So, your monitoring the plan, but what are you monitoring against – well this is the 6 aspects of Prince2 or the 6 performance targets, Time, Cost, Quality, Scope, Benefits and Risk.

The Project Manager will also manage the issues within the project as and they arise (and they will) In the case of small issues, you may choose to manage these yourself (if they are within your tolerance) and manage them using your daily log (these types of issue could be as simple as confirming your development resource arrives back from holiday and has started work) If an issue arises that could have an impact upon your project where a tolerance could be exceeded, this is a prime example of the management by exception. The Project Manager in this scenario would escalate this to the Project Board for ad-hoc direction.

The project also needs to be kept moving forward, from experience small projects move along without much management as the timescales are often very small as are the deliverables, however projects with a longer duration often need to be managed more closely to ensure they are constantly moving forward in accordance with the plan.

It is often also forgotten that a key role of the Project Manager is to identify ways to accelerate or speed up a project. These each have to be assessed for the impact on your project as they can have both a positive and a negative impact and as with all aspects of your project, the tolerances are key in the management of identified areas to speed up your project and any that could have an impact upon your project or possibly exceed an agreed tolerance should be escalated for ad-hoc direction from the project board.

The last area I would always recommend a Project Manager to spend time is at the beginning of the project, which in turn increases the chances of a successful project are the roles and responsibilities. Depending upon how mature your organisation is, you may have templates in place to support this, but remember – every project is unique and these must be reviewed and aligned to you project, in the event you do not have templates there are Roles & Responsibilities contained within Appendix C of the Prince2 2017 manual

The soft skills needed to be a Project Manager are another key to successful project management (and a successful career). Managing relationships is a crucial piece of the project management process, be mindful of this and remember you may have to work with your stakeholders on a number of projects and vice versa, so look after your stakeholders and they will look after you!

Prince2 Processes

The Prince2 Processes

If your reading this, I hope you already have some understanding of Prince2 and the Manual.

The diagram below shows how a Prince2 project starts and the steps to deliver the project. This diagram will be broken down into each of the chapters and in its whole as below shows how the whole process works to deliver a successful project.

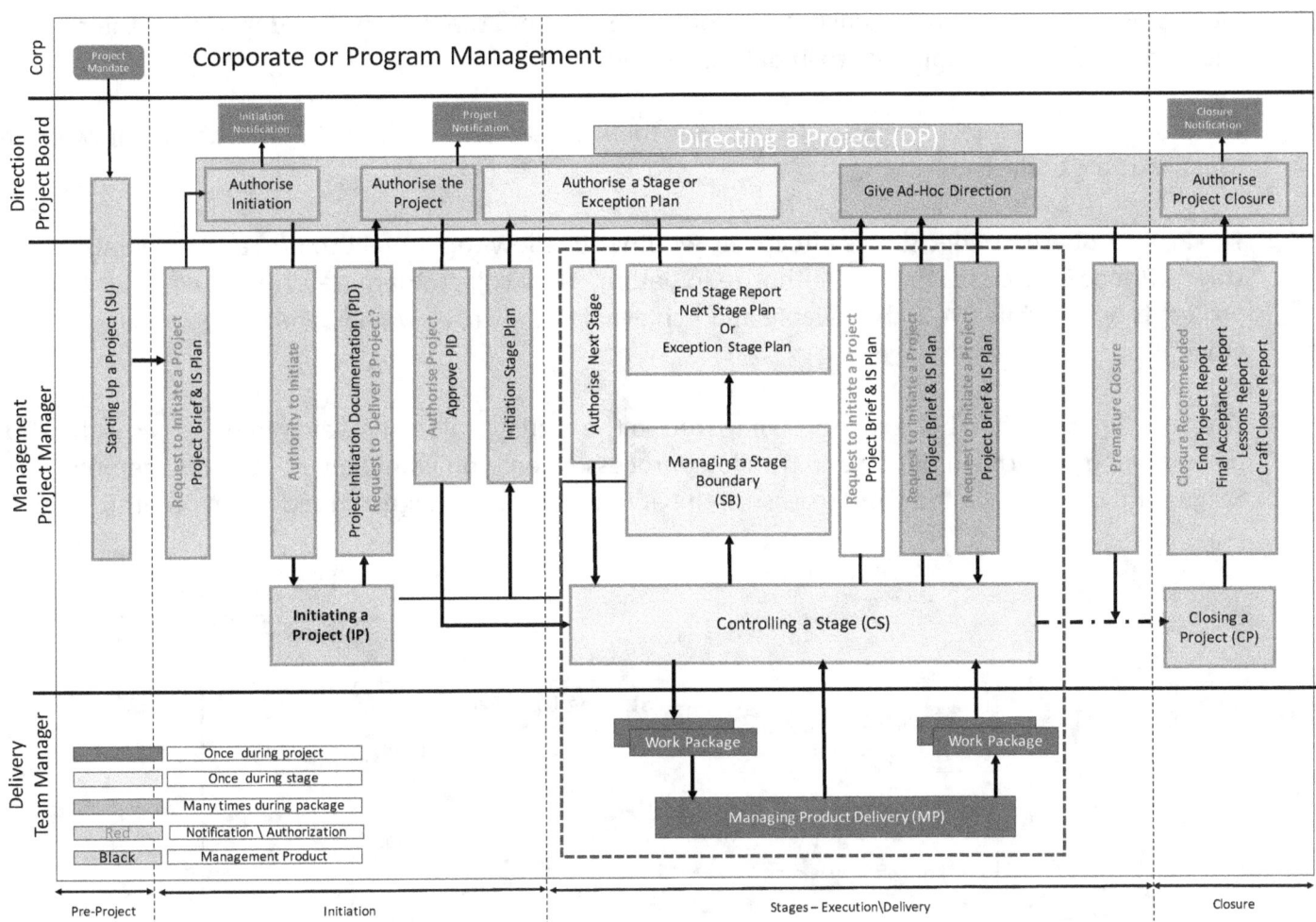

Figure 6 - Project Process

Starting Up a Project (SU)

The Trigger to starting a project is the Project Mandate. This is received from outside the project team. Prince2 states that the Project Mandate is received form either Corporate or Program Management, but in real life it can come from anywhere within your organisation where an opportunity has been identified.

Prince2 recommends that during the Starting Up a Project Process (SU) the minimum work required to effectively start up the project is completed.

Starting Up a Project Process (SU) is the first process and the following outputs are given to the Project Board to allow authorisation to proceed and Initiate the Project (IP), this decision is to "Authorise Initiation"

- Outline Business Case – a high level overview of the project, what will be delivered and the perceived benefits
- Project Brief – this contains the outline business case
- The Project Product Description (PPD)
- The Initiation Stage Plan

The Starting Up a Project Process (SU) is considered as pre-project and therefore classed as outside the project in Prince2. The actual project does not start until the Project Board has taken their first decision – which is the approval to initiate the project

The Starting Up a Project Process (SU) provides the Project Board with the information to allow them to make their 1st decision.

The Project Boards 1st decision is effectively whether to allow the project to proceed to initiation stage - Prince2 describes this as "Authorize Initiation" The Project Board determines whether the project is worthwhile (Desirable, Viable and Achievable), they review and approve the Initiation Stage Plan.

The SU stage can often be very short compared to the actual project, however in some cases it could be combined with the Initiation and be a long process where you would introduce Management Stages and break down the work to ensure the ability to both manage and report on progress.

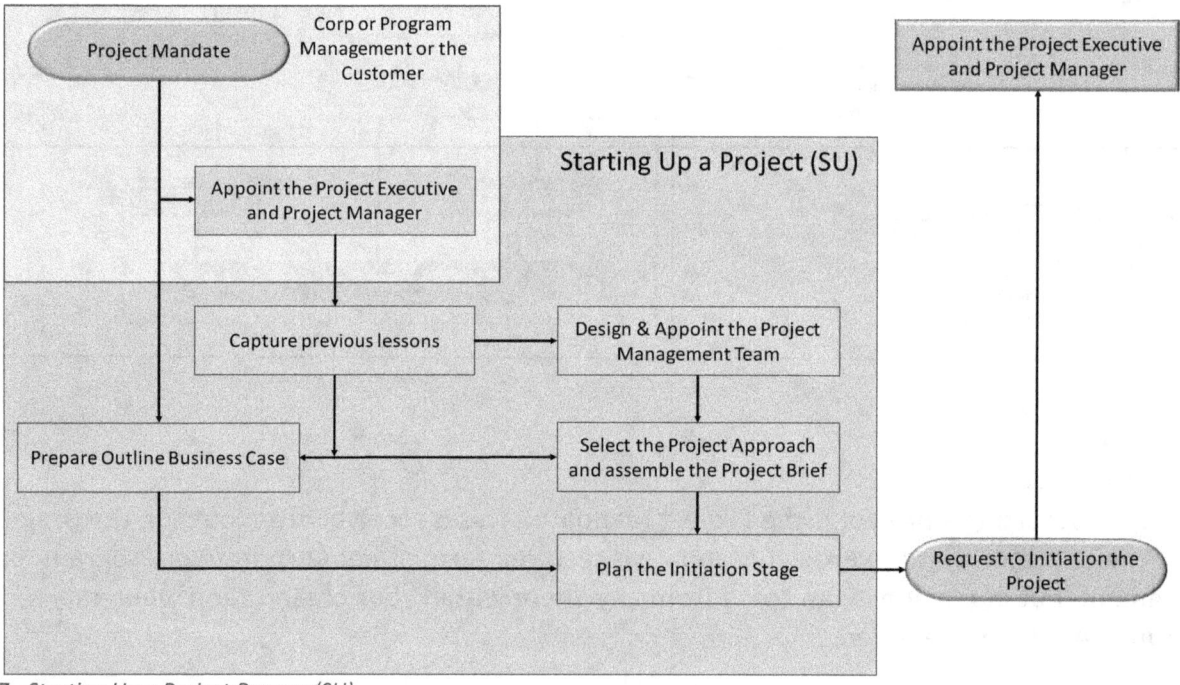

Figure 7 - Starting Up a Project Process (SU)

Initiating a Project (IP) or Initiation Stage

After the Project Board approves the Project to be initiated, the Project Manager uses the initiation stage plan to manage the delivery of this stage. In Prince2 this is the first management stage of the project.

The outputs from the Initiation Stage are:

- Detailed Business Case
  - Which is the responsibility of the Executive
  - Created with support from the Senior User and other stakeholders as needed
- The Project Plan
- The Product Descriptions
- Project Controls – describing how the project will be controlled
- Roles & Responsibilities
- Project Management Team Structure
- Project Management Approach
  - Risk Management Strategy
  - Quality Management Strategy
  - Change & control approach
  - Communication Management Strategy

These documents from the Project Initiation Documentation (PID) which is used as the baseline for the Project and reviewed at each Management Stage Boundary, it is also the starting point for any new members of the project team who join the project during its lifecycle to ensure they understand the overall project, its justification, its products and benefits.

The work at this stage is facilitated by the Project Manager (remember, if it looks like work, it is probably done by the Project Manager), however the Project Manager will possibly not have the skills or background knowledge to create and document all of the above. So, they are created with support from:

- The Project Executive – supports the development and refinement of the Business Case
- Senior User (or representative of) supports the creation of product description, requirements and quality requirements
- Senior User – Benefit Management Approach – the senior user will provide the information to support the documentation of the expected benefits. This information should include the timeline for the achievement of the benefits and the measurement of the benefits. Prince2 states that benefits should be measurable
- Specialists (Also known as Subject Matter Experts) often also help with the creation of requirements, the project planning and estimating

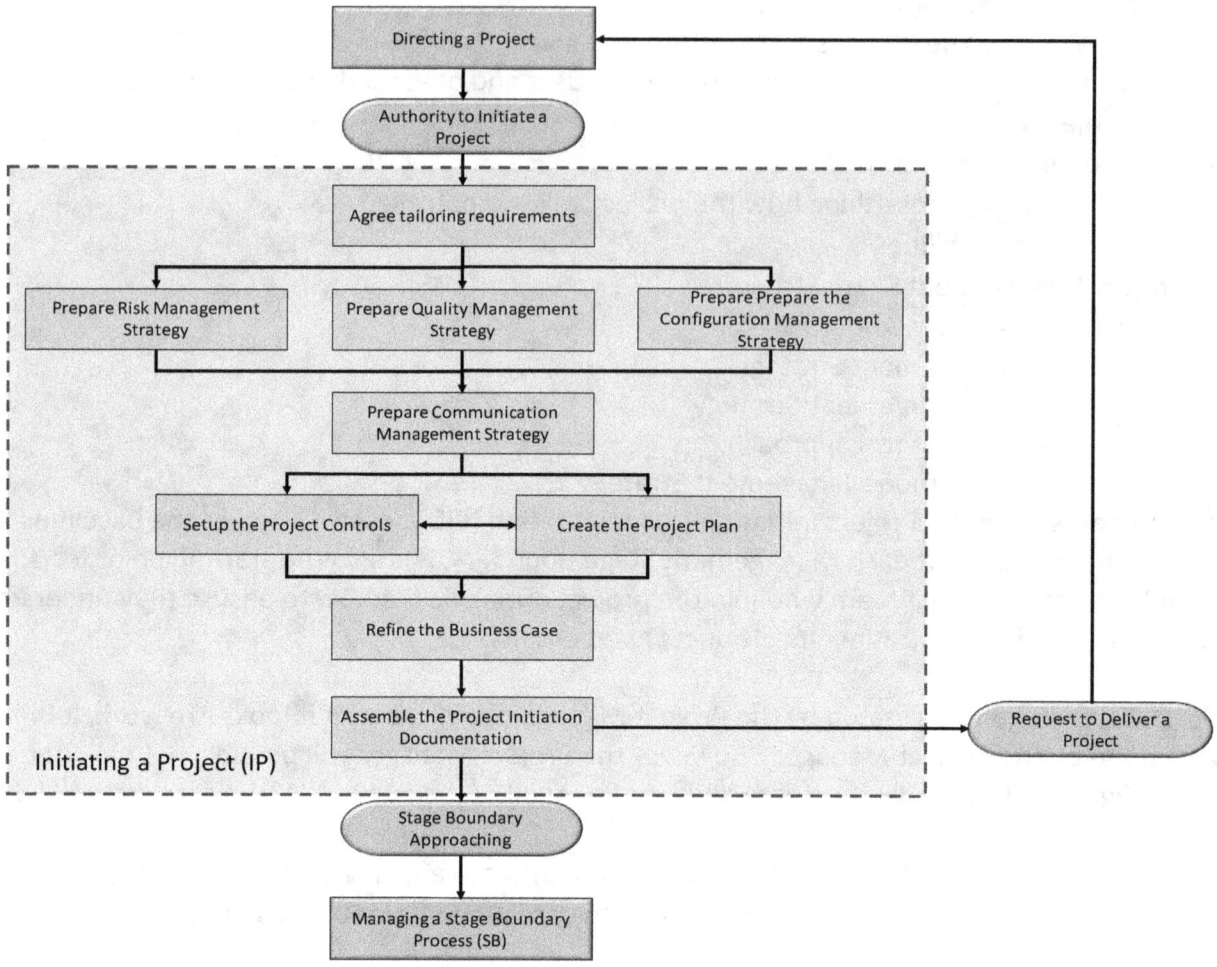

Figure 8 - Initiating a Project Process (IP)

This is all completed to enable the Project Board to make their 2nd formal decision to approve the project to proceed if it is a viable project and is approved to proceed to the 2nd stage. The Project Board will only authorise the project one stage at a time to ensure they have control and visibility of the actual progress against the forecasted progress contained in the PID.

The Project Board will review

- The Project Initiation Documentation (PID)
- The Business Case to confirm the project remains valid and viable
- A review of the risks
- A review of the Benefit Management Approach to ensure the benefits remain valid. If any benefits are forecasted to be delivered in the next stage, these need to be included in the next stage plan and the Benefit Management Approach and the benefits reporting plan aligned
- The Project Plan and next stage plan will also be reviewed

If the Project Board agrees they will approve the project to proceed, the Project Board will

- Authorise the Project – authorise the project to start
- Authorise the Next Stage Plan – enabling the first stage to commence

The timing of this is at or near the end of the Initiation Stage, however the Project Manager will commence the preparation work close to the end of the stage.

In the event that your project has a long Initiation Stage, it is advisable to break this into Management Stages, again remembering that there can only be one Management Stage but multiple Technical Stages and a Technical Stage can overlap a Management Stage.

Controlling a Stage (CS) – Delivery Stage

The Controlling a Stage (CS) is where the day-2-day work of the Project Manager begins. The Project Manager will normally complete most of the activities below

- Create and distribute work packages to Team Managers (TM), review the status of these work packages and accept work packages when completed
  - Note – the work package is delivered by the Team Manager to the Quality Review Board who will then accept or reject it based upon the defined quality acceptance criteria. Only then is the Work Package considered complete and handed back to the Project Manager
- Review stage status compared to the Project Plan and Stage Plan
- Provide regular reports to the Project Board
- Identify and capture risks and issues, and where required escalate
- Take corrective action to resolve issues within the Project Managers approved tolerance levels

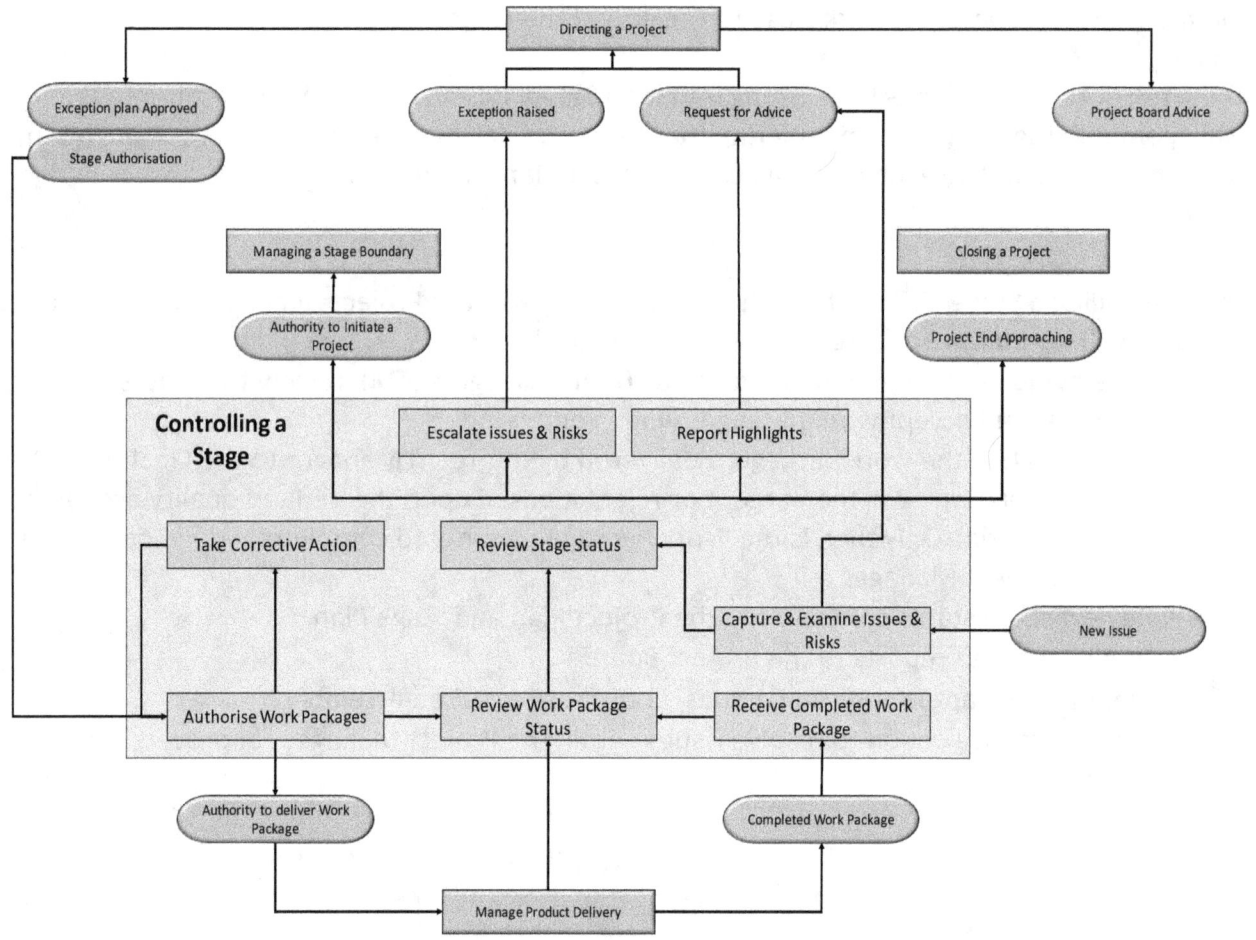

Figure 9 - Controlling a Stage Process (CS)

Managing Stage Boundary Process (SB)

The Managing Stage Boundary Process starts close to the end of the current stage. The Managing Stage Boundary Process (SB) objectives are to prepare the information for the Project Board to Authorise the Next Stage

The Project Manager will provide the following information to the Project Board:
- The End Stage Report – detailing how the stage performed against the Baselined Project Plan and the current approved Stage Plan
- The Next Stage Plan – a plan for the next management stage that will be approved by the Project Board
- The Benefit Management Approach – this will be checked to confirm if any benefits that were planned have materialised and are being measured

If the Project Board agrees they will approve the project to proceed, the Project Board will
- Review the current stage using mainly the End Stage Report, however they will also look the Business Case and Benefit Management Approach to compare forecasted against actuals and confirm the project remains viable
- Review the Next Stage Plan

This will lead to the Project Board "Authorising the Next Stage" so that the project can continue into the next Management Stage (Also known as delivery stage)

The timing of this is at the end of the current stage, however the Project Manager will start preparing the documentation close to the end of the stage

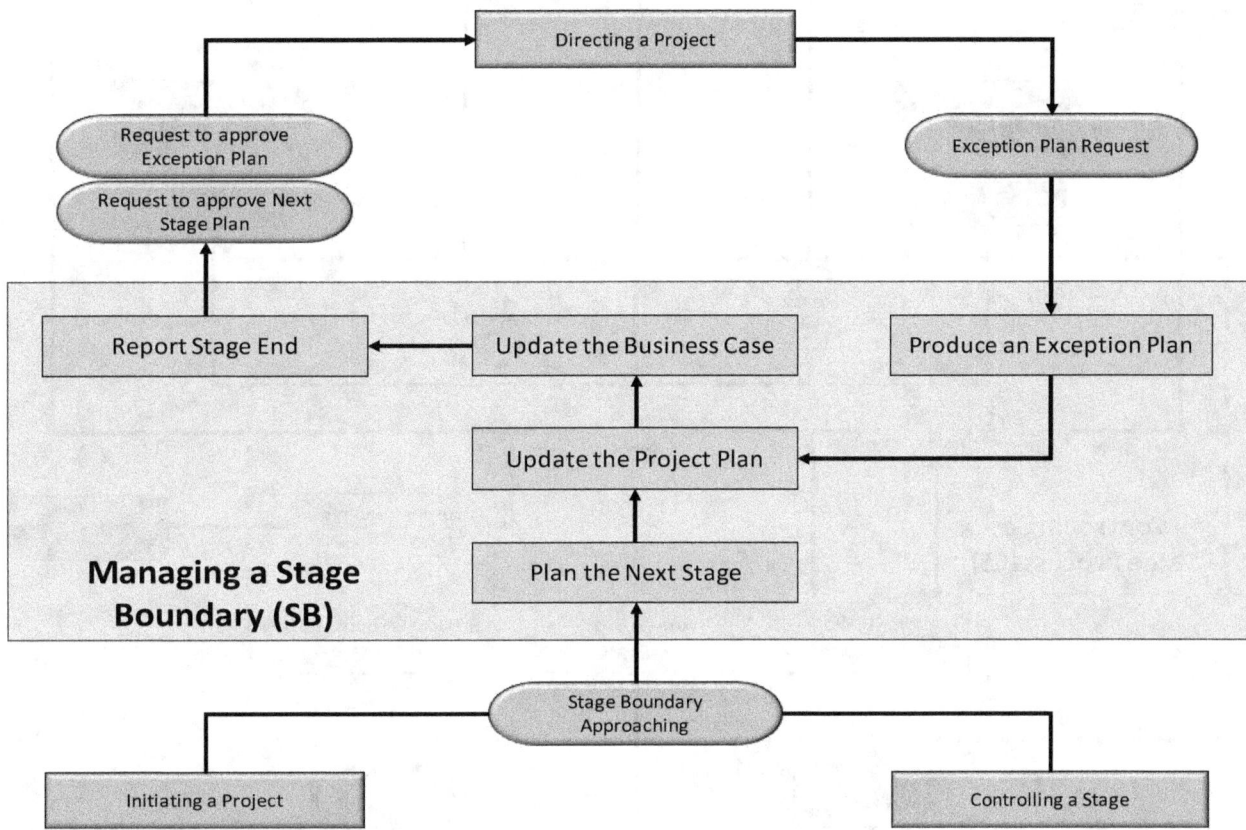

Figure 10 - Managing a Stage Boundary Process (SB)

Management (Delivery) Stages

A project can have more than one Management or Delivery Stage and they each have a decision point whereby the Project Board will authorise the following stage using the Managing Stage Boundary Process (SB)

The Project Board uses this process to ensure they maintain control of the Project and also ensure it remains viable

The end of Management Stage each stage will follow the Managing Stage Boundary Process (SB) and the Project Manager will present the information as above for the Project Board to review and approve the next stage.

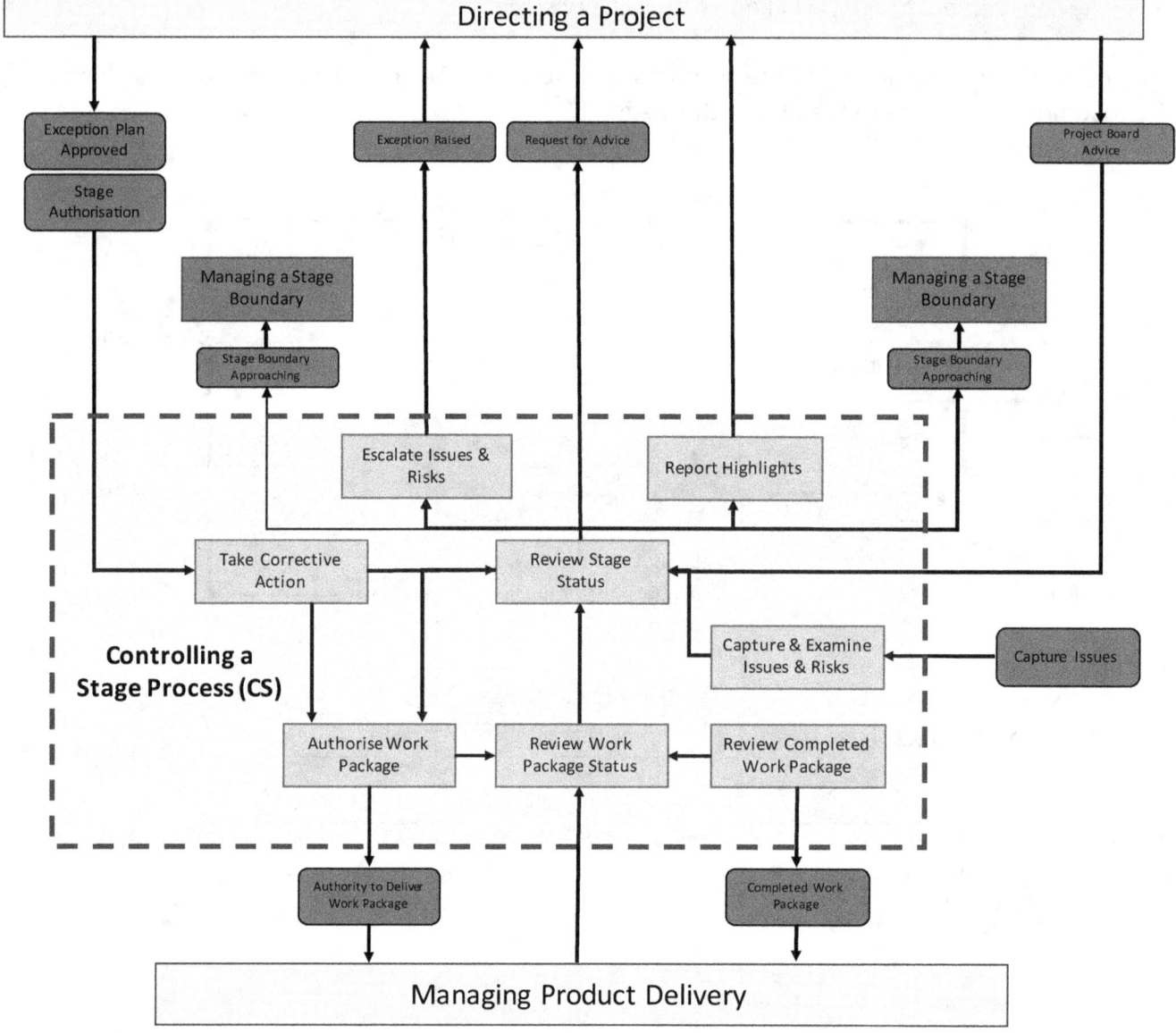

Figure 11 - Controlling a Stage Process

Final Management (Delivery) Stage and Closing a Project (CP)

The project can have multiple Management Stages to deliver the identified products and once these are complete, the project will be closed at the end of the final Management Stage. This is the Closing Project Process (CP)

"A simple way to remember this is that the Closing a Project Process is always the end of the final Management Stage"

As with the Managing Stage Boundary Process (SB) the Project Manager will start the Closing Project Process (CP) towards the end of the final Management Stage.

The Closing Project Process (CP) is the process where the Project Manager prepares the project for closure and the objectives of this process are to close the project in a controlled manner and present the Project Board with sufficient information to approve the "Authorise Project Closure"

The Project Manager will complete the following:
- Update the Project Plan to:
  - Identify what has been delivered
  - When it was delivered
  - The approval process for each product
- The handover of all products and obtain the acceptance from the Senior User or their representative(s)
- Evaluate the project and create the End Project Report, which will contain the Lessons Report
- Check and update the Benefit Management Approach and identify those benefits that have been realised and document those that have not

The Project Manager will also create the Draft Closure Report for the Project Board and present this with the recommendation to close the project. The Project Manager does not close the project, their role is to recommend the project closure to the Project Board.

The Project Board will decide to close the project and "Authorise Project Closure" based upon the following:
- A review of the following documents based upon the forecasted versus actuals to allow the Project Board to compare the delivered product against the original goals
  - Business Case
  - Project Plan
  - PID - The baselined PID from the Initiation Stage should be reviewed not the final version of the PID that will include any subsequent changes to the projects scope\times\costs etc
- Confirm that all products have been delivered, accepted and signed off
- Check the Lessons Report and hand over to Corporate or Program Management
- Review the Benefit Management Approach and compare the expected benefits against those forecasted
  - The Benefit Management Approach should also contain the following information:
    - Who will monitor the benefits?
    - When will they be reported on?
    - How will the information be obtained?
    - How long will the benefits be tracked?
    - Who needs the information?

As with the Managing Stage Boundary Process (SB) the Closing Project Process (CP) will be started towards the end of the final Management (Delivery) Stage.

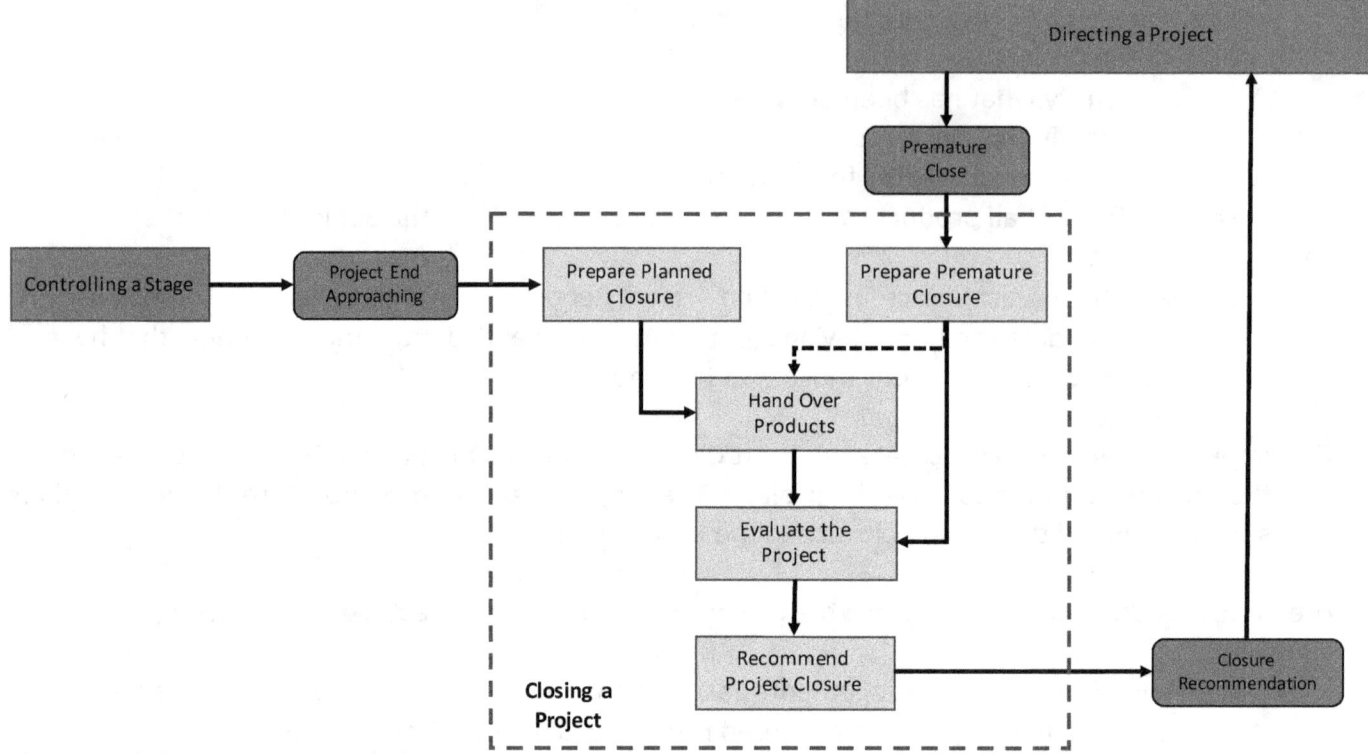

Figure 12 - Closing a Project Process (CP)

Exception Plans and Reports

In the event that an issue has arisen, and in Prince2 there are 3 types of issue

1. Off Specification – is something that should be provided by the project, but is not and is forecasted not to be provided – this could be a missing product or a product not meeting the required specification
2. Request for Change – A proposal to change an agreed baseline
3. Problem or Concern – Any issues or concerns that the Project Manager needs to manage\resolve or escalate

The Project Manager will monitor issues and in the event that a tolerance if forecasted to be exceeded and this exceeds the agreed tolerances set for the Project Manager by the Project Board, the Prince2 process is the escalation of this for Ad-Hoc direction from the Project Board.

The Project Manager creates an Exception Report, the Exception Report is used to inform the Project Board of the situation and offer options to resolve or mitigate the issue and a recommendation on how to proceed.

If an Exception Report is raised, work continues until the Project Board has approved the Exception Plan which will be requested upon acceptance of the exception report and the direction on the way to proceed.

The Project Manager will provide an Exception Plan to the Project Board, that if approved replaces the current stage plan.

The Exception Plan is a more complicated process than the Exception Report and involves

- Reviewing any changes needed to meet the quality expectations, acceptance criteria of the Senior User
- Review the Management approaches (Quality, Risk, Change, Configuration Management Strategies) and if necessary update them to ensure they remain appropriate
- Review the Product Based Plan and where necessary update this and the associated Product Descriptions and the related Configuration Item Records. The next stage should also be reviewed in relation to the upcoming products to ensure these changes have no "foreword impact"
- Providing a replacement Next Stage Plan to supersede the current stage plan

If the Project Board approves the Exception Plan, the Exception Plan replaces the current stage plan allowing the stage to be completed

The Project Board also has the ability to Authorise Premature Closure of the project in the event the project is no longer deemed viable, at this point the Project Manager will commence the premature project closure process

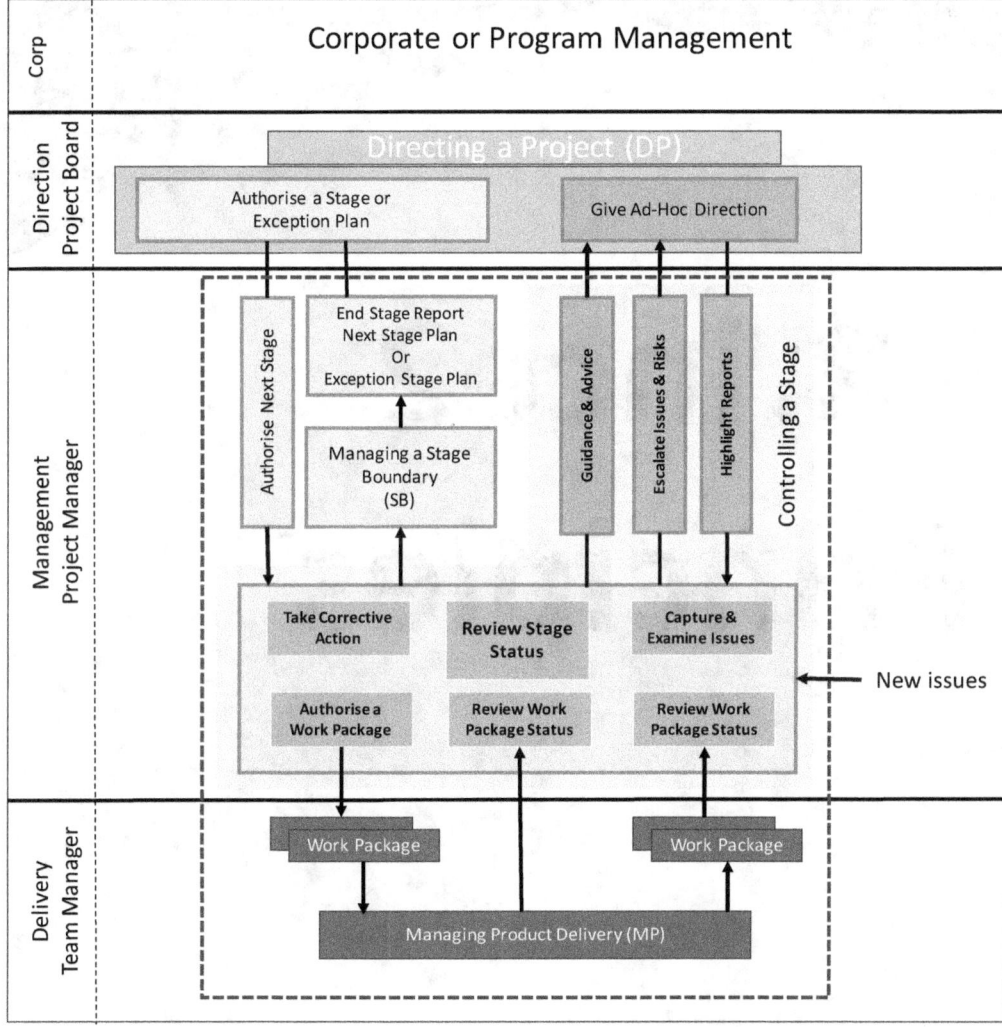

Figure 13 - Exception Plan Process

Prince2
Principles

Prince2 Principles

Prince2 is a process based methodology and the Prince2 manual states that each Prince2 Project should include the 7 Principles. If your Project is not delivering against these 7 Principles it cannot be classed as a Prince2 Project.

Prince2 defines the Principles as
- Universal in that they ca be applied to any project
- Are self-validating as they have been proven in practice over many years
- Empowering – this is explained as "giving practitioners to confidence and ability to influence the shape and how a project will be managed"

Within Prince2, the principles are a core value that **MUST** always exist within the project

The 7 Principles are:

Starting Up a Project (SU)	• Ensures the prerequisites are in place for initiating a project by answering the Question - Do we have a viable Project
Initiating a Project (IP)	• The purpose of Initiation is to establish a solid foundations for the project enabling the organization to understand the work that needs to be done to deliver the projects products before committing to a significant spend
Directing a Project (DP)	• The purpose of directing a project is to enable the Project Board to be accountable for the projects success by making key decisions and exercising overall control, whilst delegating any day-2-day management of the project to the Project Manager
Controlling a Stage (CS)	• The purpose of controlling a stage is to assign work to be done, monitor the work, deal with issues, report progress to the project board and take corrective action to ensure that the stage remains within tolerance
Managing Stage Boundaries (SB)	• The purpose of the Managing Stage boundary process is to enable the Project Board to be provided with sufficient information by the Project Manager so that it can review the success of the current stage, approve the next stage, review the updated project plan, and confirm continued business justification and acceptance of the risks
Managing Product Delivery	• The purpose of the managing product delivery process is to control the link between the Project Manager and the Team Manager(s), by placing formal requirements on accepting, executing and delivering work packages.
Closing a Project (CP)	• The purpose of the Closing a Project process is to provide a fixed point at which acceptance for the project product is confirmed and to recognize that objectives set out in the original PID have been achieved (or approved changes to the objectives have been achieved)

Figure 14 - Prince2 Principles

The 7 Principles form the guides for guaranteeing best practice when used effectively

Continued Business Justification

Prince2 defines that the Continued Business Justification of a project as:
- There is a justifiable reason to start the project
- The justification should remain valid throughout the lifecycle of the project
- The justification is documented and approved

This justification for a project in Prince2 is contained within the Business Case, which starts in the Starting up a Project Process (SU) as the Outline Business Case and is completed in Initiating a Project (IP) becoming the detailed Business Case.

The Business Case details the full justification for the project, it will document the following information:

- Why the project should be completed, what is the reason for the project
- The costs to deliver and support the project
    - (Known as Capital Costs and Operational Costs or Capex & Opex)
- The timescales to deliver the project
- The business options – The analysis and recommendations of these options along with the Prince2 options of:
    - Do nothing
    - Do the minimal
    - Do something
- The benefits that the project will deliver expressed measurable terms.
- Any expected dis-benefits
- The investment appraisal comparing the costs to deliver the project versus the benefits\dis-benefits and ongoing operational costs
- A summary of any major risks associated with the project with the supporting information on the possible impacts should they occur and the plans to mitigate or manage the risks

Learn for Experience

Prince2 Projects learn from experience based upon the Lessons Reports and Lessons Logs from previous projects. These Lessons Logs and Reports are actively sought at the Starting up a Project (SU) Stage and reviewed for any lessons that will support the current project.

The Project Manager will have a daily log and a lessons log and these should be managed and maintained throughout the lifecycle of the project.

Projects are defined as unique and no two projects are the same, Projects by their nature always deliver change to an organisation and this in turn creates risk. A Prince2 Project Manager is guided by the process and the principles to review the previous lessons learned reports and lessons logs for similar projects,

Prince2 also states that it is the responsibility of everyone involved in a project to review previous lessons learned.

Defined Roles & Responsibilities

Members of a project need to know what to do and what to expect from others, this is one of the most important and fundamental aspects of Prince2.

This is also one of the most import things to get right to avoid unforeseen confusion. Defined and agreed Roles and Responsibilities within a defined organisation structure enhances the chances of your projects success and chances of a return of investment (benefits) being achieved.

Prince2 defines 3 primary stakeholders of the project as:

Business Sponsor	• Business Users who endorse the objectives and ensure that the business investment provides clear value for money
Business Users	• Users who after the project is completed will use the products delivered by the project to enable them to gain the expected benefits
Suppliers (Internalor External)	• Suppliers who provide the resources and the expertise required by the project • These can internal or external

Figure 15 - Roles

The three primary stakeholders must be represented within the Project Management Team and be appropriately skilled and senior enough to represent and support the project.

Manage by Stages

Prince2 defines this as "A project is planned, monitored and controlled on a stage-by-stage basis"

This effectively means that the project is broken into pieces, Prince2 refers to this as Management by Stages and these are controlled by approval or decision points called Stage Boundaries where the Project Board makes the decision to approve the next stage and reviews the progress of the current stage against the forecasted plan. There can only be one Management Stage in progress at any time, however the technical stages can span more than one management stage

Upon completion of each stage, the project board reviews the performance of the project against the previous stage plan, the Business Case and other associated documents and decides if it is appropriate to proceed to the next stage.

Breaking the project into Management Stages provides the Project Board with greater control, however this can also lead an administrative burden being placed upon them. There is a fine line between just enough Management Stages and too many. Too few Management Stages and your Project Board will potentially have insufficient control, too many management stages could lead to apathy and a loss of interest in the project.

The advantages to this approach are:

- It allows the project to be divided into manageable chunks
- It provides the ability to have a high-level plan for the overall project and a detailed plan for each subsequent stage allowing a more granular management process
- Allows for the ability to learn from previous stages and increases the chances of overall project success

Prince2 states that there are minimum of 2 Management Stages. The Initiation Stage and a further Management Stage, the Closing a Project Process (CP) is part of the 2nd Management Stage

Management by Exception

A Prince2 project has defined and agreed tolerances which are set in a waterfall fashion

- Corporate or Program Management sets the Project Tolerance to the Project Board

- o The Project Board sets the Project Managers tolerance
  - The Project Manager sets the tolerance for the Team Manager

The tolerances reduce as they flow down the Project Management Structure. For Example:
- The Project Board could have a budget of $10,000,000 and a tolerance of $1,000,000
- They then set a budget of $9,000,000 and a tolerance of $500,000 with an approval limit of $50,000 on the Project Manager
- The Project Manager will then set a lower tolerance on the team manager for of $5000 and an approval limit of $2000

The same can be applied to time or resources.

Prince2 lists six aspects of quality that can be set Time, Cost, Scope, Quality, Benefits and Risk, these are also known as the 6 aspects of Project Management and each of these can have a tolerance assigned

Management by exception provides the management layers with a system to manage the project, whereby only those issues that could have a detrimental impact on any of the six aspects where the agreed and approved tolerances are forecasted to be exceed are escalated to the next higher level of management for Ad-Hoc direction

Focus on Products
Prince2 focuses upon the definition and delivery of products and also focuses upon their quality requirements.

A detailed Project Product Description (PPD) will guide the project and ensure the expectations of those involved are managed and therefore avoid any confusion. In a project, there are often numerous stakeholders within the "User" group and each has a different view upon
- What the product should be
- How it should be delivered
- How it should be used.

This often causes unnecessary meetings, delays and changes in requirements that can lead to scope creep, potentially effecting the overall quality of the final product that is delivered.

Detailed Product Descriptions ensure that all of the involved stakeholders have full clarity upon the products being delivered, their purpose, composition, quality criteria and quality method. Good Product Descriptions also make it easier to determine resource requirements, delivery times, dependencies and activities associated with the product

Tailoring to suit the Project Environment
Prince2 is tailored to suit either the project or the organisation. As stated each project is unique ad no two projects are the same, so tailoring Prince2 to suit the project is critical.

For example, if your project is small in nature, such has hosting a staff conference with 50 people compared to a large project like replacement of a company email system and migrating 20,000 email accounts. The ability to tailor Prince2 to suit the project could save time and money.

The purpose of tailoring is:
- To ensure that project methodology relates to the environment and complexity of the project
- Ensuring that the control and management of the project is based upon the projects complexity, importance, risk and costs (Capex, Opex and Benefits)

The Project Initiation Document (PID) should document where any areas of Prince2 are tailored to meet the requirements of the project

Prince2 Themes

Prince2 states that the themes are aspects of the project that must be addressed continually. Themes start at the beginning of the project and lay the foundations for the success of your project, as with the Principles and Process there are 7 Themes

These are explained below:

Business Case	• How an idea is developed into a viable investment proposition • How project management maintains its focus on the organisations objectives throughout a project
Organization	• How work is allocated to managers with clear responsibilities • How the roles and responsibilities within a Prince2 project team work together efficiently
Quality	• How the project management team ensure the requirements are delivered
Plans	• How plans are developed using Prince2 techniques • How plans are the focus for communications and control throughout the project
Risk	• How Project management handles uncertainties in its plans and the environment
Change	• How project management assesses and acts upon the need to change, either as a result of changes to requirements or to issues that arise during the project
Progress	• How to decide whether to approve a plan • How to monitor progress, and what to do when things don't go according to plan

Figure 16 - Prince2 Themes

The Prince2 Process relate to the Themes in a chronological order, the Prince2 Processes guide the typical activities of your project that are completed at the different stages during the project lifecycle and these are mostly activities that are completed once within the project

For example, the Starting up a Project Process (SU) activities and the PID are executed once and baselined. The Themes associated with these Processes will be used during the life of the project

Business Case

The Business Case answers the following questions

- Why are we doing this project?
- What are the Business reasons for this project?
- What are the benefits to the organisation in doing this project?

By completing the Outline Business Case in the Starting up a Project Process (SU) and completing the Detailed Business Case within the Initiating a Project Process (IP) this allows the Executive to review it at each Stage Boundary (SB) to revalidate that the project continues to be viable.

The Business Case is the responsibility of the Project Executive, but it will often be written with the support from other stakeholders as required.

The Project Mandate usually contains the information required for the Outline Business Case, which is expanded to create the Detailed Business Case, which then becomes part of the Project Brief and subsequently part of the Project Initiation Documentation (PID).

The Business Case is reviewed and if required updated at the end of each Management Stage as part of the Managing a Stage Boundary Process (SB) and should include the latest costs, timescales and product information to confirm the continued viability of the Project

Organisation

The purpose of the Organisation Theme is to define the projects structure of accountability and responsibility.

This is the definition of:
1. Who is in the project?
2. What are their roles within the project?
3. Who is the Project Sponsor?
4. Who is responsible for the Business Case?
5. Who is responsible for the Benefits?
6. Who represents the Users?
7. Who represents the Suppliers?
8. Who is the Project Manager?
9. What are the roles and responsibilities?

Prince2 assumes that all projects are based upon a customer and supplier environment. The supplier is responsible for the delivery of the product to the user who is responsible for the specification of the product and the quality criteria required for acceptance and in most cases, will also be responsible for paying the supplier.

Prince2 states that a Project Management Team should have the following
- Representation from the Business, User and Supplier
- A complete set of defined and agreed roles and responsibilities for the directing, managing and delivery of the project
- A Communication Management Approach to manage all communication to and from stakeholders

The Prince2 organisation structure has four defined levels of management that support the delivery of the project, support the Management by Exception Theme and allows the controlled escalation as required.

These levels are:

Corporate or Program Management	• Responsible for commissioning the Project • Outside the Project Management Team • Identifies the Executive • Sets Project Tolerances • Provides the Project Mandate
Project Board Directing	• Responsible for the overall direction & management of the Project • Accountable for the success of the Project • Approves all major plans and resources • Authorizes any deviation that exceeds or is forecasted to exceed tolerances • Authorizes the completion of each stage and authorizes the start of the next stage • Communicates with other stakeholders
Project Manager Managing	• Responsible for the day-2-day management of the Project within the constraints set by the Project Board • Ensures the project produces the required products in accordance with the performance goals for Time, Cost, Quality, Scope, Risk and Benefits
Team Manager Delivering	• Responsible for the delivery of the projects products to the required quality within the specified timescales and costs • May be responsible for planning the creation of certain products and managing a team of specialists

Figure 17 - Prince2 Management Levels

The Project Management Team Structure is defined as

"A temporary structure specifically designed to manage the project to its successful conclusion"

The Prince2 Management Structure allows for controlled communication to the right decision makers and is supported by the roles and responsibilities for all stakeholders involved within the project.

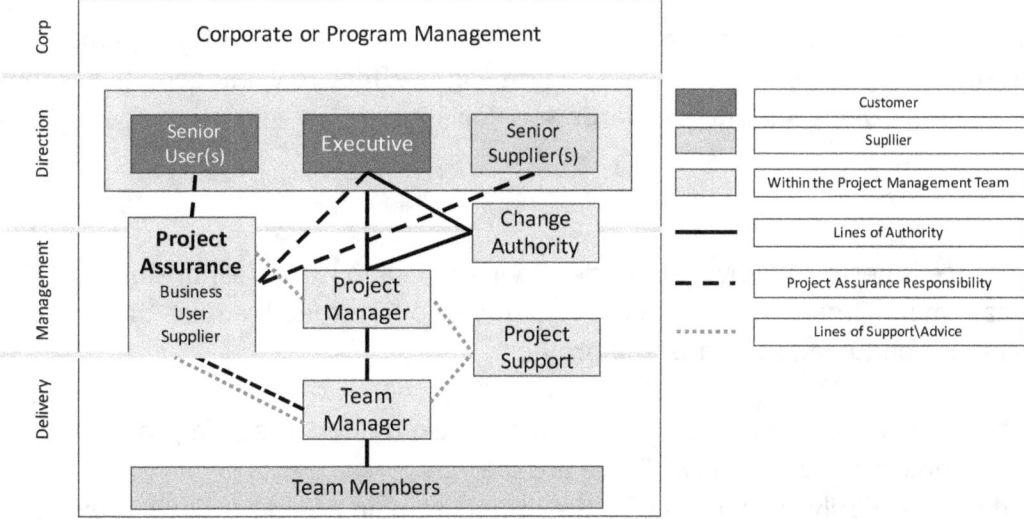

Figure 18 - Project Management Structure

The purpose of the Quality Theme is to define and implement the means by which the project will create and verify the products are fit for purpose and meet the needs of the customers\users

This effectively means that the products must meets the expectations of the users who defined the requirements and be accepted based upon this defined acceptance criteria.

The Quality Theme answers the following questions:
- What must the product be at the end of the project to ensure that it can be used as intended? – *Will it be fit for purpose?*
- What can be done by the project during its lifecycle to guarantee the levels or quality are being met and the product will be delivered to the required levels of quality defined by the users –
Will it be fit for purpose?

The Quality Theme supports the definition of Quality requirements and the approach of Prince2 is to focus upon the products as early as possible by asking questions such as
- What level of quality is required or expected of each product that is produced by the project
- Who will be responsible for the testing and acceptance of the products produced by the project

These are answered and contained in the Product Descriptions for each Product to be created by the Project

The Quality Management Strategy is used to define the following:
- How will quality work within the project?
- What standards will be applied (for example; Safety, Regulatory requirements must be met)
- The responsibilities for achieving the levels of the desired levels of quality during the project

Quality covers both Project Assurance and Quality Assurance however they both have very different purposes within Prince2

Quality Assurance provides assurance to the wider Corporate or Program Management Organisation, ensuring that the project is being conducted and managed effectively and complies with the Corporate or Program Management Standards and Policies

What does this mean?

"Quality Assurance is performed by independent personnel and is the responsibility of Corporate or Program Management Organisation, Quality Assurance would expect\require that effective Project Assurance is being conducted as part of the project"

Project Assurance provides assurance to the project's stakeholders that the project is being conducted appropriately and properly. These are the
- Executive – primarily concerned that the project remains viable and will provide a return on investment

- Senior User – Primarily concerned that the project products will meet the excepted quality, be fit for purpose and support the achievement of the benefits
- Senior Supplier – Primarily concerned that the products produced meet the customers' expectations and meet any regulatory or compliance requirements

What does this mean? Project Assurance cannot be the Project Manager, Project Support Team, Team Managers or Project Teams. Project Assurance must be independent and is the responsibility of the Project Board, each of the Project Board roles can delegate the role of Project Assurance to suitable individual or individuals to represent their interests

Plans

The purpose of the Plans Theme is to facilitate the communication and control by defining the means of delivering the products by answering
- The where
- The How
- The who
- The when
- How much
- The how long

The confusion to most people attending a Prince2 course is when the Plans Theme is first discussed, the association with the term plans is automatically linked to a Gannt chart. Prince2 Plans are not Gannt Charts, the Gannt chart is just a piece of the Project Plan

Prince2 plans are a document that contains the following information
- A brief or executive summary of the project
- The prerequisites required that must be in place to deliver the project
- Any identified dependencies (Internal or external)
- Any assumptions made during the planning process
- Any lessons from previous projects that have been incorporated
- The monitoring and control details in relation to the plan
- The budgets – covering, time, costs and including the provision for the Risk and Change budget
- Product descriptions – this may not be complete, but should cover the products being delivered by the project. The second and third level product descriptions may be created and included in the Next Stage Plans
- The schedule – this is where the Gannt Chart would potentially be included

A Prince2 project has four levels of Plan,

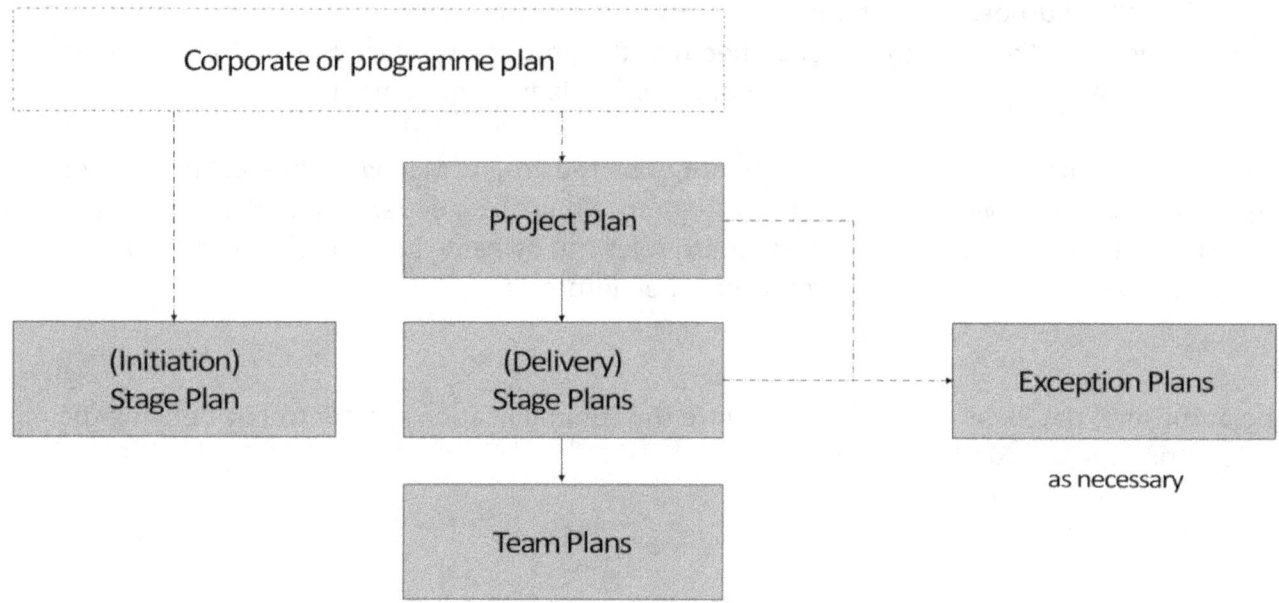

Figure 19 - Levels of Plans

These are
Project Plan
The Project Plan contains the information listed above and provides a statement of how and when the projects time, cost, quality, scope and quality performance targets will be achieved by showing the major products, activities and the resources required to enable the project to be completed.

The Project Plan is updated at the end of each stage as part of the Managing Stage Boundary Process (SB) to show what has been completed, any products that have been developed and accepted, and the Next Stage Plan is included. The purpose of updating the Project Plan is to show how well the project is doing against the original plan.

Stage Plan(s)
The Stage Plan is required for each Management Stage and is similar to the Project Plan in content but focuses only upon the Management Stage it relates to and each element of the stage plan provides sufficient detail to allow for the day-2-day control by the Project Manager

Each Next Stage Plan is produced as part of the Managing Stage Boundary Process (SB) near the end of the current stage, this allows the Next Stage Plan to:
- Be produced close to when the planned events will take place allowing for greater levels of detail enabling better control and less chances of issues arising
- Exists for a much shorter period than the Project Plan therefore overcoming the planning horizon issue
- Learns from previous Management Stages allowing continued improvement of the planning process

Team Plan(s)
A Team Plan is an optional plan in Prince2 and is produced by the Team Manager to support the execution of the assigned Work Packages.

Exception Plan(s)

An Exception Plan is prepared by the Project Manager at the request of the Project Board and contains the appropriate level of detail to show the actions required to recover from the current tolerance being exceeded or is forecasted to be exceeded.

If approved by the Project Board, the Exception Plan will replace the current stage plan and will become the new baselined Project Plan or Stage Plan as appropriate

Risk

The purpose of the Risk theme is Identify, assess and control uncertainty within the project and as a result improve the chances of the projects success.

Prince's approach to risk is based upon the Management of Risk (MoR) Guidance for Practitioners and uses the principles outlined in this as a guide for the management of risk within the project

The process for managing risk within the project is contained within the Risk Management Approach and this describes the specific risk management techniques and standards to be applied and the responsibilities for achieving effective risk management.

A risk is effectively any unforeseen or unplanned event that could have a positive or negative impact upon your project achieving its objectives

The Risk theme answers the following:
- What are the risks?
- What if the risk happens?
- How can they be identified, analysed and documented?
- How can the possibility of the risk be reduced?
- How can the risk be managed and monitored throughout the project?

Prince2 has 2 types of risk
- A threat - a threat is defined as an uncertain event that could have a negative impact upon the project,
- An opportunity - an opportunity could lead to a positive impact upon your project.

Prince2 has defined responses to both threat and opportunities and these are defined below

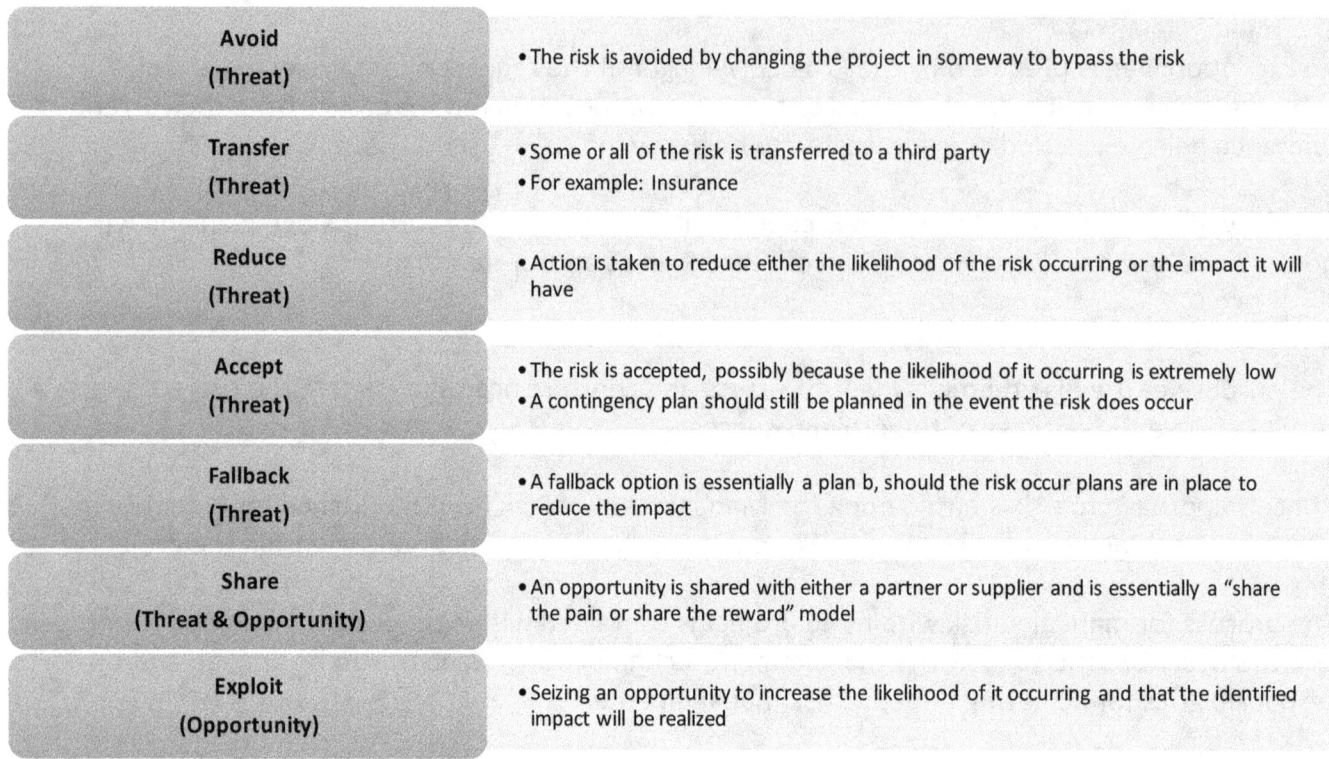

Figure 20 - Risk Responses

Risks are managed within the Risk Register, the purpose for this document it captures, manages and maintain the information on all identified threats or opportunities relating to the project

The Risk Register should contain the following as a minimum:
- Who raised the risk
- When it was raised
- Risk ID
- Risk category
- Description of the risk
  - Cause
  - Event
  - Effect
- Probability, impact and expected value
- Proximity (Strategic, Project, Current Stage, Next Stage)
- Risk response category
- Risk response actions
- Risk status
- Risk owner
- Risk actionee

The risk owner and risk actionee are named individuals assigned to monitor the risk or action the plan in the event the risk occurs

| Risk Owner | • Is a named individual who is responsible for the management, monitoring and control of all aspects of a risk assigned to them, this includes the implementation of the identified response to the identified threat or to maximize the opportunities |
| Risk Actionee | • Is a named individual assigned to carry our the response actions or actions in relation to a particular risk or set of risks.
• They support and take direction from the risk owner |

Figure 21 - Risk Roles

The risk owner and actionee can often be the same person, however the risk owner should be the person most capable of managing the risk.

It is also not recommended to assign too many risks to any one person, especially the Project Manager. This can often be counterproductive when manging both the risk or the project itself.

Change

The purpose of the Change theme is to identify, assess and control any potential and approved changes to the baseline

As projects introduce change and as each project is unique, all projects will encounter issues and most projects will at some point have a request for change

The Change Theme answers the question "What is impact of the issue?"

Prince2 defines that all changes are issues, and uses this term to cover any event that has happened

A simple way to remember the difference between a risk and issue is to remember:

"A risk is an event that could happen and an issue is an event that has happened"

Prince2 has three types of issues:

Request for Change	• The customer wants to change a requirement that has already been agreed and is signed off (Baselined)
Off Specification	• Where a product has been created\delivered and it does not meet the agreed requirements
Problem or Concern	• Anything Else – this could be a risk that has materialized into an issue and now needs management or escalation

Figure 22 - Issue Types

The Change Control Approach describes how issues and changes are handled within the project and answers the following questions:
- How should products planned, identified and controlled be verified?
- How should issues and changes be managed within the project?
- What tools are available for the project to use?
- What data should be maintained for each product's
  - Product Description
  - Configuration Item Record
  - Test Scripts (Functional and Non-Functional)

Progress

The purpose of the progress theme is to establish the mechanisms to monitor and compare the actuals versus those planned and provide a forecast of the project objectives and the projects continued viability and control any unacceptable deviations.

During the lifecycle of the project, it is monitored by the Project Manager and checks are completed to ensure that the project is progressing in line with the agreed plan.

The Progress Theme answers the following:
- How will the project be controlled?
- When will the project reporting be completed?
- Where are we compared to where we should be or compared to the plan
- Is the project still viable?

Progress is checking the development or delivery of the project when compared to the baselined or original plan, checking the continued viability of the project and controls any potential deviations.

Control is about decision making and is a central function to project management and the role of the Project Manager and enables the continued viability of the project when compared to the original business case

Prince2
Themes

Themes in Detail

The next section will take you into the detail of each theme, how it relates to Prince2, what is covered within the theme and what knowledge the theme provides, and how it supports the project lifecycle within Prince2

Business Case Theme

Introduction to the Business Case Theme

The Business Case Theme underpins the project within Prince2 and is the justification for the project.

We will cover the following areas to explain and enable you to fully understand the Business Case Theme and how it supports the project:

- The purpose of the Business Case
- What is a Business Case?
- Contents of a Business Case
- Outputs, Outcomes and Benefit's
- Business Case types
- The creation of the Business Case
- The Prince2 Business Case verification points
- Confirming benefits
- Business Case roles and responsibilities

The Purpose of the Business Case

Within Prince2 the purpose of the Business Case is provide a structure to enable the Project Board to judge whether the project is a viable, desirable, achievable and justifiable for the continued investment both during the project and after the project.

If we break up the statement above, it provides more clarity:

- Provides a structure and guidelines to follow
- Determines if the product is desirable and enables the Project Board to compare the benefits identified against the potential dis-benefits
- Determines the projects viability and clarifies if the organisation if capable of delivering the project and if the project is possible to be delivered
- Determines if the benefits identified are achievable and deliverable
- Determines if the project is worth the continued investment including the investments made both during the project and post project –

Prince2 states that if a project is longer viable, it should be stopped

Business Justification

The term "Business Justification" is popular within businesses and methodologies as well as Prince2. Business Justification means that there is a valid reason for doing the project and this remains valid thought the project lifecycle.

Continued Business Justification is also one of the Prince2 Principles

Within Prince2 the Project Executive is responsible for the creation of the Business Case, it is created within the Starting Up a Project Process (SU) as the Outline Business Case, and is maintained by the Project Manager. The Business Case is updated within the Initiating a Project Process (IP) into the Detailed Business Case that is then used to by the Project Board to Authorise the Project

The Business Case contains the following information
- The reasons for the project and why it should be completed
- The estimated costs and timescales
- The identified Benefits and Dis-Benefits
- An overview of the risks identified in relation to the project

What is the purpose of the Business Case in relation to the project
The business case is the central focal point for the information that allows the management to judge the viability of the project and if it is achievable and desirable. The Business Case is (normally) created at the start-up of the project, however in some cases the Business Case is provided by Corporate or Program Management. Once it is created, it is maintained throughout the project lifecycle.

The Business Case is constantly reviewed throughout the project, it is reviewed to confirm that the project remains viable and is justified.

Outputs, Outcomes and Benefits
Prince2 uses the Terms Outputs, Outcomes and Benefits to help describe what is delivered by the project. However, this in a term that is not widely known outside of Prince2.

How do these terms relate to the project and to each other?

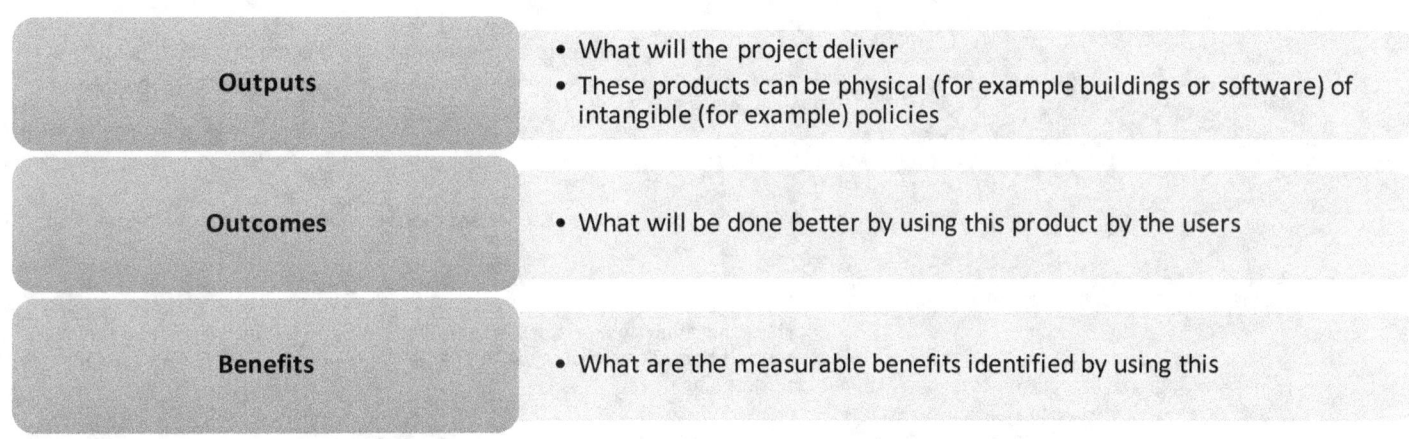

Figure 23 - Outputs, Outcomes, Benefits

The simplest way to understand how they link is

"Outputs deliver Outcomes than enable Benefits to be realized"

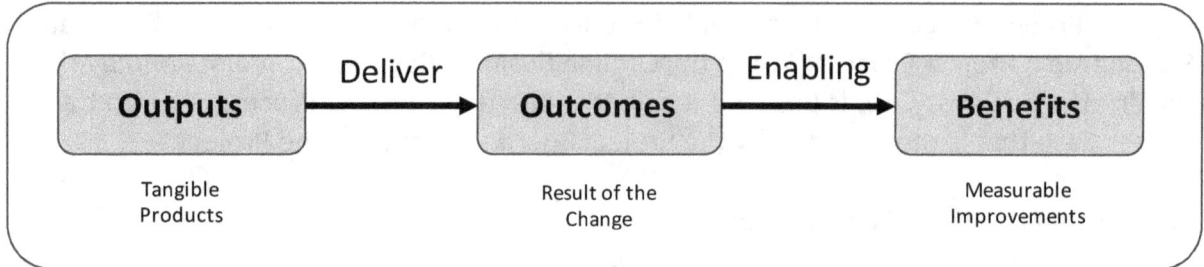

Figure 24 - Benefit Path

Outputs – The outputs of the project are the products that will be used by the users, they are also known as specialist products within Prince2 and the project is especially setup to deliver these products

Outcomes – An outcome is the result of a change, they are achieved as a result of the activities undertaken by the project to effect the change

Benefits – Within Prince2, Benefits are the measurable improvement that is the result of the outcome. Benefits can be realised or delivered both during the project and at the completion of the project, however Prince2 assumes that benefits are delivered post project in a classic customer\supplier project

Different types of Business Case

There is an assumption that a Business Case must show a return on investment, however this is not the case. Each project should have a Business Case as the approval for the delivery of the Project

There are numerous types of Business Case justifications or types, these are the types recognised by Prince2

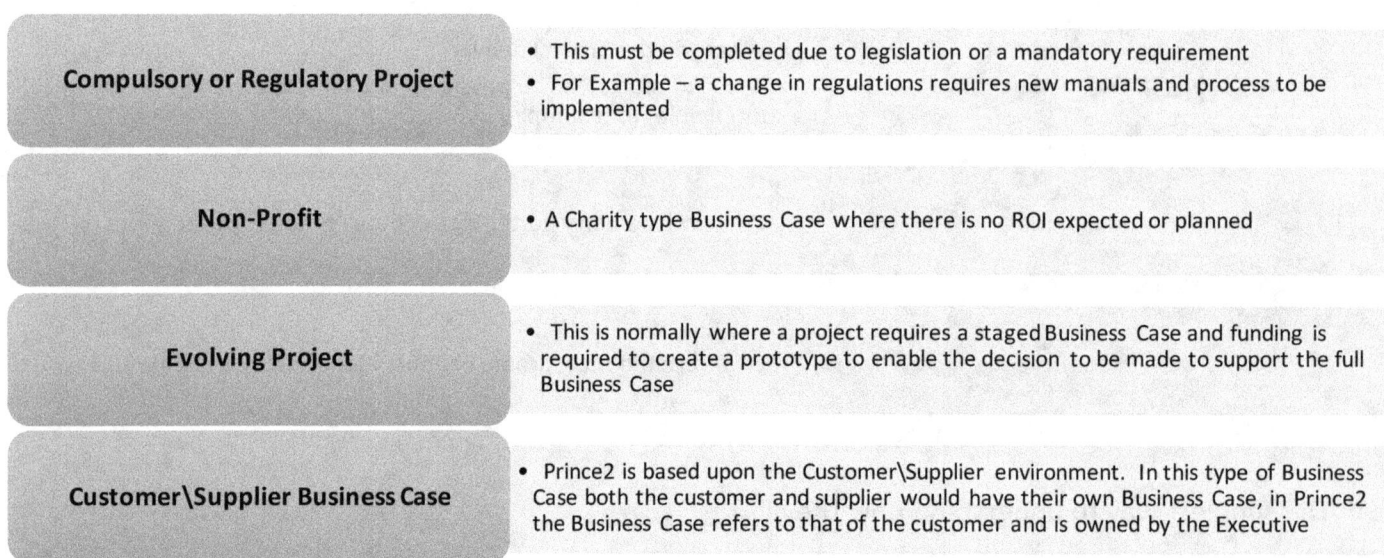

Figure 25 - Business Case Types

Creating the Business Case

The creation of the Business Case is fundamental to the Prince2 project, it underpins the foundations of the project and clarifies the need for the project, benefits to be achieved allowing the Project

Board to make the decision to proceed and allows the continued review ensuring the continued business justification for the project.

With this in mind the Business Case is started in Starting up a Project Process (SU) with the Outline Business Case and is completed with the Detailed Business Case in the Initiating a Project Process (IP).

The Business Case is then verified at each Stage Boundary by the Project Board using the Managing a Stage Boundary Process (SB)

In Prince2 there are 4 steps to creating the Business Case, these are:
1. Develop
2. Verify
3. Maintain
4. Confirm Benefits

Step 1 – Developing the Business Case

This is essentially the Create the Business Case, The Business Case as stated above is commenced in the Starting up a Projects Process (SU) and Continues into the Initiating a Project Process (IP) where it is finalised and then becomes part of the Project Initiation Documentation (PID)

The Executive is responsible for the creation of the Business Case, but it can be written by others or with the help from others (and this is often the case)

For Example, in relation to the Business Case finances and benefits, the Executive may request support from the Finance Department to review and approve the figures included as part of the assurance process.

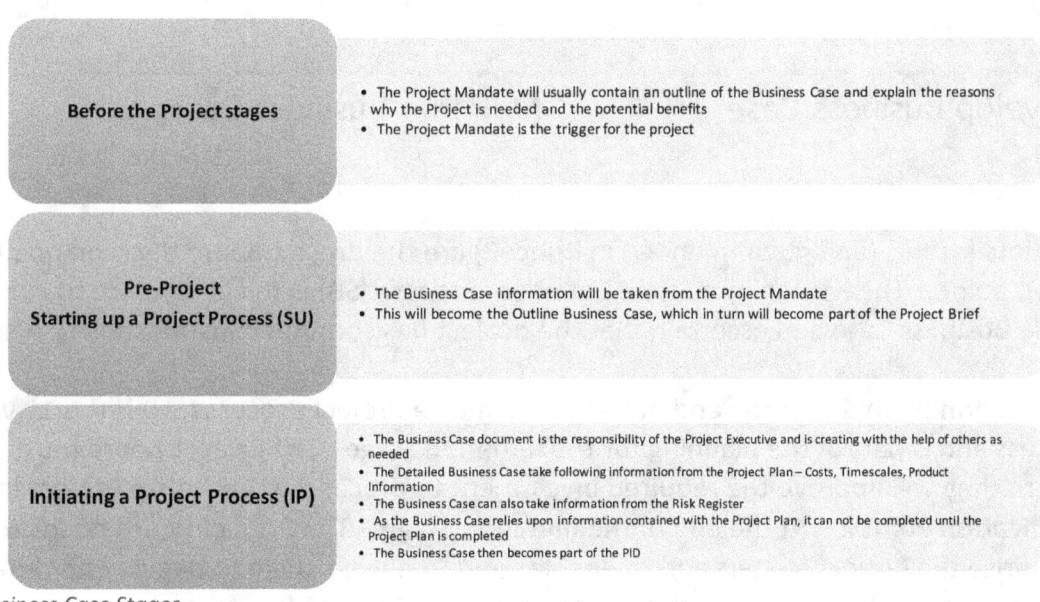

Figure 26 - Business Case Stages

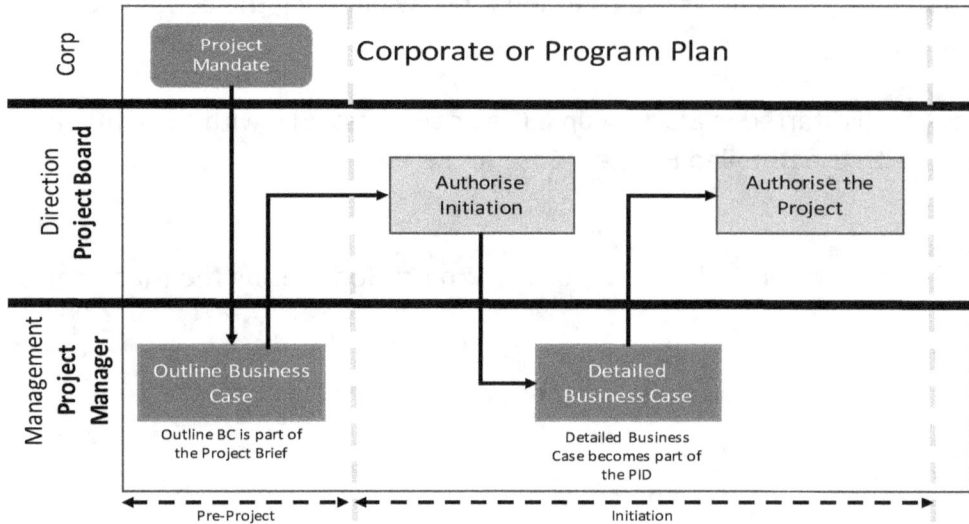

Figure 27 - Business Case Development Process

Step 2 – Verify the Business Case

Verifying the Business Case is the process of reviewing the information contained and the validity of the overall project to ensure it is worthwhile to start\authorise and the continued verification that the project should continue at it has continued justification

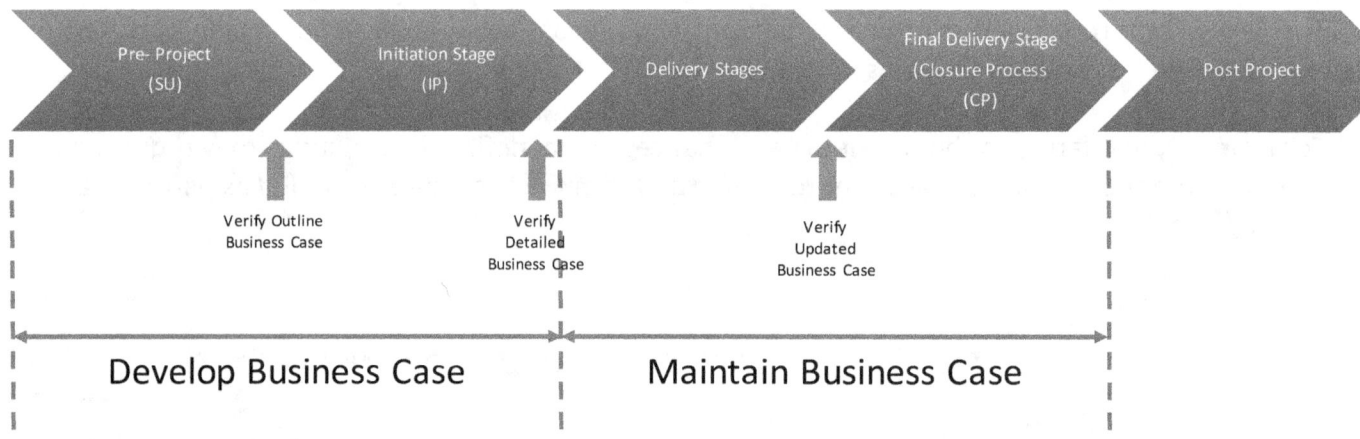

Figure 28 - Business Case Verification Points

The ideal points for this (and recommended in Prince2) are the Project Board decision points or authorisation points. The Managing a Stage Boundary Process (SB) is the ideal place to conduct a review of the Business Case and ascertain that the project has continued justification

- **Verification Point 1** – At the end of the Starting up a Project Process (SU) is the 1st verification process and is part of the planning for the Initiation Stage. The Project Board must see value before they will approve the required investment to proceed to Authorise Project Initiation
- **Verification Point 2** – At the end of the Initiation Stage – The Project Board needs to Authorise the Project to start and to enable the 1st delivery stage to begin. The Detailed Business Case will form part of the Project Initiation Documentation and is again verified at this point
- **Verification Point 3** – The is a verification by the Project Manager during the Controlling Stage Process. Any new Issues or Risks that are raised could have an impact (Positive or

Negative) upon the Business Case. The role of the Project Manager is to always ask if the Business Case is valid and if any risks\issues or changes affect the Business Case

- **Verification Point 4** – The Project Manager updates the Business Case to reflect any changes in project costs, timescales, risks or benefits.
- **Verification Point 5** – At the end of each stage and before the next stage, he Project Board will review the Business Case to confirm Continued Business Justification and Progress before any funds are released for the next stage
- **Verification Point 6** – During the Closing a Project Process (CP) the Project Manager assess the overall performance of the project against the original Business Case assessing the expected outcomes and benefits and those achieved
- **Verification Point 6** – Post Project – A review of the Benefits delivered by the project will be completed by the Corporate or Program Management Team and again verification of the Business Case for the expected Benefits. The Senior User is accountable for the benefits and the reporting of them

These are the most common areas and also those recommended in Prince2, however as always, each project is unique and the verification points may be different in your projects

Maintain the Business Case
Maintaining the Business Case is essentially the process of keeping the Business Case aligned to the project, ensuring it reflects the current state of the project. Changes may be required when assessing risks, issues, changes or progress.

The Business Case is what is known as a live document, meaning that although there is a baselined version that is approved at the commencement of the project, it continues to evolve with the project through a series of updates and the document is managed through version control.

The ideal time to update the Business Case is at the end of every stage using the Managing Stage Boundary Process (SB), as this will allow you to update the costs and progress from the current stage and include the known details of the nest stage.

In the event that you are running a phased or evolving project, it is possible some of the products have been delivered and therefore some of the identified benefits may have been materialised and are being reported upon. This information should be added to the Business Case.

The Executive has the responsibility to ensure that all stakeholders that the project maintains continued business justification and remains a viable, achievable and desirable project

Benefits
Confirming the Benefits in relation to the projects is undertaken at the beginning of the project and then as the Business Case is maintained\revalidated during the project lifecycle, these benefits and re-confirmed.

This happens in a number of steps using Prince2

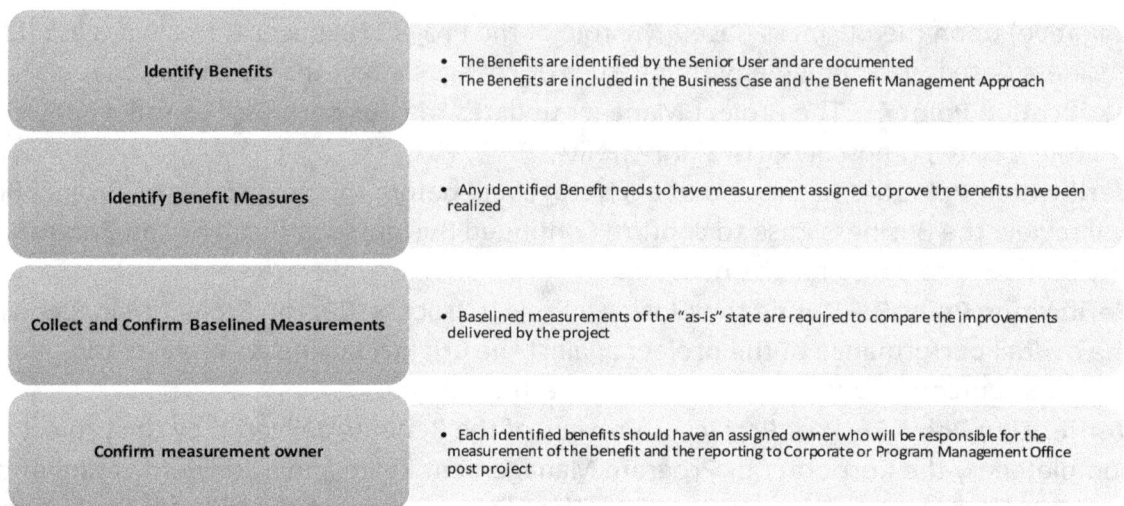

Figure 29 - Benefits Steps

Prince2 assumes that benefits are realised post-project. The Benefits Management Approach is used to define the benefits measurement process. This is created by the Project Manager during the Initiating a Project Process (IP) or Initiation Stage and is reviewed and approved by the Project Board.

The Benefit Management Approach as with the Business Case is should be reviewed and updated at the end of each management stage to reconfirm the benefits identified and in the event, any have been delivered, confirm the measurement and reporting process in in place

The ownership of the benefits post project within Prince2 are owned by the Corporate or Program Management, the reporting of these benefits to them is the responsibility of the Senior User, who will provide evidence that the benefits are being achieved

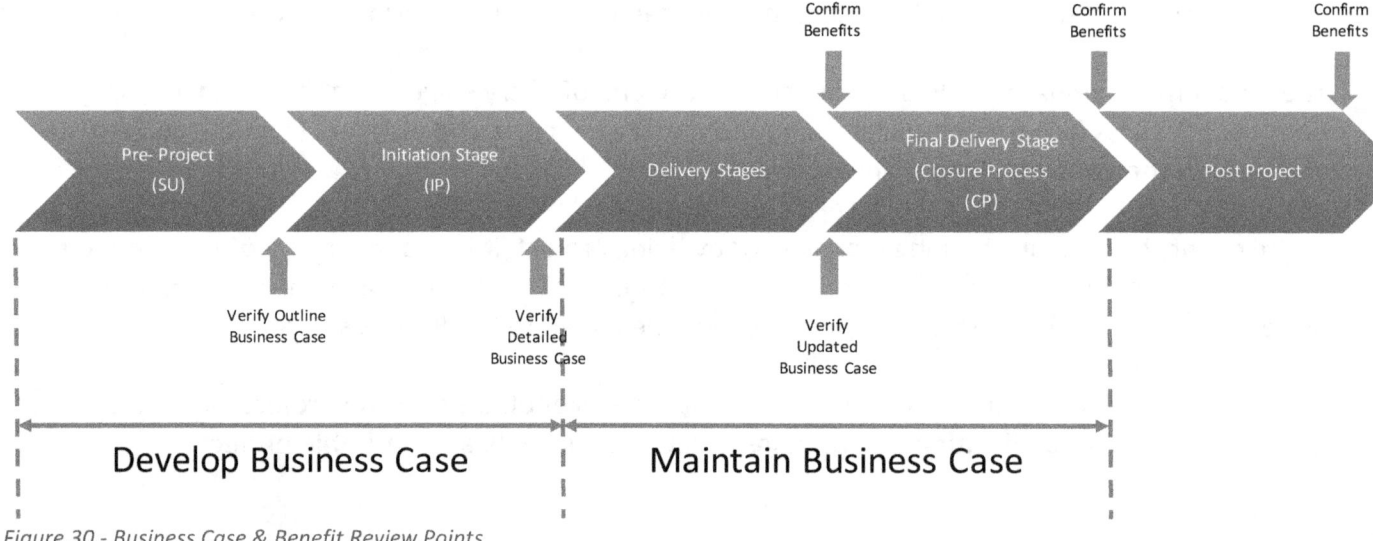

Figure 30 - Business Case & Benefit Review Points

The Benefits Management Approach
The Benefit Management Approach is used to identify the benefits, the benefit measurements and the benefit reporting process.

The Benefit Management Approach should contain the "As-Is" measurement to allow the benefits to be compared. The measurements are collected and approved by the Senior User

The timeline for the reporting of the benefits is also contained, this should include, when they will materialise, who will gather the information, how long the reporting will be required

It is essential to remember, if a benefit cannot be measured then it should not be included within the Benefit Management Approach

The responsibility for the Benefits is defined below:

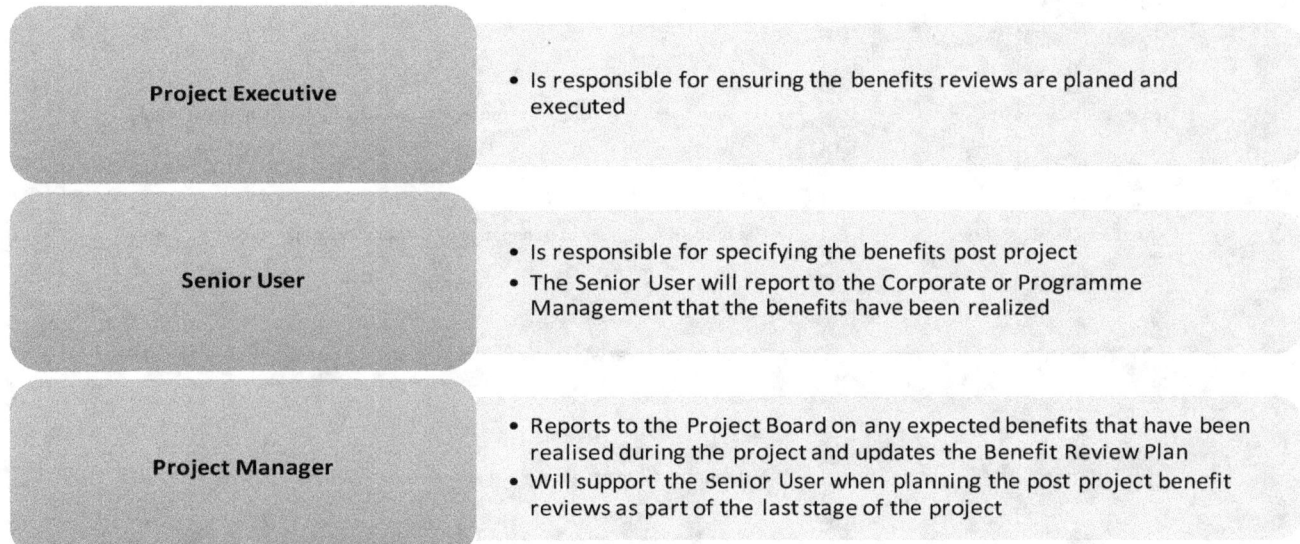

Figure 31 - Benefits Roles & Responsibilities

Contents of the Business Case
The Business Case should include the reasons for the project and the information on the estimated costs, risks, timeline and benefits.

According to Prince2 the Business Case should contain the following sections (as a minimum):

Executive Summary	• Highlights the key points within the Business Case and should include the reasons for the project, the benefits and the ROI
Reasons	• Defines the reasons for the project being undertaken and explains how the project will support the achievement of the corporate strategies and objectives
Business Options	• The analysis and recommendations for the business options - 　• Do Nothing 　• Do Minimal 　• Do Something
Expected Benefits	• The benefits that will be delivered by the project expressed in measureable terms
Expected Dis-Benefits	• The outcomes perceived as negative by one or more stakeholders.
Timescale	• The timescale over which the project will rune(A summary of the Project Plan)
Costs	• A summary of the project costs and ongoing operations
Investment Appraisal	• Compares the aggregated benefits and dis-benefits and ongoing incremental costs
Major Risks	• A summary of the major risks associated with the project

Figure 32 - Business Case Section\Details

Who is responsible for what within the Business Case?

Corporate or Program Management

Corporate or Program Management are responsible for the following information or actions in relation to the Business Case:

- Provide the Project Mandate which should or will include key information to support the Business Case
- Corporate or Program Management are primarily interested in the benefits of the project
- The Project Manager will report upon the benefits during the lifecycle of the project and update the Benefit Management Approach at key stages within the project
- Post project the Corporate or Program Management require the information in relation to the benefits and have the responsibility of monitoring the benefits ensuring they have been realised

Executive

The Executive is responsible for following in relation to the Business Case:

- Is responsible for the Business Case and the Benefit Management Approach during the project
- Is responsible for ensuring the products delivered by the project can be used as expected and meet the desired outcomes

Project Manager

The Project Manager is responsible for the following actions or information in relation to the Business Case

- Prince2 states that the Project Manager prepares the Business Case on behalf of the Executive, and this is the case in the real world, whereby the Project Manager will create and do most of the work in relation to the Business Case in relation to both the Outline and Detailed Business Case
- The Project Manager reviews the Business Case in relation to new Risks and Issues and will complete an impact analysis upon the Business Case when assessing risks or issues
- Reviews the Business Case at the end of each management stage and maintains the Benefit Management Approach during the project lifecycle

Project Assurance

Project Assurance are responsible for the following in relation to the Business Case

- Project Assurance provides an audit service to ensure that the project is proceeding as planned on behalf of the Executive
- Project Assurance can assist in the creation of the Business Case and can provide support monitoring the Business Case in relation to external events, remembering the Project Manager only monitors events internal to the project

Organisation

Introduction to the Organisation Theme

The Organisation Theme supports the establishment of the projects structure of accountability and responsibilities. It helps identify the "Who" in relation to the project

Prince2 states that a successful project should:

- Have Business, User and Supplier representation
- Have defined responsibilities for directing, managing and delivering the project
- Have regular reviews to ensure the project is on track
- Have a communication strategy to effectively manage the communication to and from stakeholders

Project Interests & Stakeholders

Prince2 states that a project should always have 3 primary stakeholders who have to be represented on the Project Board. These are the Business, User and Supplier

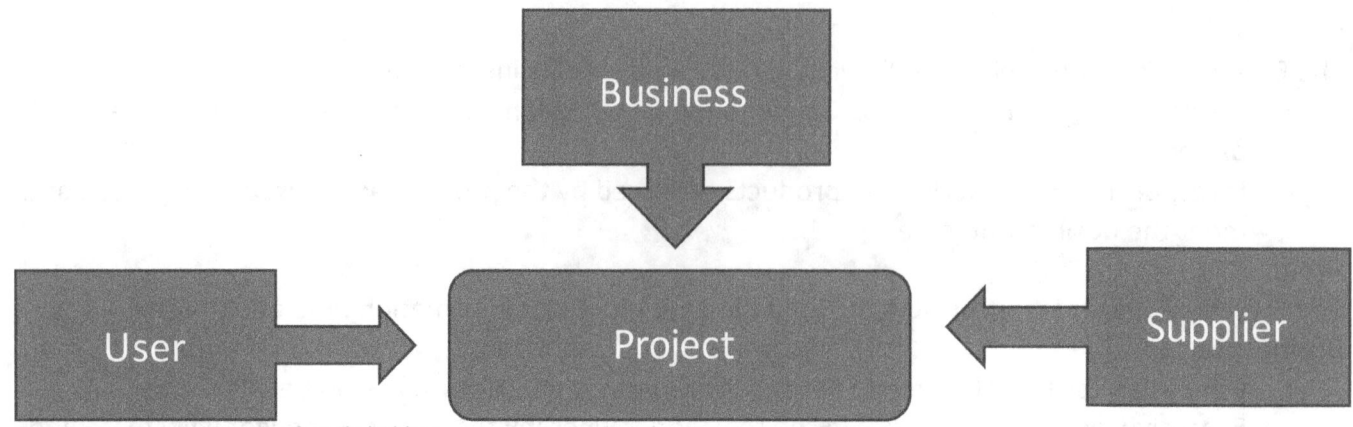

Figure 33 - Project Interests & Stakeholders

Business Interests
The Executive Role on the Project Board looks after the interests of the business and is responsible for ensuring the project is focused upon achieving its objectives and delivering a product that will achieve the forecasted benefits.

The Project Board is not a democracy, the Executive is ultimately responsible and is the decision maker supported by the Senior User and Supplier.

As with the Project Manager, there can be only one Executive assigned to the project

User Interests
The Senior User represents the user interests on the Project Board and is responsible for specifying the needs of those who will use the products delivered by the project. Within Prince2 the Users are also called customers.

The Senior User is also responsible for ensuring the product meets the needs of the users within the constraints of the Business Case in terms of quality, functionality and ease of use.

There can be more than one Senior User representing the users interests within the Project

Supplier Interests
The Supplier provides the resources and skills to create the products and can be internal of external. The Supplier is accountable for the quality of the products delivered and is responsible for the integrity of the project.

The can be more than one Supplier, and there may also be an independent person or group assigned to carry out assurance upon the products delivered by the supplier(s)

The Levels of Organisation
Within Prince2 it is crucial that you understand the difference between the Project Management Structure and the Project Management Team. Whilst the Project Management Structure has 4 levels, the Project Management Team has 3 levels

The Project Management Structure consists of:
1. Corporate or Program Management

2. Directing a Project
3. Managing a Project
4. Delivering

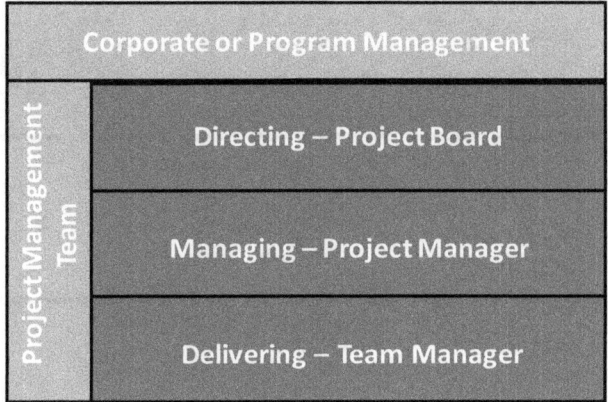

Figure 34 - Project Management Structure

The 3 levels of the Project Management Team are:
1. Directing a Project
2. Managing
3. Delivering

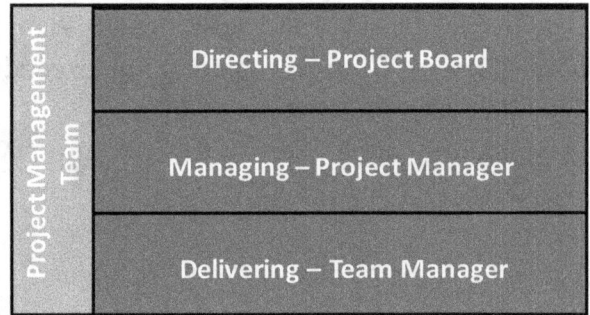

Figure 35 - Project Management Team

The only difference between the structures is that the Project Management Structure has the "Corporate or Program" who act as an escalation point for the Project Board. This is the reason Prince2 explains that the Corporate or Program Management sits outside of the Project Management Team

Corporate or Program Management
This level of management is outside the Project Management Team. The Corporate or Program Management is responsible for the commissioning of the project and identifying the Executive. They inform the Project Board how they will keep Corporate or Program Management updated and will also define the project tolerances the will apply to the project and that the Project Board will work to

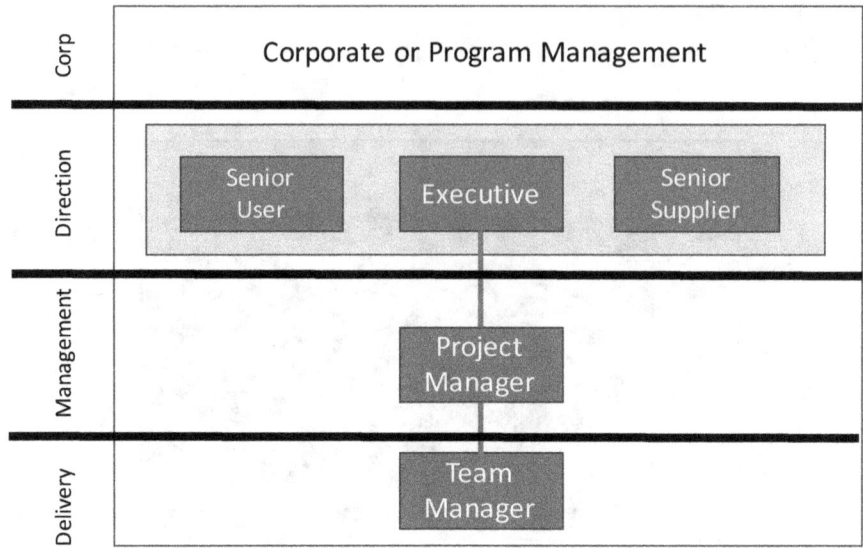

Figure 36 - Project Management Structure

The above diagram shows the simple view of the Project Management Structure

Directing Level
Within a Prince2 Project, the Project Board are responsible for providing Ad-Hoc direction and are accountable for the overall success of the project

- Approve all resources and major plans, For Example; Project Plan, Stage Plans
- Authorise any deviations if tolerances are forecasted to be exceeded or have exceeded
- Approve stage completion and authorise the next stage
- Communicate with stakeholders including Corporate or Program Management

Managing Level
The Project Manager is responsible for the overall day-2-day management of the project. The primary responsibility of the Project Manager is ensuring that the project produces the required products in accordance with the 6 aspects of the project management aligned to the Prince2 Methodology

1. Time
2. Cost
3. Quality
4. Scope
5. Risk
6. Benefits

Delivering Level
A Team Manager can have the authority to create Team Plans and manage a team to deliver the required products

The Team members are responsible for delivery of the products to the quality defined and within the timescales and costs approved.

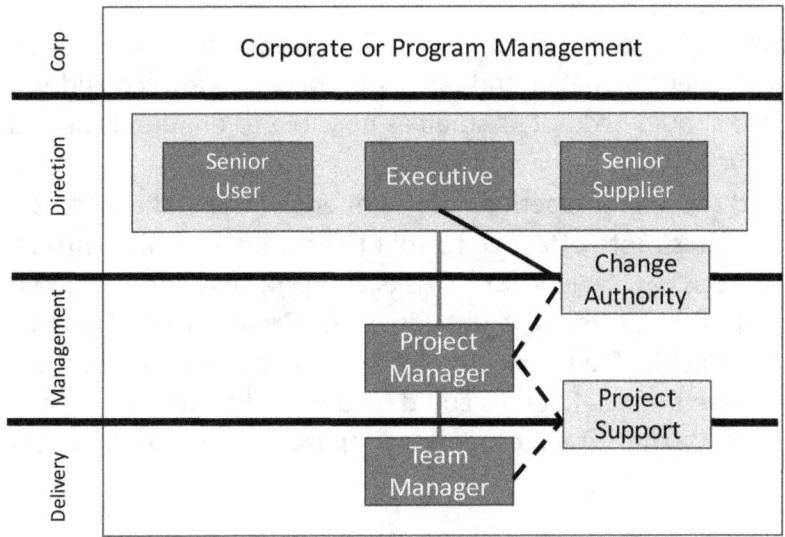

Figure 37 - Expanded Project Management Structure

Project Board

The Project Board within a Prince2 Project consists of the Executive, Senior User and Senior Supplier. As previously stated, there can only be on Project Executive assigned to a project. Senior User's and Senior Supplier's role may be assigned to multiple people, or can change during the lifecycle of the project

The Project Board has the following duties within the Project:
- Is accountable for the overall success or failure of the project
- Provides direction to the project and the Project Manager as required
- Provides the resources required and authorises the funds for the project
- Provides support to the Project Manager
- Sets the tolerances for the Project Manager in relation to Time, Cost etc
- Manages the effective communication within the project team and external stakeholders

Prince2 states that a Project Board should have 4 characteristics
1. Authority
2. Credibility
3. Ability to delegate
4. Availability – to support both the project and the Project Manager

Prince2 is very clear on these, and states that if a member of the Project Board does not meet one of these characteristics, they should be replaced.

The Project Board are usually senior people within the organisation and because of this, their time is often limited. This is where the concept of Management by Exception allows the Project Board to delegate to the Project Manager and allows them to be kept informed of progress, but more crucially only get involved when key decisions are needed.

The Project Manager communicates with the Project Board using the Highlight Report which is a regular report defined within the Communication Strategy and is a timed report providing progress updates on the current stage.

How big should the Project Board be?

Prince2 has a number of guidelines in relation to the Project Board, The Executive creates the Project Board supported by the Project Manager and takes the following into consideration:

- The Project Board should be kept as small as possible to enable decisions to be made more easily and effectively
- The Project Board should represent all of the needs of the stakeholders
- On larger projects, it is more effective to split Users and Suppliers into User Groups or Sub-Groups. These groups can review issues\risks and progress and provide recommendations to the Project Board. This is classed as outside of the Project Team Structure
- The Executive will decide if External Suppliers should be included in the Project Board. In some projects where financial details could be deemed commercially sensitive, it may be more prudent to have the Supplier meetings separate from the Project Board

Project Assurance

Project Assurance is the responsibility of the Project Board and each of the respective Project Board members are responsible for their own assurance.

The Executive is responsible for the Business Assurance:

- Ensuring that the business aspects of the project are correct
- Ensuring the project remains value for money

The Senior User is responsible for the User Assurance:

- Will the project deliver the correct products and will it meet the expected requirements?
- Ensures the products work as expected

The Senior Supplier is responsible for the Supplier Assurance:

- Are the products being delivered as expected, are the right materials and people in place to complete the work
- Ensures the products are completed within Time and Costs etc.

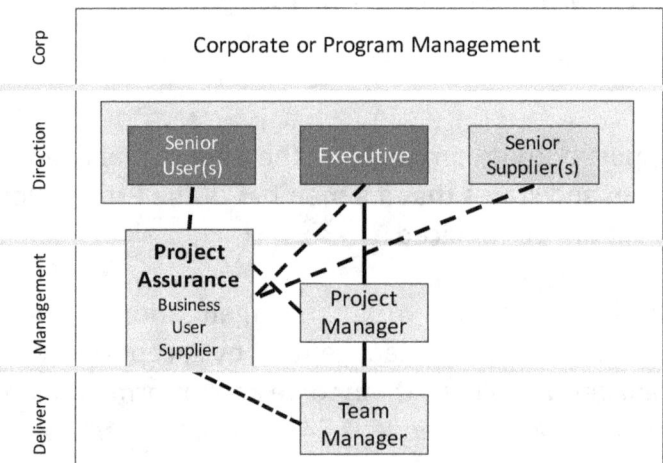

Figure 38 - Project Management Structure - Assurance Roles

The Project Board can choose to undertake the role of Project Assurance themselves, however it is more normal for this to be assigned to others within the organisation who have the necessary skills and time to support the project.

Project Assurance should not be focused on finding things the Project Manager is not doing, but should be focused upon providing support for the Project Manager ensuring they aware of additional things that could be used in the project. The Project Assurance should be available to support the Project Manager as a delegate of the Project Board

Change Authority

The Change Authority role delegated by the Project Board to a person or persons with the responsibility of considering requests for change or off-specifications. The Project Board may delegate financial authority or approval of tolerances in relation to Time, Costs, Quality, Scope.

The Change Authority can be assigned to the Project Board, a separate group or the Project Manager or a mix of the above and depending upon the severity of the change.

Other conditions can be set by the Project Board within the Managing by Exception, effectively assigning tolerances to the Project Manager or those assigned to the Change Authority

The Project Manager Role

The Project Manager primarily manages the project on a day-2-day basis and is the only person with this day-2-day focus on the project. The role can NEVER be shared, there can be Project Managers assigned to the supplier and the user, however there is only one Project Manager assigned to the project who is responsible for the control and delivery of the project

The Project Manager runs the project on behalf of the Project Board within the tolerances and constraints agreed and liaises with the Project Board and Project Assurance. The Project Manager is usually assigned from the customer or on the customers behalf and has the responsibility for all areas of the project except the "Directing a Project" and the activities with the Starting up a Project Process (SU) of assigning the Executive and the Project Manager

The Project Manager is also responsible for the Project Support and Team Manager, however in smaller projects there may be no Team Managers and this role is completed by the Project Manager. The Project Manager will manage Team Member directly. As with the Team Manager duties, if there is no Project Support function, these duties also become the responsibility of the Project Manager

Team Manager

The Team Manager role is optional, however is usually included in a project to ensure the quality of the products created and management of the specialist teams

The Team Manager role is usually used within projects if:
- The project is large and has large numbers of Team Members to manage
- If the project requires specialist skills or knowledge of the products required
- If the specialist teams are geographically dispersed, a Team Manager is key to the project success
- When the project is using external resources, the Team Manager role is often critical in managing the relationship and coordinating the resources

The Team Manager has the responsibility for the production of the products that are assigned in the Work Packages by the Project Manager. The Team Manager is also responsible for providing regular updates to the Project Manager, these can be informal however, Prince2 recommends the use of the Checkpoint Report and that this is agreed within the Work Package

The Team Manager creates the Team Plans to manage the development of the assigned products contained with the Work Packages, however again remember – the Team Plan is an optional plan within Prince2

The Team Manager reports to the Project Manager, in some instances this can mean that a Team Manager is higher within the organisation, however in this instance the Team Manager still reports to the Project Manager for the duration of the project

Project Support

The Project Support role provides key support to the Project Manager and the project, these are (but not limited to):

- Administrative support, advice, guidance on the use of the tools
- Planning support
- Risk and Issue management
- Financial Management (Processing payments etc)

Project Support is typically responsible for the Configuration Management within the project and follows the guidelines contained within the Configuration Management approach

The role of Project Support is not optional within Prince2, however in some organisations this role may not exist and it is also dependent upon the size of the project. In these scenarios, the duties of Project Support fall to the Project Manager.

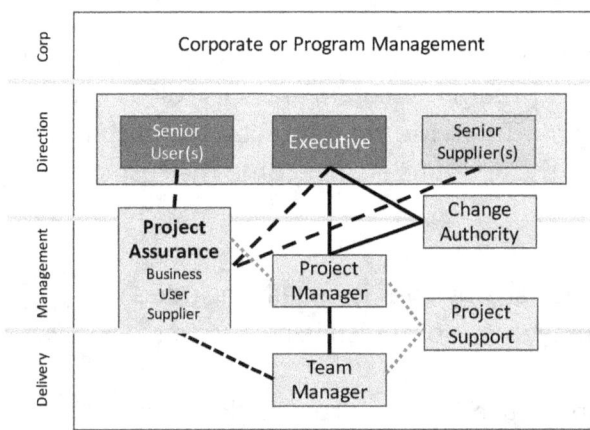

Figure 39 - Detailed Project Management Structure

Stakeholder Engagement

What is Stakeholder Engagement? Within Prince2, Stakeholder Engagement is the process of identifying and effectively communicating with those people or groups who have an interest in the projects outcome.

Managing these relationships supports achieving positive outcomes and increases the chances of the projects success.

The Communication Management Strategy
The Communication Management Strategy is a document that defines the in detail how communication will be managed during the lifecycle of the project.

- What is being communicated
- To Who
- How it will be communicated
- How often information will be communicated

The contents of the Communication Management Strategy are:

- An outline of the project
- An overview of the document and its purpose
- Reporting – the types of reports, what they should contain and when they will be sent
- Frequency of the communication
- Communication procedures and methods
- Tools & Techniques to be used
- Timing of the communication activities
- Roles & Responsibilities
- Stakeholder Analysis – types of stakeholder, positive or negative stakeholders

Organization Responsibilities
The responsibilities for the Organization Theme are:

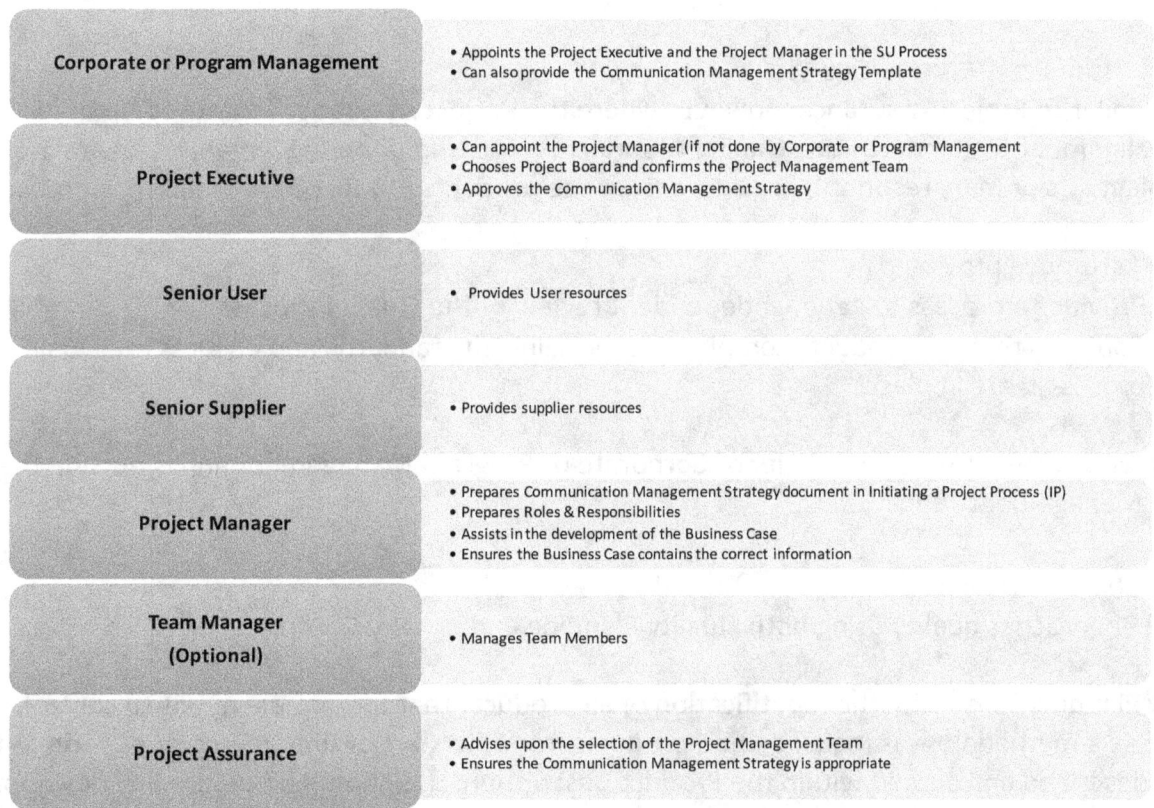

Figure 40 - Organisation Theme Responsibilities

Quality

Introduction to Quality

The definition of Quality within Prince2 is

"The total features and inherent assigned characteristics of a product, person, process, service and\or system that bears on its ability to show that it meets expectations or satisfies the needs, requirements or specification"

Which is a very long-winded way of saying "it is fit for purpose"

Prince2 approaches quality using Quality Planning and Quality Control

Quality Planning

The Project Manager must have a strategy in place that involves identifying the necessary products and the quality criteria for each of the products created, the tasks necessary for the quality control and the product acceptance criteria, including identification of those responsible for the quality control

Quality Control

Quality Control is the process of monitoring the specific project results to determine whether they comply with the relevant standards and of identifying the ways to eliminate causes of unsatisfactory performance.

Quality Control focuses upon the techniques and activities to inspect, test and approve the products created by the project. This could also include the process to improve Quality and remove areas or products that are unsatisfactory

Quality Assurance

This is similar to Project Assurance, however where the Project Assurance is focused upon Project and its alignment to standards etc, Quality Assurance is focused upon the Organisation and not just the project. Its primary responsibility is to ensure the products produced will be fit for purpose

Quality Assurance provides:

- Provides a process to get an independent review of the Quality Process
- Confirms that the products comply with the relevant standards and ensures the Quality processes are in place

Quality Assurance is the responsibility of Corporate or Program Management and is outside the Project Management Team

The Approach to Quality

Prince2 approaches quality using both Quality Planning and Quality Control

Quality Planning starts with the identification of all products that the project needs to control, Prince2 as a methodology is focused upon products from the start of the project, or as soon as they can be described and agreed within the Product Description, this should be before any development starts

A Product Description is written for each product, and this includes the Quality criteria, how each product will be assessed, what Quality methods will be used to design, develop and most importantly how the products will be accepted and the people involved including their responsibilities

Quality Control implements and tracks the Quality methods that will be used during the project

Quality Planning – an overview and introduction

Quality Planning is used to:

1. Document and agree on the overall Quality Expectations with the Project Board:
2. Document the Quality criteria
3. Document how the Quality Criteria will be checked
4. Communicate these agreements with all stakeholders
5. Ensure that all stakeholders have a common understanding of what the project will produce
6. Establish how Quality can be controlled during the project
7. Agree and document baselines and tolerances for each product

If these topics are not discussed and agreed up front, it can make for an entertaining project, that risks changes in scope, delays or even a potentially cancelled project

The following questions should be asked in Quality Planning:

1. What are the Quality Expectations of the customer?
2. How can the project prove that each specification has been met?
3. What is the Acceptance Criteria that the Customer will use to accept products during or at the end of the project?

Quality Planning - The path to Quality

The Quality Planning process ensures that the projects chances of success are increased by defining what these quality expectations are, the Quality Planning steps are listed below:

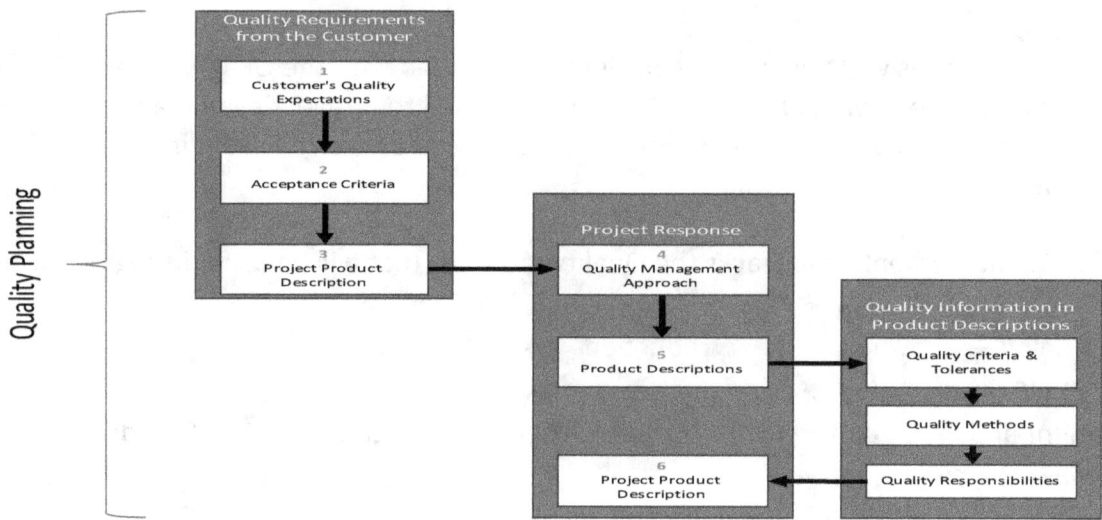

Figure 41 - The Path to Quality

The steps Quality Planning are:

1. Gather the customers Quality Expectations: This is a very general, high-level definition of the customer expectations and:
   a. The Key Requirements for the main product (**Project Product**) to be produced
   b. Identify standards that must be met and the Quality Management System to use.
   c. Measurements that can be used to assess Quality
2. Document the Acceptance Criteria and include these in the Project Product Description
3. Document the Project Product Description and include:
   a. The Project Level Tolerances in relation to the main product
   b. The Acceptance methods that will be used defining how main project product will be accepted
   c. The Acceptance Responsibilities documenting who will be responsible for the acceptance of the main product
4. Create the Quality Management Approach
5. Document the Product Descriptions for each of the main products and all products that make up the main product and include:
   a. The Quality Criteria for each product
   b. The Quality Method that will be used for each product
   c. The Quality Responsibilities for creating, quality checking and the approval of the product
6. Setup the Quality Register

Customer's Quality Expectation

The customers quality expectations are a clear statement upon which the quality levels are defined and should include the following:

- Key quality requirements for the main product being delivered by the project
- Any standards or process that must be met to ensure acceptance
- Any measures that will support the acceptance of the product and could also be used to assess the overall success of the project

These requirements will support the choice of the overall solution being delivered and in turn could influence the Time, Costs, Scope, Risk and Benefits relating to the project

Where possible these expectations should be prioritized to support the tolerances in relation to the main product

Whilst Prince2 does not specify any techniques, a common technique used for prioritisation is the MoSCoW technique

1. M – Must have
2. S – Should have
3. C – Could have
4. W – Won't have for now

Or the simple High, Medium and Low prioritisation method could be used

Listing Acceptance Criteria

The Acceptance Criteria are a list of requirements, attributes or statements that the project product must have upon completion. This is agreed between the customer and the supplier as early as possible within the project process and documented within the Project Product Description.

Once the Acceptance Criteria is complete, it will become part of the Project Brief. It is important that the Acceptance Criteria are also prioritised to ensure the right areas are focused upon, again the MoSCoW technique can be used for this

The Project Product Description

The Project Product Description is the product description of the main product that will be delivered by the project upon completion of all sub products that make up the product.

A simpler way of understanding this is a car

The Project Product Description for a car would be at a much higher level than that of the components for example it would contain high level information like:

- The car should have 4 wheels and a spare wheel in the event of emergencies
- Should have a minimum of 4 seats with 2 in the front
- Should meet all safety and regulatory requirements
- Should have a minimum of 3 engine choices
- Should come in petrol, diesel and hybrid models
- Should come in 2 & 4 door option with the investigation into a convertible model

Note these are high or helicopter level requirements and don't go into much detail compared to a Product Description

Each of the above statements could be turned into acceptance criteria and also prioritised

Quality Management approach

The Quality Management approach is a plan of action defining the Quality requirements and the Quality methods that will form the controls for the products that will be created by the project. This document also details the Quality Systems, any Quality Standards that are required to be met from both the customer and the supplier

The Quality Management approach defines how Quality will be met within the project, it is created during the Initiation Stage and then forms part of the Project Initiation Documentation

Product Descriptions

The Product Descriptions are created for each of the sub products that will be created by the project that when completed will form the main product that is being delivered, if we go back to the car example.

The high-level requirement of "Should have a minimum of 4 seats with 2 in the front" would be broken into a level of detail that would enable the actual creation of the product, the testing of it and subsequently the acceptance upon completion of its development

The Product Descriptions are not always created at the beginning of the project as there is insufficient detail and Prince2 allows for this by using the Managing Stage Boundary Process (SB), Product Descriptions are either created or updated within the Stage Boundary Process and these Product Descriptions must be agreed and baselined before any development commences

Quality Register

The Quality Register is a log of the Quality events that will occur during the project. These could be workshops, brainstorming sessions, reviews, unit testing, functional testing, non-functional testing or acceptance tests.

At the beginning of the project the Quality Register will be a blank document, however it is a crucial document that should be managed and the information to support this will come from areas within the Project Plan, the Project Product Description and the Product Descriptions

The Quality Register should contain at the minimum the following information:
1. Product ID — A unique id no assigned to each product
2. Product Name — A simple common name for each product
3. Quality Method — A description of how the testing will be completed upon the product once it
   is completed
4. Target Review Date — When the product should be reviewed
5. Actual Approval Date —When the product was actually approved
6. Results — Pass or Fail
7. Remarks — Any remarks ascertaining to the product or its development

The Quality Register will also have the information in relation to the roles of the Producer, the Quality Reviewer and the Approver who will be used within the Quality Review process for the acceptance of the product

The Quality Register is a live document and is updated throughout the project to provide a full audit trail of all Quality related activities

Quality Control

Quality Control is the process of carrying out any activities that control Quality as defined within the Quality Management Approach. Prince2 defines Quality Control as having 3 parts

1. Carrying out the Quality Method's – Quality Reviews etc
2. Maintaining Quality and Approval Records – The Quality Management Approach and Quality Register
3. Acceptance and Approval Records and providing the customer with the Acceptance Records

All of this information is contained (as stated in No2) within the Quality Management Strategy and the Quality Register

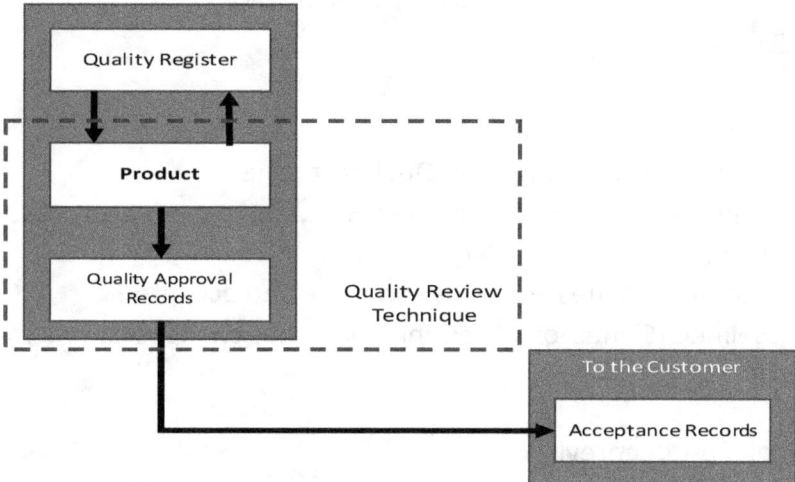

Figure 42 - - Quality Review Method\Technique

Quality Review Technique

Prince2 has a Quality Review Technique that has defined roles and responsibilities and defined structure to be followed. This is ensuring that products are inspected and they meet the expectations of the customers and that they meet the Quality criteria defined within the Product Description

These roles are the Chairperson, Presenter, Reviewer and the Administrator

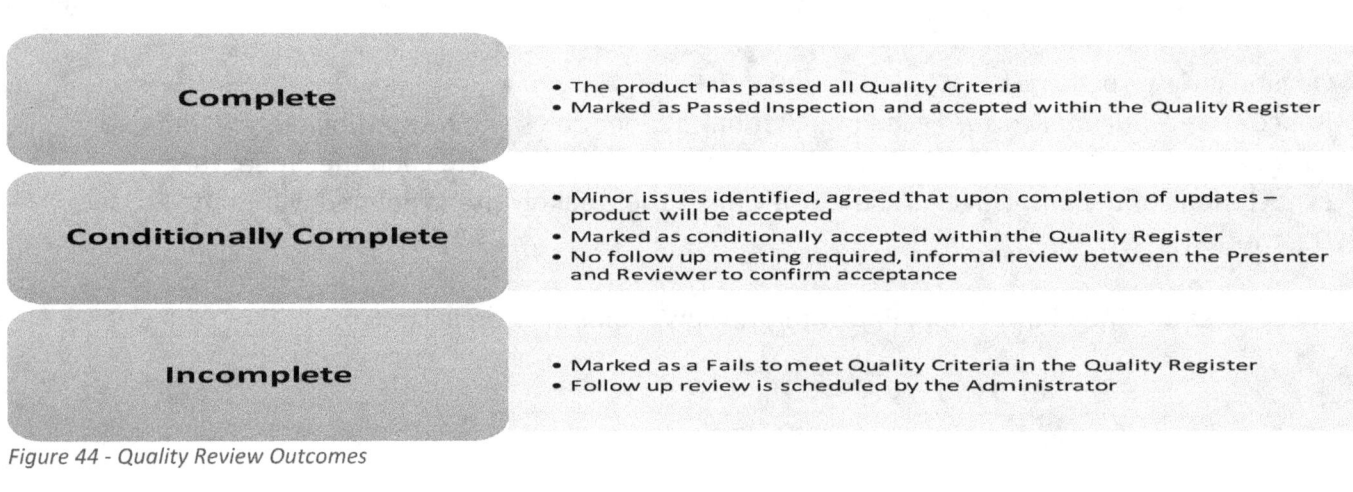

Chair	• Responsible for chairing the review meeting • Can be anyone who is capable of managing the meeting and controlling the process
Presenter	• Presents the products and represents the interests of those who produced the products • Normally from the Supplier Team or Team Manager
Reviewer	• Suppliers who provide the resources and the expertise required by the project • Reviews the products, submits questions or queries, confirms acceptance or rejection • Suggest improvements
Administrator	• Provides admin support for the chairperson • Arranges the meeting, takes minutes and circulates meeting minutes and any approvals\rejections

Figure 43 - Quality Review Roles & Responsibilities

The objectives of the Quality Review Technique are to:

- Assess the products against their agreed Quality criteria
- Ensures key stakeholders are involved in the review and approval process ensuring continued Quality within the project
- Provides confirmation that the product is complete and accepted
- Products are baselined (Signed-off) ensuring no further changes can be made without agreement

There are 3 outcomes of a product review

Complete	• The product has passed all Quality Criteria • Marked as Passed Inspection and accepted within the Quality Register
Conditionally Complete	• Minor issues identified, agreed that upon completion of updates – product will be accepted • Marked as conditionally accepted within the Quality Register • No follow up meeting required, informal review between the Presenter and Reviewer to confirm acceptance
Incomplete	• Marked as a Fails to meet Quality Criteria in the Quality Register • Follow up review is scheduled by the Administrator

Figure 44 - Quality Review Outcomes

Quality Responsibilities

Quality is a Theme that underpins the project and is key to ensuring the overall success of the project. The responsibilities for Quality are listed below:

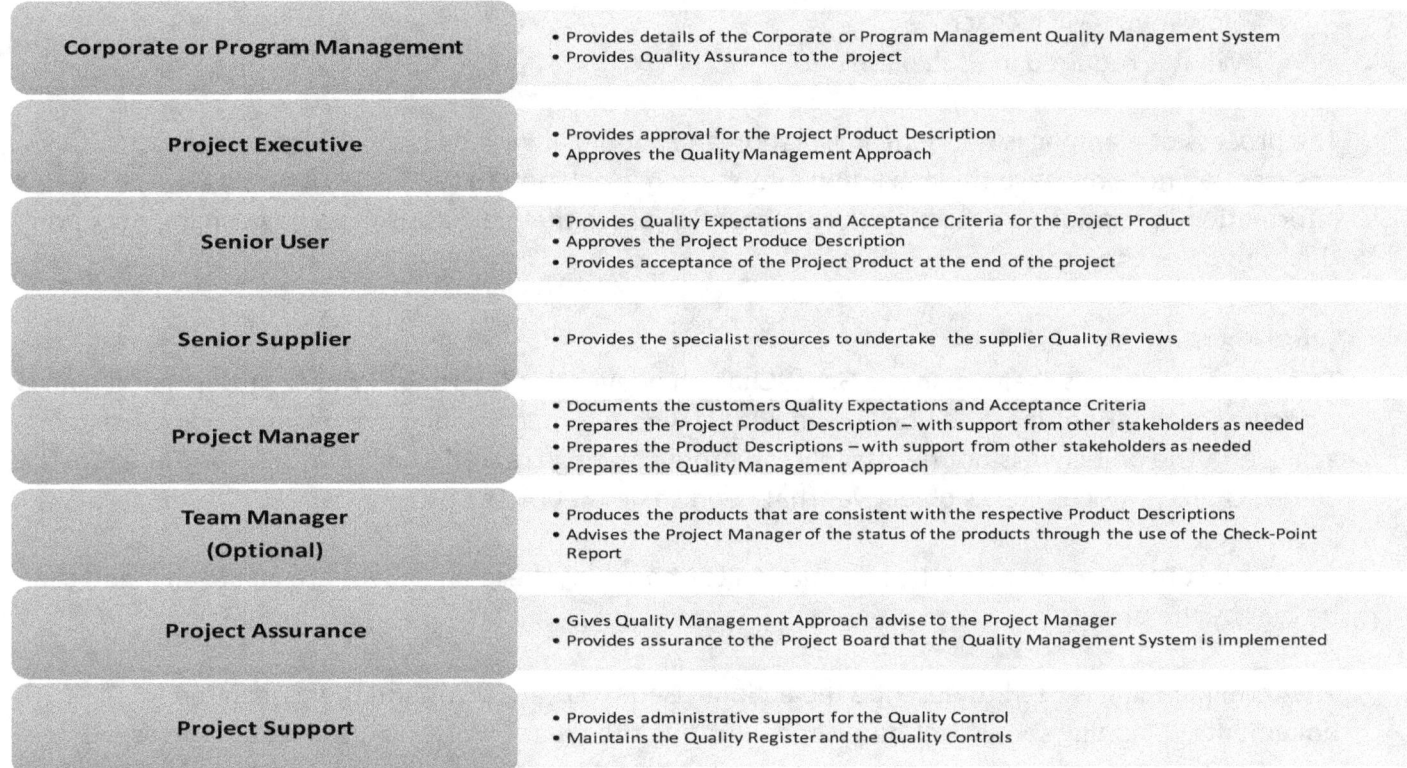

Corporate or Program Management	• Provides details of the Corporate or Program Management Quality Management System • Provides Quality Assurance to the project
Project Executive	• Provides approval for the Project Product Description • Approves the Quality Management Approach
Senior User	• Provides Quality Expectations and Acceptance Criteria for the Project Product • Approves the Project Produce Description • Provides acceptance of the Project Product at the end of the project
Senior Supplier	• Provides the specialist resources to undertake the supplier Quality Reviews
Project Manager	• Documents the customers Quality Expectations and Acceptance Criteria • Prepares the Project Product Description – with support from other stakeholders as needed • Prepares the Product Descriptions – with support from other stakeholders as needed • Prepares the Quality Management Approach
Team Manager (Optional)	• Produces the products that are consistent with the respective Product Descriptions • Advises the Project Manager of the status of the products through the use of the Check-Point Report
Project Assurance	• Gives Quality Management Approach advise to the Project Manager • Provides assurance to the Project Board that the Quality Management System is implemented
Project Support	• Provides administrative support for the Quality Control • Maintains the Quality Register and the Quality Controls

Figure 45 - Quality Roles & Responsibilities

Plans

Introduction to the Plans Theme

The purpose of the Plans Theme is to facilitate the communication and control of the project by defining the means of delivering the products (the where, the how and the by who) and estimating the when and how much

Planning in Pricne2 is perceived to be very rigid however it is the opposite, Prince2 allows you to create a helicopter Project Plan within the Initiation Stage and then allows the constant refresh of this Plan and the creation of Stage Plans for the subsequent delivery stages.

This is often called "rolling wave planning" whereby we only plan in detail for what we now and then we plan in detail for the next stage when we know more

The Plans Theme provides a framework to design, develop and maintain the Project Plans, which are
- Project Plan
- Stage Plan or Exception Plan
- Team Plan

It helps answer the following questions
- What is required?
- When is it required?
- How will be achieved and by whom?
- How will the products be created and by whom?
- What are the steps required to create the products?
- What levels of Quality must be achieved to ensure acceptance?

- How much will it cost?
- What is required in each plan?

The process of planning is not done in isolation and should always be a collaborative approach, this ensures you not only have the maximum information in relation to the plan but also have information in relation to possible risks or potential issues that could arise and have an impact upon the product or the project

What is a plan?

This misconception is that a plan is a Gantt Chart, however this is wrong. Prince2 states that a plan is a document that describes the how, when and by whom a specific objective or set of objectives are achieved. The objective is not necessarily the product being created, there may also be Time, Cost, Scope, Quality, Risk, Benefits objectives that need to be met by the project

A plan must therefore contain the information to show that these objectives are achievable and can be met by the project

The term planning is used to describe the actions used to create plans and the associated documents. Planning should not be rushed. Rushing the creation of a plan will result is missed information, over ambitious schedules that cannot be achieved causing perceived delays when in effect it is not a delay as the project was incorrectly planned in the beginning by rushing

The three levels of a plan

As mentioned previously, there are 3 levels of plan within Prince2, the use of these three levels supports the real-world fact that in very rare cases can you plan a complete project at the beginning, you can only plan a short distance ahead in time. This is called the Planning Horizon – i.e. only as far ahead as you can see

The three levels of plan within Prince2 are

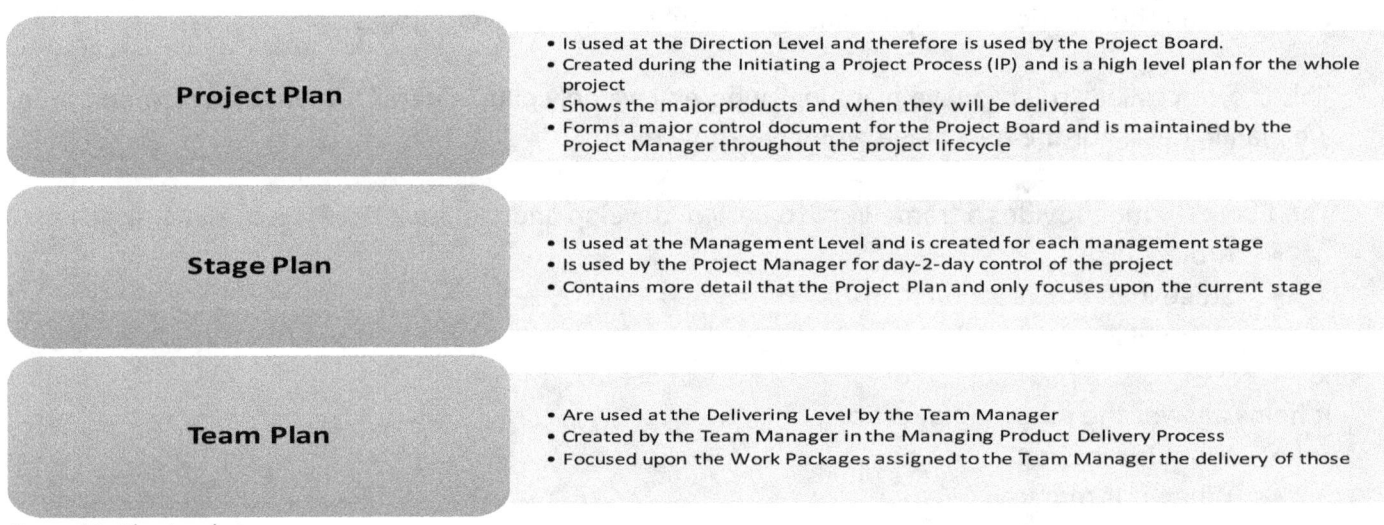

Project Plan
- Is used at the Direction Level and therefore is used by the Project Board.
- Created during the Initiating a Project Process (IP) and is a high level plan for the whole project
- Shows the major products and when they will be delivered
- Forms a major control document for the Project Board and is maintained by the Project Manager throughout the project lifecycle

Stage Plan
- Is used at the Management Level and is created for each management stage
- Is used by the Project Manager for day-2-day control of the project
- Contains more detail that the Project Plan and only focuses upon the current stage

Team Plan
- Are used at the Delivering Level by the Team Manager
- Created by the Team Manager in the Managing Product Delivery Process
- Focused upon the Work Packages assigned to the Team Manager the delivery of those

Figure 46 - Plan Levels

The other plan mentioned in Prince2 is the Exception Plan, which is created at the request of the Project Board in response to a forecasted tolerance being exceeded or in the event a tolerance has been exceeded. An Exception Report will be provided with a recommendation upon which the Project Board if accepted will request an Exception Plan

The Exception Plan will replace the Project Plan, Stage Plan or Benefit Management Approach as appropriate.

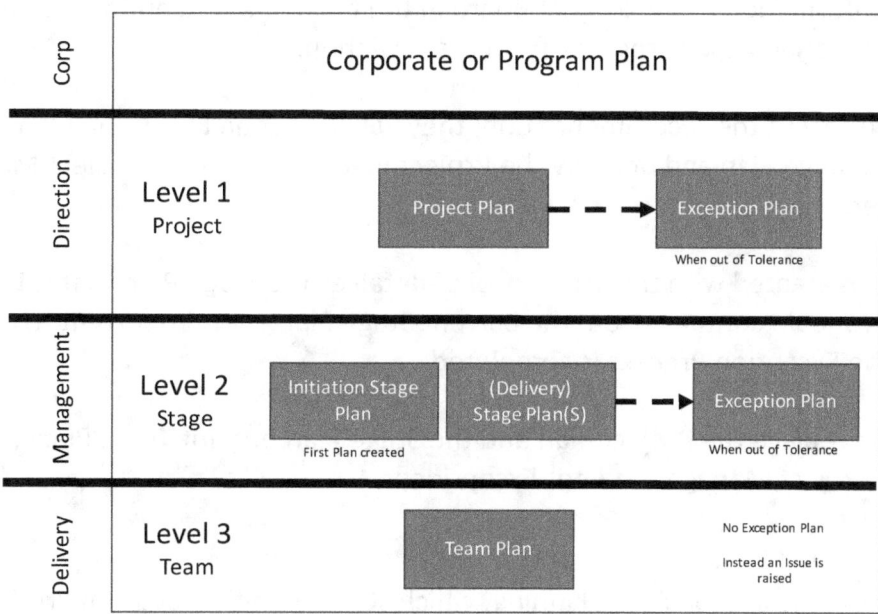

Figure 47- Plan Levels

The Project Plan, Stage Plan and Team Plan

The Project Plan

The Project Plan is a high-level plan (a Helicopter Level plan is a description often used) and used mainly by the Project Board. It provides a clear statement of the how and when a projects time, cost, scope and quality targets are going to be achieved. It also shows the major products, the activities and the resources required to the project

It is used as a baseline to monitor the progress stage-by-stage, allowing the review at the end of each stage against the forecasted plan

The Stage Plan

Is required for each stage of the project. The Stage is similar in content to the Project Plan but contains much more detail to allow the Project Manager to manage and monitor the progress on a day-2-day level. The Project Plan is the high level and the Stage Plans are the low-level plans

Each Stage Plan is created near the end of the current management stage – note the wording! It is not created at the end of the stage, but NEAR THE END OF THE STAGE. The advantages of using stages and numerous but some of the more obvious ones are

- Allows larger projects to be broken into manageable chunks allowing more control
- Breaking into stages often de-risks the projects by allowing more focused management of the deliverables
- Allows the planning of the next stage using the lessons learned from the current stage

Team Plans

Whilst listed as option in Prince2, Team Plans are often crucial to the success of the project by allowing the Project Manager to liaise with the Team Manager and monitor the progress of the associated Work Package.

The Team Manager is responsible for the creation of the Team Plan, Team Plans can be from internal suppliers or external suppliers depending upon the configuration of your project

The Exception Plan – Tolerance

The Exception Plan is used to recover from the impact or effect of a deviation of Tolerance.

For example – If the Project Manager has forecasted that the delivery of a key product will be delayed by 3 weeks and the allocated tolerance only allows for a 1 week delay, the Project Manager must provide this information to the Project Board in the form of an Exception Report which will include a recommendation how to recover from the deviation.

If the Project Board accept the recommendation, they will ask for an Exception Plan which will replace the current Stage Plan and possibly the Project Plan and allow the Project Manager to complete the current stage

The Exception Plan is created with the same level of detail as the Stage Plan that is being replaced, The Exception plan should continue from the current Stage Plan – it is important to note that work continues whilst the Exception Process is completed.

Exception Plans can replace the Project Plan and the Stage Plan but not Team Plans, Team Manager raise issues to the Project Manager and not Exceptions

The Prince2 Approach to Planning

Prince2 has a very unique approach to planning, which starts with the focus on Products. It starts with the identification of the Products required and then considers the activities, resources and dependencies required to deliver the products.

Prince2 uses a 7-step approach to planning

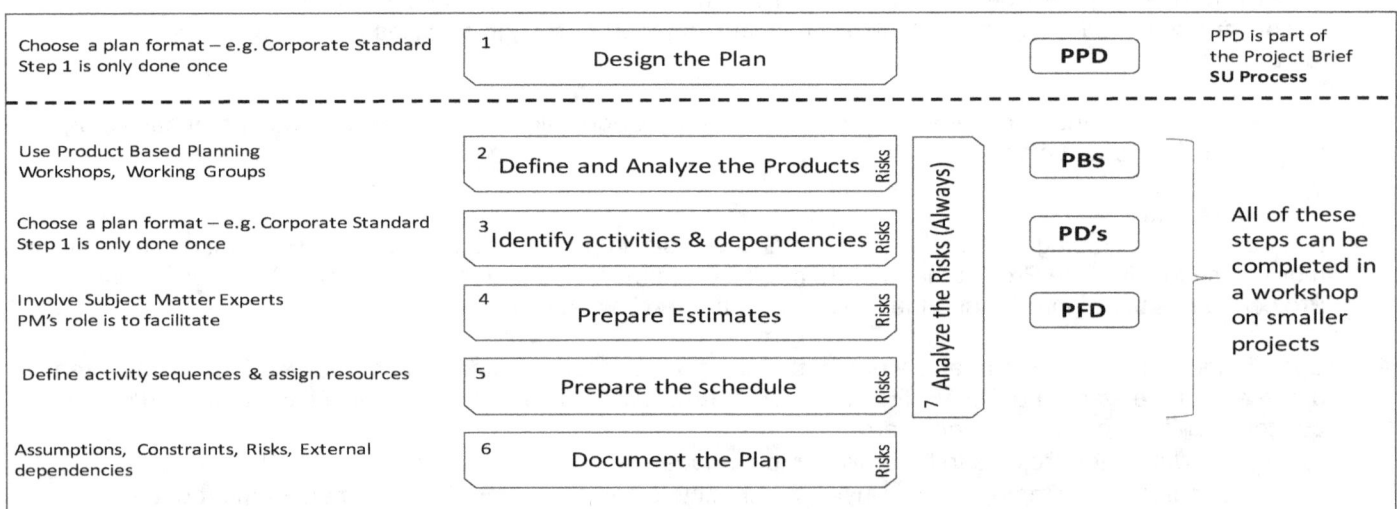

Figure 48 - Approach to Planning

These steps are taken to create the Project Plan, Stage Plan and can support the creation of the Team Plan

The 7-Steps to Planning

Step 1 – Designing the Plan

This depends upon the maturity of your organisation, in essence if your organisation has mature process that is embedded. Designing the plan is simply using the provided template.

Some guidance on designing the Plan
- Think about how the data will be accessed and who will be using it
- Think about the tools available to you and your stakeholders, not all member of the project will have access to MS Project for example
- Consider the tools you will use for the tasks such as estimating, planning and monitoring
- The use of planning tools can save time and also highlight potential issues within the project

Step 2 – Product Based Planning

Prince2 uses a technique called Product Based Planning to identify and analyse the product's that are planned within the project.

There are 3 steps to Product Based Planning – These are:

1. Write the Project Product Description   Describe the main product (in SU)
2. Create the Product Breakdown Structure   List all products that need to be created
3. Create the Product Description   Required for all products needed to make the

    Project Product

4. Create the Product Flow Diagram   Shows the Product development path and inter-

    dependencies

Product Based Planning is an iterative process and has a number of benefits, it allows the following:
- Clearly identifies all products required to form the main Project Product
- Highlights the inter-dependencies within the products
- Clearly shows what is involved and required to deliver the Project Product and therefore manages expectations
- Involves all stakeholders
- Clarifies the scope – what is in scope and what is out of scope
- Makes it easier to gain approval of what is needed

| High Level Description with quality requirements & acceptance criteria | 1 Write the Project Product Description | PPD | PPD is part of the Project Brief **SU Process** |

A diagram showing an overview of the products be created during the project	2 Create the Product Breakdown Structure	PBS	
Write the Product Descriptions for major products and include the Quality information	3 Write the Product Description's	PD's	All of these steps can be completed in a workshop on smaller projects
A diagram showing the sequence of events * inter-dependencies	4 Create the Product Flow Diagrams	PFD	

Figure 49 - Product Based Planning

Step 3 - The Project Product Description (PPD)

The Project Product Description (PPD) is the first step in the Product Based Planning technique, this is a description of the main product that the project will produce (For example a new car). This is crucial and links to the Quality Theme allowing everyone on the Project to understand what the project will produce and understand the required level of quality to be accepted

The Senior User is responsible for providing the information to support the creation of the Project Product Description. The Project Manager will coordinate the work required to prepare this document. The Executive, Senior User and other stakeholders will be consulted to ensure the Project Product Description is as detailed and complete as possible.

It is not always possible to fully define and document the Project Product Description at the start of the project, so it is not unusual for it to be refined during the Initiation Stage. New Product Descriptions can be created during the project and this will form part of the Stage Boundary Process as part of the planning the next stage. Product Descriptions need to be baselined before any development can start.

Step 4 - Create the Product Breakdown Structure

By breaking the project down into the major products being created and then taking them down a further level to give a hierarchical view of the project is called the Product Breakdown Structure (PBS)

(See Appendix C for more information on Product Breakdown Structures)

A MindMap can also be used for this purpose, it is often recommended to start with a MindMap and then use the information to create the Product Descriptions

When creating the Product Breakdown Structure is it worth considering the following:
- Involving a group of people in a workshop environment to represent the different interests of the project. For example, stakeholders such as the Senior User, Supplier, Subject Matter Experts

- Use facilitation techniques like post-its, whiteboards, to gather information to support the create of the Product Breakdown Structure

An example of a Product Breakdown Structure is below again using the car example

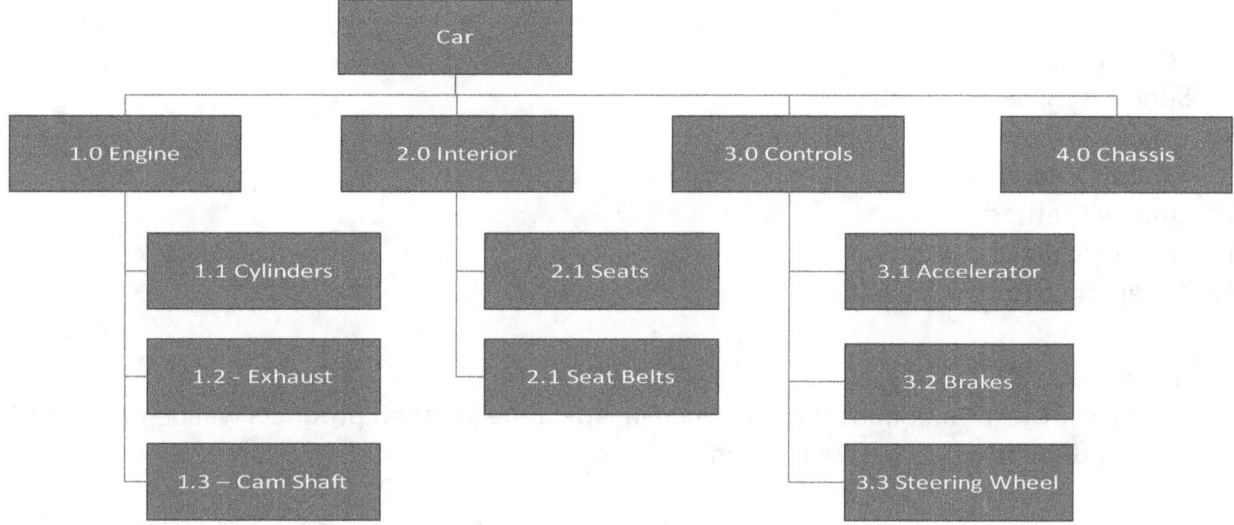

Figure 50 - Example Product Breakdown Structure

Note that when creating Product Breakdown Structure the number sequence is sequential, so the process is as follows

The Engine is Product Description 1.0
The Cylinders are Product Description 1.1
The Exhaust is Product Description 1.2
Etc

This denotes that all Product Descriptions with numerical sequence starting with a 1 are related to the Product that is the engine, this enables the project to understand the dependencies relating to the engine and the products that must be competed to complete the engine

Step 5 - Writing Product Descriptions
A Product Description is written for each of the identified products in the Product Breakdown Structure. When writing them some useful points to consider are below:
- Writing the Product Descriptions should be completed as soon as the products are identified and should involve the necessary stakeholders to ensure as much information and the Quality Criteria is documented
- Upon completion of the Project Plan, the Product Descriptions are baselined and are then under change control to ensure the project scope is managed
- The Users should be represented and involved in defining the Quality Criteria for each of the Products identified
- In Projects where Products have been developed or delivered previously and are classed as standard or off-the-shelf products that require no change, the existing Product Descriptions could be used
- For smaller projects, it may be possible to only write the Project Product Description

The Product Description should contain the following information as a minimum:
1. Unique Product ID
2. Title
3. Purpose
4. Composition
5. Source Products
6. Format
7. Specialist Skills Required
8. Quality Criteria
9. Quality Tolerance
10. Quality Method
11. Quality Skills Required
12. Acceptance Responsibilities

Product Flow Diagram

The Product Flow Diagram defines the sequence in which the planned products will be developed and shows the dependencies between them

The diagram shows the products that are outside the scope of the plan as dependencies or external products

The Product Flow Diagram supports the planning activities that are required as well as the estimating and scheduling activities (see Appendix C for more information on Product Flow Diagrams)

Identify Activities and Dependencies

The objective is to make a list of all activities that are required, the Product Based Planning Techniques support this and enable a much simpler process of documenting these activities and the sequence of the products and their development

The dependencies between the activities should be identified and noted. There are two types of dependencies – Internal and External

Internal Dependencies are those within the project and External Dependencies are outside of the project

Prepare Estimates

Estimating is the decision upon how much time and how many resources are required to complete the required work to an acceptable standard ensuring it meets the required Quality Criteria. The Project Manager should do as little of the estimating as possible, it is better to have the subject matter experts provide the estimates.

The Project Manager can facilitate this by using workshops and this can be completed in the same workshop as the Product Based Planning under ideal circumstances

Estimating involves identifying the type of resource required, the specific skills, specialist equipment and approximating the effort required for each activity

Prepare the Schedule

Preparing the schedule often means using a computer based tool. The Project Manager should have a list of activities, the dependencies and the approximate duration of the effort required to complete the activity.

This information supports the schedule creation and the Project Manager will use some of the steps below carry out this process:

1. A defined list of activities
2. Assessment of resources and their availability
3. Assign resources
4. Level the resource usage (using the required tools)
5. Agree control points
6. Define the milestones
7. Define the critical path
8. Calculate the total resource requirements and costs associated
9. Present the schedule for approval

If like most Project Managers you have done this before the ideal tool for the job is MS Project, and most of the tasks and reporting can be automated

Step 6 - Document the Plan

The objective of documenting the plan is text to explain the plan

1.	Plan Description	A description of the plan
2.	Pre-Requisites	A List of dependencies that will influence the plan
3.	Assumptions	Any assumptions that have been made during the production of the plan
4.	Lessons	Lessons are incorporated from previous projects
5.	Monitoring and Control	A description of how the plan will be monitored and controlled
6.	Budget Information	Cost & Time provisions for the project including the Risk & Change Budget
7.	Tolerances	An overview of the tolerances for the 6 aspects Time, Costs, Scope, Quality Risks & Benefits
8.	Risks	An overview of the identified major risks

The Product Checklist

The Product Checklist is a list of all major products contained within the plan, plus the key delivery dates.

The Product Checklist may contain the following information (but could include more if required)

1.	Product ID	Number & Product Title
2.	Product Description	A description of the product
3.	Schedule	Plan and Date when this will be ready and the actual date
4.	Product Draft	Product Dates for the draft versions of the product
5.	Quality Check place	Plan and Dates when the Quality Checks or Reviews will take

6. Approved date   Plan and Actual approval dates
7. Handover date   Plan and Actual handover dates

Responsibilities

The responsibilities in relation to the Plans Theme are listed below:

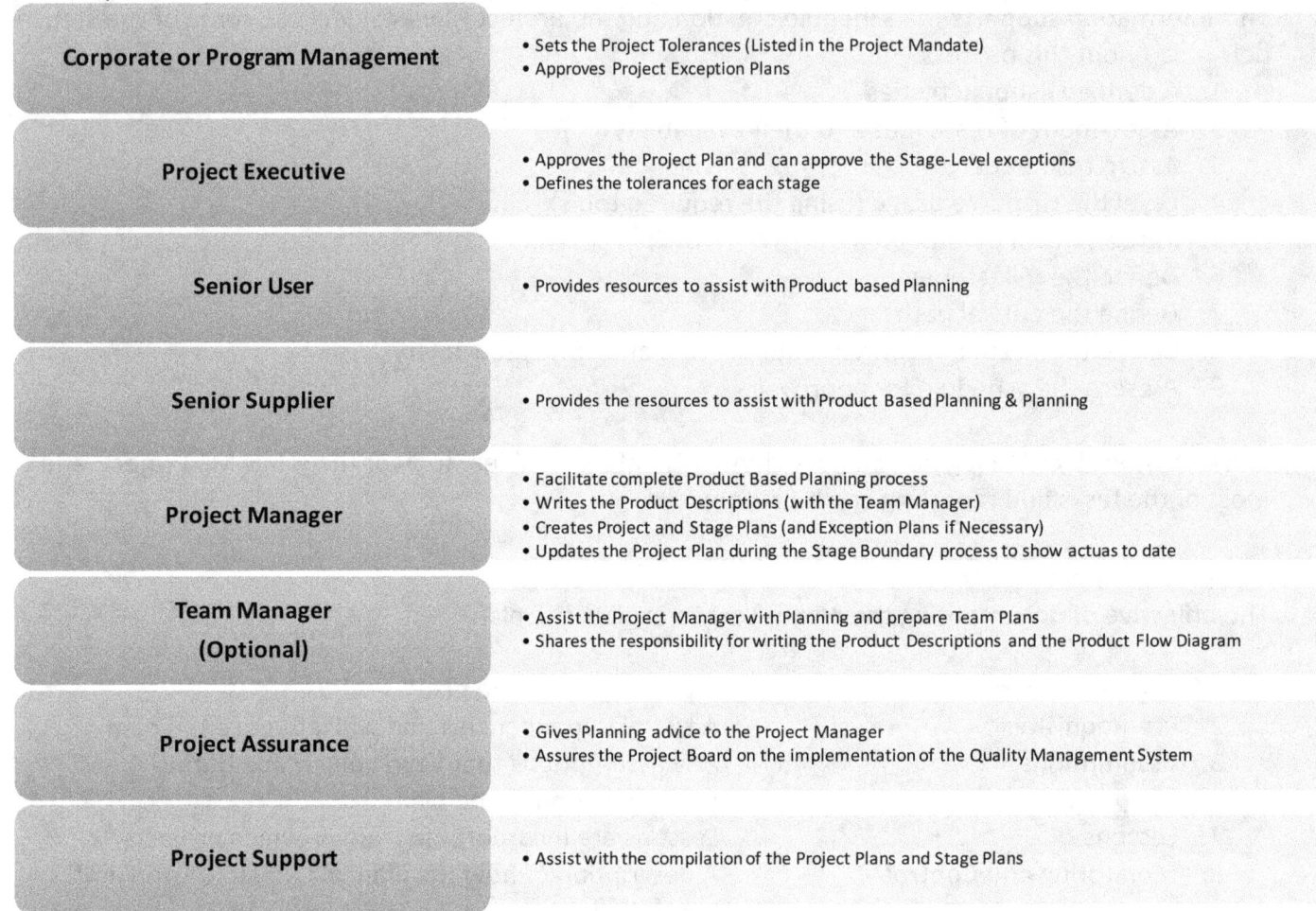

Corporate or Program Management
- Sets the Project Tolerances (Listed in the Project Mandate)
- Approves Project Exception Plans

Project Executive
- Approves the Project Plan and can approve the Stage-Level exceptions
- Defines the tolerances for each stage

Senior User
- Provides resources to assist with Product based Planning

Senior Supplier
- Provides the resources to assist with Product Based Planning & Planning

Project Manager
- Facilitate complete Product Based Planning process
- Writes the Product Descriptions (with the Team Manager)
- Creates Project and Stage Plans (and Exception Plans if Necessary)
- Updates the Project Plan during the Stage Boundary process to show actuas to date

Team Manager (Optional)
- Assist the Project Manager with Planning and prepare Team Plans
- Shares the responsibility for writing the Product Descriptions and the Product Flow Diagram

Project Assurance
- Gives Planning advice to the Project Manager
- Assures the Project Board on the implementation of the Quality Management System

Project Support
- Assist with the compilation of the Project Plans and Stage Plans

Figure 51 - Planning Roles & Responsibilities

Risk

An Introduction to the Risk Theme

The purpose of the Risk Theme is to identify, assess and control uncertainty and as a result improve the chances of the project to succeed.

So, what are risks?, in Prince2 there is a very specific definition of a risk which is taken from the Management of Risk (MoR) methodology.

"A Risk is a set of events that should it occur, will have an impact on achieving the project objectives"

In essence,

"A Risk is any event that could happen and have an impact (Positive or Negative) upon your project"

Which is easy to remember, and in truth we all deal with risks on an everyday basis and unknown to you, you analyse them and determine a way round them subconsciously.

For Example, if you need to drive from London to Manchester and you would normally use the M1 Motorway, however you know that on a Friday evening it will be heavily congested, so you decide to take the A1 – this is in essence a risk that you have identified, analysed and then planned a mitigation that enables you to meet your objective of arriving in Manchester and your risk response was to avoid the risk.

Risk can be seen as both positive and negative, which is easier explained as a Risk can be either a threat or an opportunity.

Risk Terms
Risk has its own language, much like the Prince2 Methodology. The Risk Theme has lots of new language to understand especially if your new to both Prince2 and the management of Risk. These terms are explained in the coming pages.

Risk Management
Risk Management is the steps taken that will enable you to:
- Identify and describe the Risk
- Assess the Risk and understand the likelihood of the Risk occurring, its impact upon the projects objectives and when it could occur
- Control the Risk enables you to determine how best to respond to the Risk and assign a risk owner to execute the responses and monitor the risk

Risk Management is done throughout the lifecycle of the project, in essence a new Risk or Issue can arise at any point during the lifecycle of the project. When any new risk arises the first question that the Project Manager should ask is "how will this impact the objectives of the project or any of the identified benefits"

Risk Context and the Management of Risk
Prince2 uses the Management of Risk (MoR) methodology as a guide to the management of risks, it takes advantage of the processes and procedures of the methodology that have already been defined rather than try to reinvent the wheel

The approach to Risk is:
- Understand the Risk and its context in relation to the project and its objectives
- Involve the Stakeholders, Users, Suppliers and Teams
- Establish an approach for the Project and document this approach within the Risk Management Approach
- Provide regular reports upon the Risks within the Project

- Defined and agree the Roles and Responsibilities in relation to the management of Risks within the project

Risk Context

Understanding the Projects Context means understanding how the risk could affect the project or the project achieving its objectives.

The first step is to obtain the information upon the risk and the project objectives that are at risk and then formulate the Risk Management Approach for the project

When first considering the Risk, you also need to understand what policies are in place within the Organisation or within the Program so that they can be used, reducing the need to recreate them therefore saving the need to recreate work un-necessarily

This will provide the following information:
- The organisations attitude towards Risk or the organisations risk appetite
- The agreed Risk Tolerances
- Procedures for escalation
- Roles & Responsibilities
- A Risk Management Approach Template to be tailored for use within the Project

Using a common approach will also ensure that the Stakeholders involved in the Project should already be familiar with the approach and should have an understanding of how Risks will be managed within the Project

The attitude towards Risk within the Project also needs to be taken into account in relation to the Project Board. If you have three "thrill seekers or risk seekers" you will have to ensure that you have an approved approach to define, measure and manage risks to ensure you can control risks within you Project

The Risk Management Approach defines the procedures for Risk Management, including how Risks will be identified, assessed, controlled and communicated within the Project.

Risk Register

The Risk Register is the central document that enables the control and management of Risks within the Project. It captures and maintains the Risk information for both Threats and Opportunities. It includes a record of all risks including their current status and history whether open or closed

Prince2 recommends the Risk Register contents as a minimum are:

1. Unique Risk Identifier — A unique ID for each Risk raised
2. Risk Author — The Person who raised the Risk
3. Date Registered — The date the Risk was registered into the Risk Register
4. Risk Category — Each Project should have its own unique categories and these should be defined within the Risk Management Approach
5. Risk Description — This is written as "Cause, Event, Effect" to explain the Risk and its impacts upon the Project Objectives
6. Probability & Impact — The chances of the Risk occurring and the Impact upon the

Project
7. Risk Response Category
   a. Threats – Avoid, Reduce, Contingency, Transfer, Accept or Share
   b. Opportunities – Enhance, Exploit, Reject or Share
8. Risk Response   The actions to resolve the Risk in the event it occurs
9. Risk Statues   The status of the Risk – Active\Closed
10. Risk Owner   The person who is responsible the management of the Risk
11. Risk Actionee   The person who will carry out the actions contained within the
              Risk Response (This can be the same person as the Risk Owner)

The Project Manager is responsible for the Risk Register, it should be maintained by the Project Support role (when available). The management\maintenance & use of the Risk Register is defined in the Risk Management Approach

Risk Management

There are three steps to managing Risks
1. Identification
2. Assessment
3. Control

The Risk Management Procedure is a series of 5 steps,
1. Identify
2. Assess
3. Plan
4. Implement
5. Communicate

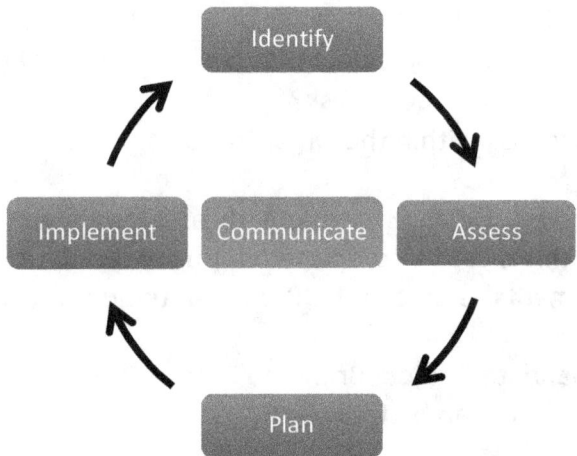

Figure 52 - Risk Management Cycle

Step 1 is Identify
- Understanding how the Project perceives Risk and complete the Risk Management Approach
- Does the Project have a High, Medium or Low Tolerance for Risks?
- Identify the Risks that could affect the Project's objectives (Threats and Opportunities)

Step 2 is Assess
- Assess the risks in relation to their probability and impact upon the objectives

Step 3 is Plan

- Once you have understood the Risk, its probability and possible impact, you need to plan the steps for the response to the threats (Avoid, Reduce etc) or the opportunities

Step 4 is Implement
- Implement the planned response as identified in Step 3

Step 5 is Communicate
- Step 5 is to ensure the Project Manager communicates to the stakeholders, this should be documented within the Risk Management approach
- This can be done using an existing management reports, the Highlight Report or the End Stage Report

Identify the Risk

The identification of the Risk can be broken into smaller steps

Identify the Context

Identifying the risk is the first step in the Risk Management Procedure - **Identify**, Assess, Plan, Implement and Communicate

A number of questions need to be asked when understanding the Project and the completion of the Risk Management Approach

- What type of Project is this in relation to the Risk Tolerance, can the Project accept a high level of tolerance in relation to risks or if it has very little room for risk within the Project
- What are the Customer's Quality Expectations- will the product need to have a very high level of functionality with no room for error – Low tolerance to Customer Quality Expectations
- How will the project be delivered, how many suppliers, in-house, external or a mix of both?
- What is scale and complexity of the project, has it been completed before or a Project like it has been completed before within the organisation
- Have the resources within the Project worked on similar or any Projects previously
- What is the Project Boards attitude to Risk?
- What is the approach to Risk within the Organisation

These questions need to be asked and answered as early as possible within the Project to define the Risk Management Approach, this must be completed during the Initiation Stage with the 3 other Management Approach documents as part of the Project Initiation Documentation (PID).

Whilst creating the Project Mandate, Project Brief and Project Product Description most if not all of the answers to the questions above can be found

The Risk Management Approach should contain the following information
- The Risk Management Procedures to be followed by the Project
- Tools & Techniques (Workshops, Risk Meeting etc)
- The structure of the Risk Register and what information it will contain
- Risk Management activities
- Roles & Responsibilities
- Risk Scales (Likelihood, Proximity, Impact etc)
- Scale Categories

- Risk Tolerances and how they will be used
- Risk Budget information
- Dashboard or Early Warning Indicators

The identification and management of risks can be undertaken using a number of techniques, as previously stated whilst Prince2 does not specify specialist techniques, it does recommend the use of them.

In relation to Risk Identification, the following are excellent techniques to be used:

- **Review Lessons** – Review lessons from similar projects and understand the threats and opportunities experienced and the mitigations planned
- **Risk Checklists** – These are checklists created by the Project, they are used to help identify Risks, the proximity, impacts and plan the responses or mitigations
- **Brainstorming** – Use working groups to involve stakeholders or subject matter experts to help identify risks or if they have been identified, to help plan the responses

Understanding the Risk or Expressing the Risk

Expressing a risk is the process of breaking the risk down into its component pieces.

Figure 53 - Risk - Cause-Event-Effect

An example of a Risk using the above is:

An airstrike in France may mean that delegates are unable to attend the conference meaning the conference will not proceed

The **Cause** is that there may be an Air Strike in France – this is the possible event that may occur
The **Effect** is that the attendees of the conference will not be able to attend
The **Event** is that conference will not proceed

This is the example from the Prince2 Manual

The Farmers crops might get damaged due to the heavy rains, as the fields will get flooded.

The **Cause** is - The Heavy rain
The **Event** is - The fields might get flooded
The **Effect** is – If the event occurs (the heavy rain causes the fields to flood) the crops will get damaged

The correct way to describe the risk if

Cause – Due to the rain is very there is a threat that
Event - The fields may become flooded and

Effect - The crops will become damaged

An opportunity can be broken down using the same process

The ideal way to write a risk is
Cause - Due to
Event - There is a risk of
Effect - That could result in

Assessing the Risk

Assessing the Risk is the 2nd part of the Risk Management Procedure- Identify, **Assess**, Plan, Implement, Communicate

Assessing the Risk covers two important actions, the estimating and evaluating the Risk

Estimating

Estimating is assessing the probability, the impact and the proximity of each threat or opportunity. These are all listed as separate columns within the Risk Register

There are a number of techniques for the estimation of the Risks,
- Probability Trees
- Expected value
- Probability Impact Grids

Within Prince2 it is recommended that the probability of the risk (the likelihood of it occurring) and the impact of the risk is used as a standard

The probability grid is the simplest way to understand the risk in terms of probability and impact and also present them in an easily understandable format

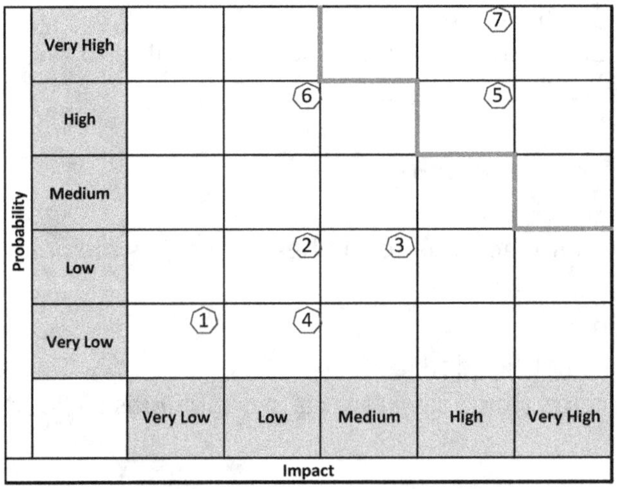

Figure 54 - Risk Summary Profile

Prince2 recommends plotting the estimates on a Summary Risk Profile diagram, this is a probability versus impact grid that is a simpler way to express the risks and compare them against each other

The advantages of using the diagram are:
- It is easy to get an overview and use this as a way to communicate the risk profile to the stakeholders
- The use of the grid highlights those risks that should be managed and need more focus or attention
- You can highlight the Risk Tolerance line to highlight any risks that are above this line have a higher probability or impact (or worse both)
- All Risks above the tolerance line require closer monitoring

The Summary Risk Profile or Probability Grid is a snapshot of the risks, and these will keep changing during the lifecycle of the project

The Project Manager is expected to provide Risk information to the Executive and the Project Board, this can be done using the Highlight Reports or at the end of each stage using the Managing Stage Boundary Process (SB) and using the End Stage Report

The Project Manager will immediately inform the Executive if a risk moves into above or below the Risk Tolerance Line

The 2nd step in the "Assess the Risk" is the Evaluate

Evaluate

The objective of evaluating is to evaluate the risks together understand the overall Risk Value for the project. The purpose of understanding the is to allow the Corporate or Program Management Team, Project Board to understand the Risk Value for the project as a whole. This allows them to understand if the Project is viable and should proceed.

The easiest way to understand the total value of the Risk Value is to use the expected monetary value

An example of this technique is:

The Project requires the purchase of a specialist piece of computer equipment which is valued at $160,000, there is a risk that this equipment could be damaged in transit or installation
- The financial impact would be an additional $160,000
- The probability of this happening is 10%
- The expected value of the risk is 10% of $160,000 = $16,000

This would be represented within the Risk Register and the Risk Value is the total of the project risks financial impact or expected monetary value

Planning the response

Planning the response to the Risk is the 3rd step in the Risk Management Procedure - Identify, Assess, **Plan**, Implement and Communicate

The objective is to plan the specific responses to the identified threats and opportunities within the project

The Management of Risk is in effect being prepared to manage the Risk in the event it occurs

The management or responses to the Risk do not remove the risk, the Risk Response actions within the project are done to reduce the impact of the Risk. Within Prince2 there are 6 responses to threats and four responses for opportunities

These are:

Threats	Oppurtunities
Avoid	Exploit
Reduce (Probability and\or Impact)	Enhance
Fallback (Reduces the Impact only)	
Transfer (Reduces the impact only and often only t financial impact)	
Share	
Accept	Reject

Figure 55 - Risk Responses (Threats & Opportunities)

To help decide the type of responses that are best to reduce the impact of the risk. Using the lessons learned from previous projects that have already been completed could support this process

Threat Responses
The Threat Responses are Avoid, Reduce, Fall-back, Transfer, Accept and Share

Avoid
This involves changing something within the project so that the identified threat no longer has an impact or can no longer happen – therefore you have avoided the risk

The Prince2 Manual example is:
A critical meeting could be threatened by air travel disruption so the project chooses to hold the meeting by conference call instead – This avoids the possibility of the risk occurring by removing the need to use air travel

Reduce
The threat actions are to
  * Reduce the probability of the risk
  * Reduce the impact of the risk

The objective of the Reduce is to reduce the probability of the impact risk happening an example of this is:

To reduce the likelihood of the users not using the new software application, the number of training sessions has been increased to maximise the training and awareness

The risk still exists however the planned response aims to reduce the probability of the risk occurring

Reducing the Impact is to reduce the impact of the risk in the event it occurs an example of this is below:

The impact of a prototype being damaged in transit would mean a delay to the launch of the new product, to reduce this risk, multiple prototypes will be created and shipped using different shipping methods

This reduces the chances of the risk occurring

Fallback
The Fallback response is also known as contingency or Plan B, the fallback is a plan of actions that will be implemented in the event the risk occurs, which will then become an issue. These actions will reduce the impact of the threat

An example of a fallback or contingency is below:

The testing facility is only available to the project for the month of August and loss of access could delay the launch of the product, as a contingency a second testing facility has been hired and placed on standby if required

The fallback or contingency is only implemented if the risk occurs and is not implemented or actioned if not required

Transfer
The objective of the transfer response is to transfer the financial risk to a third party, for example using an insurance policy in the event the risk occurs the costs could be recovered. An example is below:

The impact of a prototype being damaged or lost to the project financially is transferred to a 3rd party insurance company

Accept
The decision is taken to accept the risk and not take any action or response in relation to it, the mitigation may be too expensive or there may be no mitigation to implement.

However, the risk is monitored and the status remains open.

An example is below:
A competitor is potentially bringing a product out on the same day as our planned launch, however it is too late to change our launch or the product details. The project proceeds as planned and the risk is accepted

Share
Share is both a threat response and an opportunity response. Share is a common response in a customer\supplier project where both parties agree to share the gain or the pain. In essence both

parties agree to share the gain if the costs are less than planned or share the pain if the costs are exceeded

An example of this is below:

Share the Gain - The cost of the steel needed for the bridge is forecasted to be $150 per tonne, in the event that the costs drop to $125 it is agreed between the customer and the supplier to split the reduced costs by 50\50

Share the Pain - The cost of the steel needed for the bridge is forecasted to be $150 per tonne, in the event that the costs increase to above $225 it is agreed between the customer and the supplier to share the increased costs by 50\50

The 6 Threat Responses are listed above, for more information the Management of Risk (MoR) is the specifically focused on Risk Management within Programs and Projects

Responses to Opportunities
The responses to opportunities are Share, Exploit, Enhance and Reject

Share
The response to Share in relation to opportunities is the same as the threat response above

Exploit
Exploit is the process of taking advantage of the opportunity if it does occur. An example of this is below

If the project is delayed, the next release of the operating system for the phone will be released which has the features we originally planned to use. The project will take advantage of this and delay

Enhance
The Enhance response is where actions are taken to increase the likelihood of the vent occurring and the impact of the opportunity is enhanced should it occur. This is not the same as exploit but doing things proactively to increase the chance of the opportunity occurring

An example of this is below:
If the product passes the testing in 2 cycles instead of 4, the launch can be brought forward beating our rivals to market. The Project Board has approved increased training and testing resources to ensure the product passes testing within 2 cycles

The difference between Exploit and Enhance are:
- With Exploit, in the event the Risk occurs you will take advantage of it
- With Enhance, the project attempts to increase the chances of the Risk occurring

Reject
The Reject response to the opportunity is where the opportunity is identified and analysed but the Project Board decides to Reject the response and decides to take no action. There can be many

reasons for this, for example the return financially does not warrant the effort compared to the originally planned benefits

An example for this is below:
It is possible that the products complete testing in 2 cycles rather than 4, however the cost to provide additional resources and training to complete the testing are more expensive than the benefits achieved, therefore the Project Board rejects opportunity and proceeds as planned

The 4 responses in relation to Opportunity are Share, Exploit, Enhance and Reject

Implementing the Responses

Implementing the responses is the 4th step in the Risk Management Procedure, the aim of this is to ensure that the Planned Responses to the risk are completed

The main decision points are:
- Who will carry the planned Risk Response?
- Who will monitor the Risks?

There 2 specific roles in relation to the Risk Management Procedure, the Risk Owner and the Risk Actionee

The Risk Owner is the person responsible for managing and monitoring the aspects of the risk, tey can also be the Risk Actionee

The Risk Actionee is someone who is assigned to carry out the actions and support the Risk Owner, they are not responsible for monitoring the Risk

In many cases the Risk Owner and the Risk Actionee can be the same person, however assigning too many Risks to one individual can be counter productive

Communicate

The 5th step in the Risk Management Procedure is to Communicate, however this is actually done throughout the project and the whole Risk Management Procedure. The purpose of the Communication is to ensure that the information in relation to the threats and opportunities is communicated within the project to all involved stakeholders

Management reports are used to communicate Risk Information, these are:
- The Project Brief
- Highlight Report
- End Stage Report
- Lessons Learned Reports

The guidelines for reporting in relation to the project and risks are documented within in the Communication Management Approach

The Project Manager will ask questions such as, what has changed since the last report? As risks within the project are never static. Risks can move in relation to the Probability Grid, they can increase and decrease and move above or below the tolerance line.

Risk Management is dependent on communication. The more the Project Manager communicates with the Project Stakeholders, the more effective the Risk Management is and the more trust within the Project

The Risk Budget

A Risk Budget is an optional amount agreed to deal with the specific responses to threats or opportunities. It cannot be used for anything else. Responses to Risk will require actions to be done, and this can cost money for resources etc, this will be funded from the Risk Budget

Calculating the value of Risk Budget requires the risks to be analysed and a value assigned. This is based upon the likelihood and the cost of the response. Using this method, it is possible to calculate the value of the risk budget. If you review the Expected Monetary Value, this method can be used to calculate the value of the Risk Budget

The Risk Budget is allocated at the at the start of the project, however as explained Risks can occur at any point within the project lifecycle, this can mean the Risk Budget is reviewed and possibly increased.

Roles & Responsibilities

Role	Responsibilities
Corporate or Program Management	• Provides the Risk Management Policy and information
Project Executive	• Accountable for all aspects of Risk Management • Ensures that a Risk Management Approach exists • Ensures that all Risks associated with the Business Case are identified, assessed and controlled • Escalates Risk to the Corporate or Program Management as necessary
Senior User	• Ensures that risks to the supplier are identified, assessed and controlled • Encourages users to identify risks and provide information to the Project Manager and reviews reports provided by the Project Manager
Senior Supplier	• Ensures that risks to the supplier are identified, assessed and controlled
Project Manager	• Create the Risk Management Approach Document • Create and Maintain the Risk Register with assistance from Project Support • Ensures that risks are continually identified, assessed and controlled throughout the project lifecycle
Team Manager (Optional)	• Identifies, assesses and controls risks within the project supporting the Project Manager • Participates in workshops supporting the identification of risks
Project Assurance	• Reviews the Risk Management Procedures to ensure they perform within the Risk Management Approach for the project
Project Support	• Assist with the maintenance of the Risk Register

Change

Introduction to the Change Theme

The purpose of the Change Theme is to identify, assess and control potential changes to the products that are approved and baselined. It is not just about handling change requests but also manages the issues that arise during the project. The Change Theme provides a structured approach the management of issues and changes to the products

No project exists without change, it is inevitable that at some point there will be a change. All projects need a structured approach to how these changes are managed

When does Issue and Change Control occur?

The objective of Change is to manage the changes within the project, not stop them. For this reason, change occurs during the full lifecycle of the project

The Configuration Management System tracks the products, records when they are approved and baselined, helps to ensure that the correct versions are being used during the project and is delivered to the customers

Change Terminology

As with the Risk Theme, Change has its own language that can often be confusing. The next section will break down the Change Theme and its components

Configuration Management

What the manual says

"Configuration Management is the technical and administrative activity concerned with the creation, maintenance and controlled change of the configuration of a product"

This is essentially saying that Configuration Management is about the management pf the products within the project

What is a Configuration Item?

- A configuration item is the name to an entity (item) that is managed by Configuration Management. This may be a component of a product or a set of products that form a release. For example:
    - If we go back to the car example, the Distributor, Spark Plugs, Radiator would all be components of the engine or if we were to use a computer as example: The hard drive, the memory, the processor would all be components of the computer
    - A release is a complete and consistent set of products that are managed and deployed as a single entity. For example: The computer could be released with a new operating system, hard drive, graphics card and new version of a game which together would form a release

Issues

Prince2 uses the term Issue to cover any relevant event that has happened. If you think back to Risk – it is often easier to think of a Risk and Issue as being related

"A *Risk* if something that could occur and have a positive or negative impact upon your project, whereas an *Issue* is something that has occurred"

There are 3 types of issues within a project, these are:
1. Request for Change
2. Off-Specification
3. Problem or Concern (which could also be a question)

The definition of these is:

Request for Change: Is a proposal to a baselined product. A product that has already been agreed and approved and has an agreed product description is a baselined product. Any subsequent modification to this is a Request for Change

Off-Specification: This is something that has been agreed but is not provided by the supplier or is forecasted not to the be provided. For example: The supplier of a new website could not provide the ability to create subscription box pop-up for requesting email addresses, therefore we will not be able to create a mainlining list for future promotions

Problem or Concern: Is any other issue that needs to be managed, resolved or escalated by the Project Manager. For example: Your plumber can no longer be on the building site for 2 weeks, which will have a knock-on effect to the schedule

The Approach to Change

The management of Issues, Changes and Change Management will be defined early within the project, during the Initiating a Project Process (IP), which is the first stage of the project. This should be reviewed as part of the Managing a Stage Boundary Process (SB)

There are 6 management products within Prince2 that are used to control issues, changes and Configuration Management. The Change Control Approach establishes the project controls and is supported by the remaining documents to help maintain the project controls

The five management products are:
1. Configuration Item Records
2. Product Status Account(s)
3. Daily Log
4. Issue Register
5. Issue Reports

Change Control Approach: The Change Control Approach contains the strategy\process on how issues and changes will be managed within the project. It contains information such as how to identify the products, how to control the products and how to do status accounting and verification

Configuration Item Records: These provide a set of data for each product used in the project. This is a set of data that provides the status of the product, its stage of quality, version number, who is responsible for the product and its relation to any other products (Cross reference data), Its relation to any issues that have arisen. This information is gathered from the Product Breakdown Structure,

Stage Plan, Team Plan and Work Package – a simple way is to think of this as the meta-data for a product

Product Status Account: This is a report on the status of the products being created by the project at any point in time

Daily Log: This is the Project Managers log and is used as a diary and for the informal management of issues and changes, the use of the term Register is used to imply a more formal product or process

Issue Register: This is the central register that contains all of the information relating to any Issues that are under formal management, it contains information such as: Issue ID, Issue type, Date raised, Raised by, Issue description, Priority, Severity, Status, Remarks, Closure Date

Issue Report: This report contains the description of an issues, which could be a Request for Change, an Off-Specification or a Problem\Concern

Change Control Approach

The Change Control Approach contains the approach that will be used for the management of issues and changes within the project. If there are existing standards for the management of Issues and Change Control within the Organisation, this could be modified to support the project.

This document will answer the following questions:
- How will the products be planned and controlled?
- How will the products be verified?
- How will Issue and Change Control be managed within the Project?
  - Capture, Examine, Propose, Decision, Implement
- What tools are available for use by the project to track Issues and Product information
- What data will be kept for each product
- How will the Project Manager review, change & Issue control?
- How are Issues and Changes prioritised – What scale will be used and how will it be displayed

Prioritising Issues and tracking severity

Issues are Change Requests, Off-Specifications and Problems\Concerns. As we have explained previously Prince2 is not concerned with specialist techniques, there are many ways to prioritise Issues and Change Requests and Prince2 explains the **MoSCoW** technique.

Using the **MoSCoW** approach is a good basis when starting to prioritise Issues and Change Requests, whilst asking questions like
- How will this change effect the overall project?
- Will this change effect the project objectives?
- How will the Business Case be affected?
- Will the timeline be effected?
- Will the Change require additional funding to be completed?

Priority & Severity

Whilst **MoSCoW** is an excellent tool for enabling the prioritisation and the classification of changes, it is limited in relation to Issues and their severity

A simple scale of Very High, High, Medium, Low and Very Low or Critical, Major, Significant, Minor can be used to classify Issues, however the meaning of the classification is unique to the project or organisation and must be documented within the Change Control Approach

The Tolerances agreed during the Starting Up a Project Process (SU) and Initiating a Project Process (IP) allow the Project Manager to deal with minor issues, the Change Authority are tasked with managing or dealing with major issues and the Corporate or Program Management can manage or deal with critical issues.

A critical issue that could for example take a project completely out of any agreed tolerance, whereas an issue rated as low could virtually no impact upon the project but needs to be managed, this means that each issue must have its severity rated. This severity rating will be classified by the Project Manager with the support of Subject Matter Experts

Change Authority and Change Budget

The Change Authority considers the requests for change and off-specifications. This can be a person or a group depending upon the size, complexity and risk of the project. The Project Board has the responsibility so this can be managed at the level of the Project Board, which is a common approach in smaller projects where minimal change is expected. In projects where considerable change is expected it is recommended to have a change authority and delegate this responsibility on behalf of the Project Board again this is part of the Management by Exception Principle

The role of the Change Authority can be assigned to a person or persons, and dependent upon the budget agreed that can be spent by the Change Authority and other Tolerances agreed\delegated dictates the level of the person who can be assigned as the Change Authority.

A Change Authority would normally include a financial representative and a representative of the Project Executive, the Change Authority will act on the instructions of the Project Board

The budget assigned to the Change Authority, is agreed by the customer and the supplier to fund the costs related to Requests for Change. It is advisable to always have an agreed Change Budget unless you are sure there will be no change requests. The Project Board can still enforce control upon the project as they can put a limit upon the cost of a single change or the spent within a stage for example

The Change Control Process is a crucial tool used by the Project Manager. Using this can be a way to manage the changes and control the changes, for example the use of the Change Control Process when requests for change from senior executives are requesting something to be added that will place the project or its objectives at risk.

The Project Manager can use the Change Control Process to control the change and request that all of the information in relation to the change is logged upon the appropriate form to enable it to be assessed as to the impact upon the project, its objectives, the Business Case and its identified benefits. This allows the project to never outright reject a change whilst keeping the project on track

Management Products
The Product Descriptions for all of the Management Products are contained within the Prince2 Manual in Appendix A:

Configuration Item Records
The Configuration Item Record is a set of records that describes the products of the project.

If you think of the Configuration Item Record as a single page that contains the details or metadata that when combined make up the project product

The Configuration Item Record should contain the following information as a minimum
- Project ID
- Item Identifier
- Current Version
- Item Title
- Date last changed
- Owner
- Location
- Item Type
- Item Details or attributes
- Stage
- Users
- Status
- Producer
- Date allocated
- Source
- Relationship (Dependencies)
- Cross Reference

Product Status Accounting
The Product Status Account provides information about the status of products during the project. This is a report upon the on product or a group of products or all of the products created during a stage.

An example, of you are sending out the invites by email for a corporate event and the version used is out of date and contains what are now competitors, so it is important that the right list is used.

The Product Status Account ensures the right product is in place at the right time.

Daily Log
The Daily Log is used by the Project Manager to record informal issues, actions or events that are not captured in other documents. The Daily Log is effectively a diary for the Project Manager and contains information such as the Date, Comments, Raised by, Date of Follow-Up and Remarks

When the Project Manager is first informed of an issue, the information or details may not be sufficient to make an informed decision as to whether it requires formal management. The Project Manager will enter the data into the Daily Log and if more information is learned or the issues becomes more serious and requires follow-up, it will be transferred to the Issue Register.

Excel is an ideal tool to use a Daily Log in the event that your organisation does not have a centrally managed tool.

Issue Register
The Issue Register is used to capture, manage and maintain the issues raised during the project. The Issue Register should contain information such as:
- Issue No
- Issue Identifier
- Issue Type
  - Request for Change
  - Off-Specification
  - Problem or Concern
- Priority
- Severity
- Date Raised
- Raised by
- Issue Description
- Status
- Closure Date

Issue Reports
The Issue Report is a description of an issue that has been raised

It also contains the impact assessment of the issue raised. The report is normally created when the issue is first raised or registered into the Risk Register. The basic information contained is the Issue Identifier, Issue Type, Date Raised, and Raised By. It should be updated after the issue has been reviewed and solution proposed or chosen. The final Issue Report update is when the Issue Status changes to closed and the date of closure is added

Configuration Management Procedure
Configuration Management are the activities that control, maintain and control changes for each product during the life of the project and post project completion, the focus of Configuration Management is looking after the products created by the project

Prince2 suggests 5 activities within Configuration Management that should be followed, these are: Planning, Identification, Control, Status Accounting, Verification and Audit

Planning
Planning is undertaken at the start of the project; each project is unique. The first questions asked is what level of Configuration Management is to be used within the project. What level of detail is needed for each product.

Identification

It is important that all products that will be used within the project are identified and a system of identification is selected, each product should have a unique identifier. For example, a product could be identified using a numerical value, its project code and the version number.

Control

The control of changes is crucial within projects. When a product has been baselined and it is updated or a change is approved, a new version is created and requires approval to become the new baseline. Prince2
States:

"Nothing moves and nothing changes without authorisation"

Baselined products are used to compare the current situation with the previous objectives, an example of this is the Managing Stage Boundary Process, at the End Stage Assessment the Stage Plan will be reviewed against the approved Next Stage Plan to assess the actuals versus the forecast

Control is also about the management, distribution, access control, archiving activities for the management and specialist products during the project

Status Accounting

Status Accounting, is the reporting of the current and the historical data for each product using the Product Status Account Report. The report provides information upon the current status of the product and how it has changed with each new revision. The Status Account should include the following information:

- Identifier
- Version
- Last Update
- Status
- Owner
- Changes since last update
- Users
- Next Baseline
- Related items

Verification and Audit

Verification and Audit is the verification that the products are in line with the data contained within the Configuration Item Records. For example: Do the correct people have access to the correct products? and the correct versions? are the products in the correct locations? are they using the correct identifiers? are they secure?

Verification and Audit also ensures that the change control procedure as outlined within the Change Control Approach is being followed within the Project

Issue and Change Control Procedure

The Issue and Change Control Procedure is the management of issues within the project, which could be

- Requests for Change
- Off-Specification
- Problem or Change

There are 5 steps within Prince2 in relation to the management of Issues and Change Control, these are:

- Capture
- Examine
- Propose
- Decide
- Implement

Capture – Determines the type of issues, formal or informal, request for change and off-specification

Examine – Assess the impact of the issue against the projects objectives

Propose – The actions to be taken – Identify the options, evaluate the options and recommend

Decide – Is the decision to approve or reject the "proposal" and is undertaken by a higher authority within the project

Implement – The recommended\proposed solution. This is also known as taking corrective action, it can also involve updating a Work Package or creating an Exception Plan

The Project Manager has approved tolerances in relation to the 6 aspects within Prince2 (Time, Cost, Quality, Risk, Scope and Benefits) as long as the project remains within tolerance, the Project Manager can take decisions to ensure this. In the event a recommendation could mean that a tolerance could be exceeded, this is escalated to the Project Board for Ad-Hoc direction.

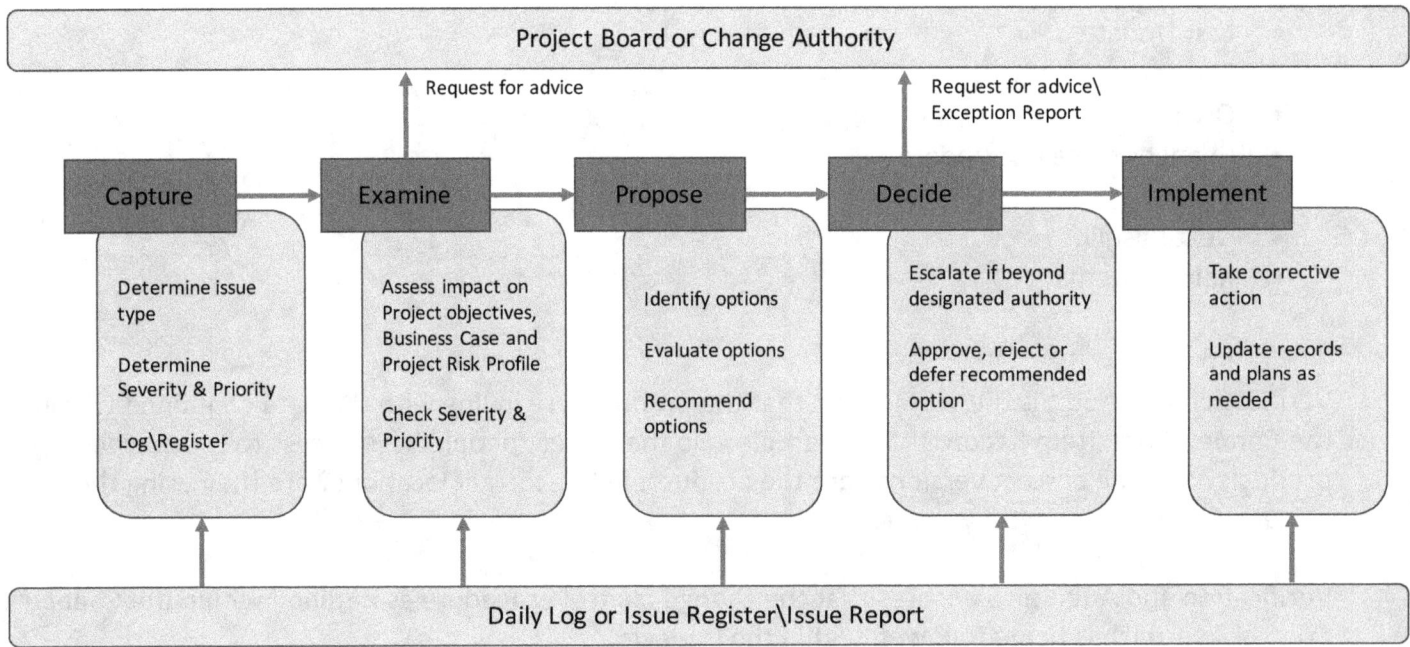

Figure 56 - Issue & Change Control Procedure

Capture

Capture is the first step within the Issue and Change Control Procedure, the objective of this step is to determine the type of issue (Request for Change, Off-Specification or Problem\Change), its severity and if it should be treated formally. If this is the case then it is added to the Issue Register. If the issue does not need to be managed formally then it can be managed informally within the Daily Log by the Project Manager

During the life of the project, there will be many issues raised, some of which can be solved immediately by the Project Manager within the agreed tolerances and without the need for formal management.

Understanding the difference between formal and informal issues has many advantages
- Some issues can be managed immediately, however there is a management burden to managing every small issue raised and managing these formally (the management of issues within the Issue Register and the creation of an Issue Report)
- Effective management of Issues avoids the Project Board being overwhelmed and creating apathy in relation to the project, meaning the Project Board can focus upon the issues that do need their attention

An Issue that should be managed formally and entered within the Issue Register for example may have a high severity impact upon the project and only the Project Board can take the necessary decision

Examine

The second step within the Issue and Control Procedure is Examine, and involves the examination of the issue by completing an Impact Analysis where the effect the identified issue will have upon the project objectives are understood

The Impact Analysis should consider as a minimum
- The projects performance targets or objectives – Time, Cost, Quality, Scope Risk and Benefits
- The project Business Case, especially in relation to the identified benefits
- The projects exposure to risk

The Project Manager, depending upon the issue will decide the level of detail required for the Impact Analysis, If the Issue only requires a small amount of work to solve, there is little or no benefit to completing a long winded and protracted Impact Analysis

Upon completion of the Impact Analysis, the Project Manager can add any other information to the Issue Register, including the severity and also as required update the Issue Report and also ensure the person who raised the Issue is kept informed

Propose

The third step within the Issue and Change Control Procedure is Propose, upon completion of the Impact Analysis, there is much more information and understanding in relation to the issue. The next step for the Project Manager is to propose the actions needed to deal with the issue.

The Project Manager will consider the options available and propose an appropriate course of action. The options must balance the cost when compared to the benefit of doing a certain action when compared to others. It will also look at the effect of each option upon the projects objectives of Time, Cost, Quality, Scope, Risks and Benefits

If any of the options investigated are forecasted to put the stage or project out of tolerance, the Project Manager should create an Exception Report and include this with the option, the Project Board or higher-level management need to authorise the continuation of the project. Prince2 states that the Project Manager should present more than one option and that they should obtain advice from other sources when defining these options

Decide
The fourth step in the Issue and Control Procedure and dependent upon the issue, the relevant authority (Higher Authority, Project Board or Project Manager) decides what action if any should be taken. For issues that do not take the project out of tolerance and are within the scope of the Change Control Approach, or the agreed tolerances assigned to the Project Manager, the Project Manager can approve the option selected without the need to escalate to the higher authority

Implement
The fifth step is to decide (approve\reject or defer) the selected option and Implement is where the Project Manager will either
- Take the respective corrective action, for example the update of a Work Package or the issue of a new Work Package
- Create an Exception Plan that will require the approval of the Project Board

Upon completion of the implementation, it must be checked and accepted for the issue to be closed. The Project Manager will update the Issue Register and Issue Report changing the status of the issue to "Closed" and ensure the person who raised the issue is informed

Roles and Responsibilities

Role	Responsibilities
Corporate or Program Management	• Provides the Corporate or Program Management Strategy for Change Control, Issue Resolution and Configuration Management.
Project Executive	• Determines the Change Authority and change budget • Defines the scales for Severity, Issues and Priority rating • Responds to requests for advice from the Project Manager during the project • Makes decisions on issues that are escalated by the Project Manager
Senior User	• Respond to requests for advice from Project Manager • Makes decisions upon issues escalated from the Project Manager
Senior Supplier	• Respond to requests for advice from Project Manager • Makes decisions upon issues escalated from the Project Manager
Project Manager (Can be assisted by Project Support)	• Manages the Configuration Management Procedure • Manage Issues and Change Control Procedure • Creates and maintains the Issue Register • Implements corrective actions
Team Manager (Optional)	• Implement corrective actions that were assigned by the Project Manager
Project Assurance	• Provides advice on examining and resolving issues • Checks that procedures within the Configuration Management Strategy Documents are being followed
Project Support	• Administer the Configuration Management • Maintain Project Products and complete administrative tasks for issue and change control procedures

Figure 57 - Change - Roles & Responsibilities

Progress

Introduction to the Progress Theme

The purpose of Progress Theme is to establish the mechanisms to monitor and compare actual achievements against those planned, provide a forecast for the project objectives and the projects continued viability and control any unacceptable deviations

Progress is all about how to control the project and know where you are against the current plan, this is a question to be raised for the Project Board – How to best keep them informed of the progress of the project? This answer will answer a lot in relation to how mature the organisation is in relation to Project Management

The most important points that a Project Manager should provide be aware of are:
- The type of reports and how often the information should be provided to the Project Board
- How to manage Issues, Risks and Changes
- Review the current progress against the current baselined project plan

The most common mistakes made are:

- There is not a system in place to effectively track progress
- The Project Manager becomes a firefighter and feels ownership or responsibility for the issues that are raised and fails to manage the project
- Is not confident enough to escalate issues
- The Project Board does not understand their role in relation to Issues

The Progress Theme can be explained simply as follows:
- Establishes how to monitor and compare actual achievements against those planned during the project
- Provides a forecast for the project objectives and the projects continued viability
- Control any unacceptable deviations

Progress is essentially about checking progress when compared to the plan, checking the projects viability and controlling deviations

Three of the seven principles are represented within the Progress Theme:

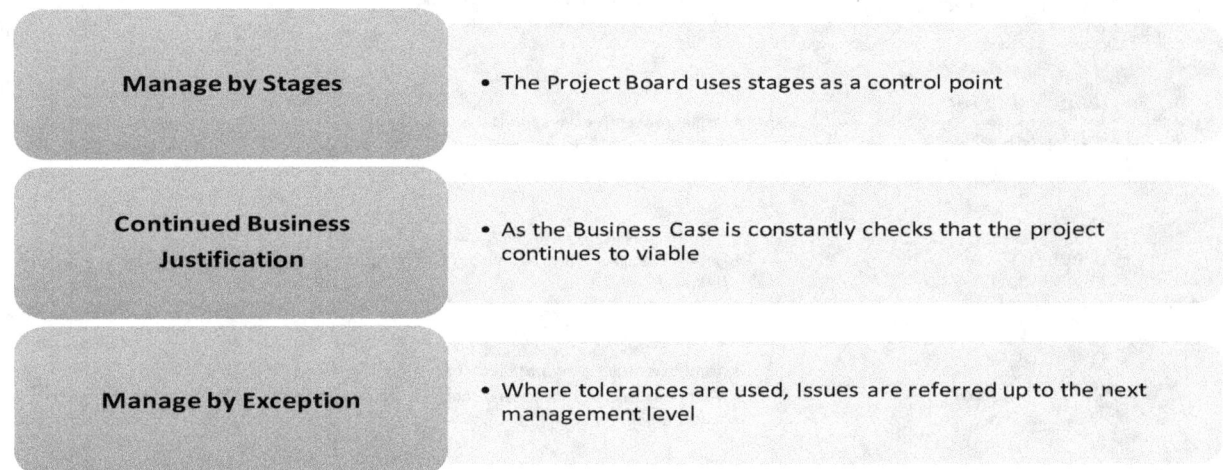

Figure 58 - Principles within the Progress Theme

There are four levels of control within a Project Organisation, and three levels in a Project Team. Each Level above has management control over the level below, which translates to there are 3 levels of control in the Project Organisation and two levels of control in the Project Team

Control in relation to the progress is about the decision-making and is central to project management ensuring that the project continues to remain viable when reviewed against its Business Case

Progress, Progress Controls, Exceptions and Tolerances

What is Progress?

Progress is the checking and controlling where the project is in relation to the plan, this is undertaken for the Project Plan, Stage Plan and Work Package

What are the Progress Controls?

Progress controls are used by the laver above to manage the layer below, which essentially means that the layer above manages and monitors the team below, the layer above does the following to manage progress:

- Monitor actual progress against the plans
- Review plans with the forecast
- Detects problems and identify risks
- Initiate corrective actions to fix issues
- Authorise work as required, The Project can authorise a next stage and a Project Manager can authorise a new Work Package

Exceptions and Tolerances

Within Prince2 an Exception is a situation where it can be forecasted that there will be a deviation beyond the agreed tolerance levels

Tolerances are the deviation above or below a plans target. Tolerance levels could be set for all six of the aspects – Time, Cost, Quality, Scope, Risk and Benefits.

These are often known as Project Variables or Contingency

If tolerances are not used, every small issue that occurs would need to be escalated by the Project Manager to the Project Board, which would essentially mean that a Project Board Escalation meeting would be needed every day almost guaranteeing project apathy from both the Project Board and the Project Manager!

The Project Board are normally senior people within and organisation, setting tolerances allows the Project Manager to manage the smaller issues and only escalate those issues that need the direction of the Project Board

Project Tolerances can be allocated to or on the following:

Tolerance Areas	Project Level Tolerances	Stage Level Tolerances	Work Package Level Tolerances
Time - +/- Days, Weeks	Project Plan	Stage Plan	Work Package
Costs - +/- % of budget	Project Plan	Stage Plan	Work Package
Quality – Quality Criteria	Project Product Description	NA	NA
Scope – MoSCoW	Project Plan	Stage Plan (Agile)	Work Package
Benefits	Business Case	NA	NA
Risk	Risk Management Strategy	Stage Plan (Agile)	Work Package

Figure 59 - Tolerances Matrix

The Prince2 Approach to Progress

Prince2 provides control using the processes below:

1. Delegating Authority from one level to the next for example the Project Board will delegate to the Project Manager and the Project Manager will delegate to the Team Manager
2. Dividing the Project into Management Stages and authorising one Management Stage at a time

3. Time driven and event driven reporting
4. Management by Exception – raising exceptions as a method to alert the layer above

The use of these controls is documented early within the Project and is documented within the Project Initiation Documentation (PID)

Delegating Control

Corporate or Program Management

- Corporate or Program Management is external to the project and they set the overall requirements and tolerance levels for the project.
- If the project tolerances are exceeded, this should be escalated to Corporate or Program Management

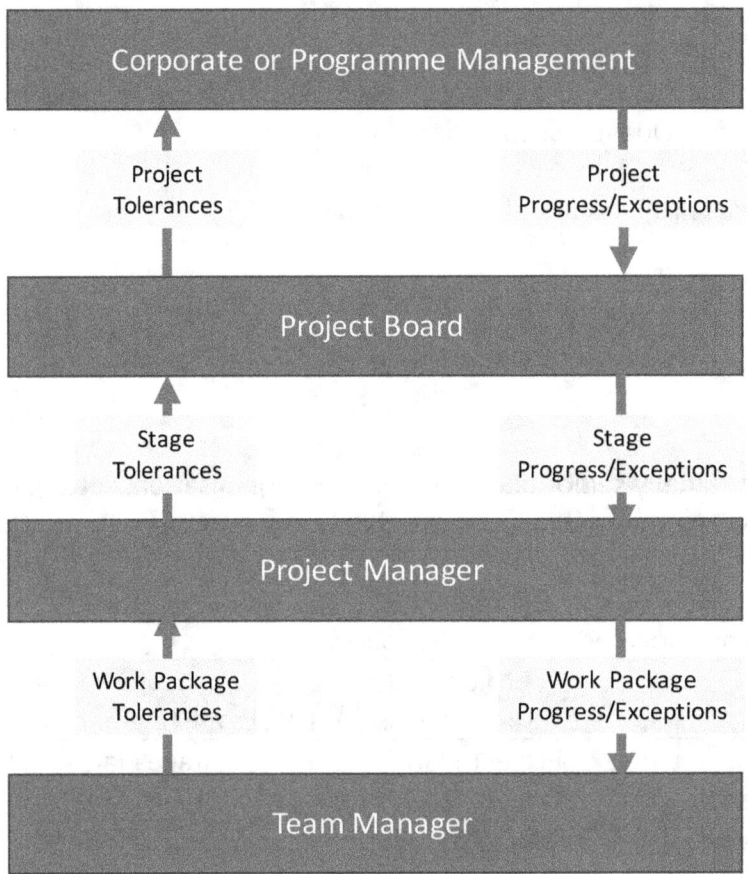

Figure 60 - Progress Reporting & Tolerance Delegation

The Project Board

- Sets the tolerances for the stages, therefore the Project Manager will escalate any issues to them in the event the issue is identified to go outside of tolerance in relation to any of the 6 aspects
- If the exception affects the projects tolerance, the Project Board should escalate this to Corporate or Program Management

The Project Manager

- The Project Managers whilst having day-2-day control over the stage and works within the tolerances defined by the Project Board

- The Project Manager also sets and agrees tolerances in relation to the Work Packages

The Team Manager
- The Team Manager controls the Work Package and works within the tolerances defined and agreed with the Project Manager

The Project Board Controls
The Project Board has 3 main controls available to support the management of the levels below, these are:
- Authorisation – They authorise the next management stage
- Progress Updates – The receive regular reports from the Project Manager
- Exceptions & Changes – They can receive Exception Reports and Issue Reports

Project Board Authorisations
- Authorises Project Initiation
- Authorises the Project so that the first management stage can commence
- Authorises each subsequent Management Stage
- Authorise Project Closure the last decision from the Project Board

Project Board Progress Updates
- Highlight Reports, End Stage Reports are sent regularly by the Project Manager to the Project Board and provide information on how the stage is progressing according the plan

Exceptions and Changes
- Exception Reports and Issue Reports
- Exception Reports advise the Project Board that the stage is out of tolerance, providing the Project Board with information to continue controlling the project and provide direction as required
- Issue Reports provide a reporting mechanism to gather information and report upon Requests for Change, Off-Specification or a Problem\Concern

If all of the above are used effectively, the Project Board has strong control and this should not encroach upon their time, the effective management of issues means that upon an issue being identified or a forecasted breach of tolerance they should be informed

Project Manager Controls
The Project Manager has the same controls assigned to the Project Board, but are within smaller boundaries defined by the agreed tolerances
1. Authorisations:
   a. The Project Manager authorises the Work Package to the Team Manager as part of the Controlling a Stage Process (CS)
2. Progress Updates:
   a. Checkpoint Reports are provided by the Team Manager or Team Members
3. Exceptions and Changes
   a. Project Managers use the Registers and Logs to review and monitor progress

b. The Project Manager uses the Registers and Logs to identify issues that may need to be resolved

c. Changes will be managed using the Issue and Change Control Procedure

Management Stages (Management Control)

Management Stages allow the project to be broken into smaller portions providing decision points allowing the Project Board to maintain control of the project.

The management stage is a collection of activities to produce products and is managed on a day-2-day basis by the Project Manager

Management Stages allow the Project Board to:

- Provide review and decision points at the end of each stage and allow the approval of the plan for the next stage
- Allows the conformation of continued viability
- Allows the Project Board to authorise one Management Stage at a time, or in the event it is now longer viable to stop the project
- Review the End Stage Report for the current stage and review the stage plan for the next stage
- Check the projects progress compared with the baselined Project Plan at the end of each Management Stage

The Management Stages are a key to the success of the Project. With tolerances set by the Project Board, day-2day authority of the management stage is delegated to the Project Manager. The Project Manager uses the Highlight Reports to ensure the Project Board are informed of the stage progress according to the Stage Plan, and otherwise only communicates with them if the stage has gone or is forecasted to go out of tolerance

How many stages within a Project

Prince2 states that the use of Management Stages is mandatory and minimum number of stages is two.

The Initiation Stage to allow the definition and agree upon what is required, and at least one more stage to produce the products.

The decision on the number of stages, can be determined by the complexity of the project, risk and number of products to be produced by the project. This can be a tricky process; considered the following when determining the number of stages:

- How far ahead can be planned effectively – for example if you are developing software you may not wish to plan more than 2 months ahead to ensure you remain on track
- Where are the key decision points within the project – these can be payment milestones or product acceptance points
- How much risk is there within the project – have you delivered a project like this before, have the resources assigned to the project worked on projects before etc

- How much control does the Project Board require – how much is the administrative overhead using several smaller stages versus longer stages compared with more control – this decision is crucial to ensuring the continued support from the Project Board
- What is the confidence level of the Project Board and the Project Manager – have either worked on a similar project previously, or is this a totally new Project with new resources

The Project Board and the Project Manager will choose or decide how many stages are required within the project, which can be a tricky process.

How long should a stage be?

The main decision or consideration in relation the length of a management stage, is the level of risk or complexity. If the project is classed as a high-risk project it could be considered that stages should be short and ensure that the Project Board maintains control. If there is less risk and the project is not complex, the stages could be longer

Prince2 states that the following points should be considered when deciding the length of the stage:
- The planning horizon at any point with the project – how far ahead can you safely plan?
- The Technical Stages within a project
- Is there any alignment with program activities – do you require input from other projects
- The level of risk

What are Technical Stages

Technical Stages allow the grouping of work together by the techniques required or by the products to be delivered. This results on stages covering the design, build and implementation. Technical Stages differ from Management Stages in the following way:
- Technical Stages can overlap Management Stages (But there can only be one active Management Stage)
- Technical Stages are normally aligned to specialist skills such as the completion of Analysis, Design or Build, whereas Management Stages are more focused upon decision points or authority to spend project funds

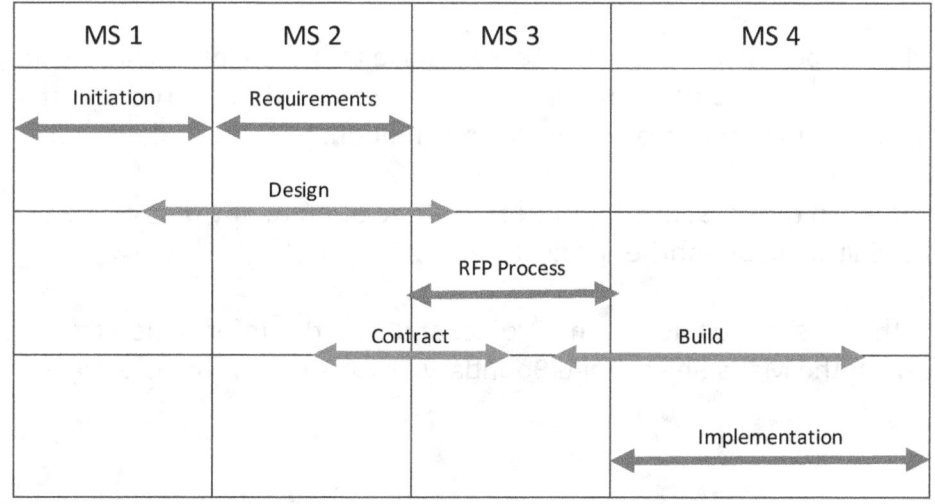

This diagram shows the Management Stages compared to Technical Stages

The Design and Contract Technical Stages cross multiple Management Stages

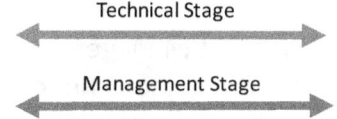

Figure 61 - Technical Stages

Controls – Event and Time Driven

Within Prince2 all controls are divided into 2 types – Event Driven and Time Driven

Event Driven Controls take place when something happens, when an event happens within the project this triggers a report, for example an End Stage Report or an Exception Report

Time Driven Controls take place at pre-agreed or defined intervals. The Project Board will agree with the Project Manager when to send the Highlight Report to the Project Board, The Project Manager as part of the Work Package will agree with the Team Manager when to send the Checkpoint Reports – Time Driven Reports don't wait for a trigger or event to happen

The frequency of the reporting is defined within the Communication Management Strategy which is documented during the Initiation Stage and forms part of the Project Initiation Documentation (PID)

These can however be changed by the Project Board, this would normally happen during the Stage Boundary Process and be part of the approval of the Next Stage Plan

Reviewing Progress

As part of the Controlling a Stage Process (CS) the Project Manager will regularly review the Progress using the Checkpoint Reports and maintain the registers and logs. This information will be used to maintain or update the Stage Plan with the actual progress achieved to date on the project.

Within the Controlling a Stage Process (CS) a number of Management Products support in reviewing progress, these are
- Daily Log – useful for recording actions, ad-hoc conversations or tasks
- Issue Register – contains the details of all issues under management within the project
- Product Status Account – provides a snapshot of the products within the project, management stage or an area of the project
- Quality Register – records all planned and implemented quality activities
- Risk Register – contains a record of all identified risks and their status

Lessons

The Prince2 Principle of Learn from experience means that Lessons have to be sought, recorded and actioned during the life of the project. Prince2 uses the term sought to ensure that everyone within the project checks for previous lessons that may provide useful information.

Any useful experiences are recorded in the Lessons Log, this can be in relation to any part of the project that could help in a following stage or another project.

The Project Manager maintains the Lessons Log during the Project and uses this information to create the Lessons Report as part of the Managing a Stage Boundary Process (SB) or the Closing a Project Process (CP)

Reporting Progress

There are three reports used by the Project Manager when reporting upon project Progress

1. Highlight Report
2. End Stage Report
3. End Project Report

Highlight Report

The Highlight Report is used by the Project Manager to report on the status of the current stage when compared to the approved Stage Plan. The Highlight Report allows the Project Board to manage by exception during the current stage, as they are aware of the agreed tolerances the information in relation to these should be included (Time, Cost, Quality, Scope, Risk and Benefits)

The frequency of the Highlight Report is agreed within the Communication Management Strategy, however this can be updated during the Managing a Stage Boundary Process

End Stage Report

The End Stage Report is created by the Project Manager near the end of the current Management Stage and is used to compare performance of the stage against the approved Stage Plan

End Project Report

The End Project Report is produced by the Project Manager near the end of the project as part of the Closing a Project Process and is used by the Project Board to evaluate the project allowing them to take the decision to Authorise Project Closure

Raising Exceptions

An exception is raised when an agreed tolerance is either forecasted to be exceeded or is exceeded. This is raised to the management level above

Work Package Tolerances are agreed between the Project Manager and the Team Manager when the Team Manager accepts the Work Package. In the event an agreed tolerance is forecasted to exceed or has been exceeded, the Team Manager will raise the issue to the Project Manager. This could be formally or informally raised. The Project Manager will enter this into the Issue Register and an Issue Report is created (if the Issue needs to be handled formally)

The Team Manager does not create the Exception Report, the Team Manager only informs the Project Manager by raising the issue

Stage Tolerances are agreed between the Project Board and the Project Manager. If the stage is forecasted or has gone out of tolerance, the Project Manager will create and Exception Report to capture the information and allows the analyse why. This information is then provided to the Project Board

The Exception Report should include a number of options with a recommendation, the Project Board can do the following:

- Adjust the agreed tolerance level
- Remove the cause (if possible)

- Request more time to consider the issue and the response
- Request and exception plan

Project Tolerances are set between the Corporate or Program Management and the Project Board. If the project tolerance is forecasted or has gone out of tolerance then the Project Board will advise the Corporate or Program Management and can provide the Exception Plan to provide information on how the issue can be handled and the stage completed (if possible)

Progress Responsibilities

Corporate or Program Management	• Provides the Project Tolerances within the Project Mandate • Makes decisions on the Exception Plan when Project Tolerances are forecasted to be exceeded as the Project Board can not do this
Project Executive	• Provides Stage Tolerances • Makes decisions on Exception Plans when stage tolerances are forecasted to be exceeded • Ensures that progress remains consistent from the business perspective
Senior User **Senior Supplier**	• Ensures that progress remains consistent from the business perspective
Project Manager **(Can be assisted by Project Support)**	• Authorizes Work Packages • Monitors the progress of Stage Plans • Produces Highlight Reports, End Stage Reports, Lessons Reports & End Project Reports • Produces Exception Reports for the Project Board as required • Maintains the project using the registers and logs
Team Manager **(Optional)**	• Agrees on Work Packages • Produces Checkpoint Reports • Notifies the Project Manager of any forecasted deviation from the agreed Work Packages tolerances
Project Assurance	• Verifying the Business Case against external events and project progress • Confirming stage and project progress against agreed tolerances ensuring the Project Manager is following process and procedures
Project Support	• Assists with the creation of reports • Assists in maintaining the registers and logs

Figure 62 - Progress Roles & Responsibilities

Prince2
Processes

Processes

Within Prince2 the Processes are defined as a structured set of activities designed to accomplish a specific objective. As with the Themes and Principles, there are 7 Processes that guide you through the project and each provides a set of activities.

These activities help to direct, manage and deliver the project, like any process the Prince2 Process take inputs from multiple sources, acts upon this information and provides defined outputs

The 7 Prince2 Processes are:
- Starting Up a Project (SU)
- Initiating a Project (IP)
- Directing a Project (DP)
- Controlling a Stage (CS)
- Managing Product Delivery (PD)
- Managing a Stage Boundary (SB)
- Closing a Project (CP)

Pre-Project

The work that is undertaken before the project starts is known a Pre-Project.

The first step undertaken is the creation of the Project Mandate, this is the trigger for the project.

There are a number of activities that are completed as part of the Starting Up a project (SU) Process. The main objective is to verify that the project is worthwhile and prevents poor projects from starting. The Project Mandate is expanded into the Project Brief and a plan is created for the Initiation Stage.

After this process is complete, the Project Board reviews the Project Brief and makes the decision to Authorise the Initiation of the Project, this is the first decision undertaken by the Project Board

Initiation Stage

The Initiation Stage is the first stage of the Project and the activities undertaken are contained within the Initiating a Project Process (IP), as explained earlier there are a minimum of two project stages for each project. The Initiation Stage and the Next Stage where the products will be created.

The natural question at this point is "where is the Closing a Project, is that a stage?"

Closing a Project is a process and is part of the last stage of the project, put simply – the Closing a Project Process is the last part of the last Management Stage within the Project and replaces the Stage Boundary Process as there are no further stages

The objectives of the Initiation Stage are:
- To create the Detailed Business Case describing the project objectives and the benefits
- Prepare the Benefit Management Approach describing how and when the benefits will materialise and be reviewed

- Define the Project Product Quality, the timeline, costs, risks analysis and commitment of the required resources. This is then assembled into the Project Initiation Documentation (PID).
- The Project Plan at this stage is a high-level plan for the whole project, the Stage Plan is created for the first management stage which is more detailed

At the end of the Initiation Stage the Project Board will review the Project Initiation Documentation and decide whether to Authorise the Project. If authorised, the Project Initiation Documentation is baselined to enable reviews or comparisons against the project objectives

Next Stage

The Project Manager has day-2-day responsibility for the project and reports to the Project Board, the Project Manager completes the following:
- Assigns work to be completed
- Checks all deliverables have passed the required quality tests and met the required quality criteria
- Checks that the project is progressing in line with the agreed Project Plan
- Checks that forecasts are within project tolerances

All of the above activities are completed as part of the Controlling a Stage Process, the Project Manager maintains a number of documents, such as the Daily Log, the Registers and the Configuration Item Record

The Project Manager maintains the flow of information to the Project Board ensuring they are kept informed about the progress of the project using the Highlight Report

Work Packages are produced as part of the Managing Product Delivery Process, the Checkpoint Reports are used to ensure the Project Manager is kept up-to date in relation to the progress of the Work Package

Near the end of a stage in Managing a Stage Boundary Process, the Project Manager will request permission to proceed to the next stage and will provide the Project Board with the updated Business Case, End Stage Report and the Next Stage Plan

The Project Board will review this information to assess the continued viability of the project and decide whether to authorise the next stage

Final Delivery Stage

During the final management stage, the Project Manager will be accepting and obtaining the relevant approvals for the last products and will focus on closing the project

The Project Board will review the products created by the project owned by the relevant users, and also check that the support is in place for when the project has been closed

The Closing a Project Process (CP) is always the last part of the final management stage and includes the following activities:
- Assessing the project against the original plan

- The End Project Report is written by the Project Manager
- Planning the post project benefit reviews
- The Project Manager writes the Lessons Learned Report

The Project Board will review and where needed revise the data provided by the Project Manager and take the decision to Authorise the Project Closure. The Project Managers role is then completed

The Seven Processes

The seven management processes within Prince are aligned to one of the management levels within the Project Organisation (The Project Board, The Project Manager and the Team Manager)

Directing a Project Process

Directing a Project is the responsibility of the Project Board. The process runs from the Starting UP a Project Process until the Closing a Project Process is completed and authorisation to close the project is reviewed. The Objective of Directing a Project is to enable the Project Board to be accountable for the project's success by making key decisions and exercising overall control, whilst delegating day-2-day management of the project to the Project Manager

The Starting Up a Project Process

The Starting Up a Project Process (SU) is the responsibility of both the Project Executive and the Project Manager. This the very first process and is classed as Pre-Project within Prince2. This term is used as the project is not officially started until Initiation Stage has begun.

The reasons for the project as established and documented and the Project Management Team is assigned and a plan is created for the Initiation Stage

Initiating a Project Process

The Initiating a Project Process is the process that defines the Project Product, Product Quality, Project Timeline, Costs, Risks, Risks Analysis, commitment of resources and the Project Initiation Documentation (PID) is assembled by the Project Manager.

The Project Plan is created and the Detailed Business Case is completed.

The Objective of the Initiating a Project Process (IP) is to establish the solid foundations for the project enabling the organisation to understand the work required to complete the delivery of the projects products before the commitment of significant funds and resources

Controlling a Stage Process

The Controlling a Stage Process (CS) is the stage where the Project Manager does most of the work. The Project Manager monitors the work, takes corrective action as required, observes changes and communicates with stakeholders. This includes reporting and receiving reports.

These processes can be completed many times by the Project Manager until the stage is completed, the project is broken into stages to ensure management and control. The Controlling a Stage Process monitors each stage and repeated for each stage during the project

The objective of the Controlling a Stage Process (CS) is to assign the work to be completed, monitor the work, deal with issues and report progress to the Project Board. Take corrective action where required to ensure the stage remains with tolerance

Managing Product Delivery Process

The Managing Product Delivery Process is the reporting process for a stage enabling the Project Board to check on the stages progress against the plans.

The objective of the Managing Product Delivery Process is to control the link between the Project Manager and the Team Manager by placing formal requirements for the acceptance, execution and deliver the project work

Managing Stage Boundary Process

The Managing Stage Boundary Process (SB) is the reporting process for a stage, enabling the Project Board can check on the stage and how well the stage has done when compared against the plans. The process evaluates the stage and prepares the plan for the next stage, the End Stage Report and the Next Stage Plan are submitted to the Project Board

The Objective of the Managing Stage Boundary Process is to enable the Project Board to be provided with sufficient information by the Project Manager so that it can review the success of the current stage, approve the stage plan, review the updated stage plan and confirm the continued business justification for the project and the acceptance of the risks

The Closing a Project Process

The Closing a Project Process covers the process of closing the project and is the last part of the final stage. Pricne2 suggests a number of activities are completed when preparing for project closure, such as the End Project Report, Lessons Learned Report and the Acceptance Record

The Output of this process will be the basis for the Project Boards approval for closure, The Project Manager recommends the closure and the Project Board is responsible for the closure of the project within the Directing a Project Process. The Project Manager recommends closure only

The Objective of the Closing a Project Process is to provide a fixed point at which acceptance for the project product is confirmed and to recognize that the original objects as defined in the Project Initiation Documentation (PID) have been achieved or the approved changes to the objectives have been achieved or that the project has nothing to contribute

Starting Up a Project Process

The purpose or objective of this process is to answer the primary question

"Do we have a worthwhile and viable project"

The Project Mandate is normally the only document that exists at this point in the project and is not sufficient to answer the above question by the Project Board

The Starting Up a Project Process provides the Project Board with the necessary information to make the assessment if the project is worthwhile. They use the Project Brief which contains the information from the Outline Business Case. This prevents poorly defined projects from starting and wasting funds and resources

The Objectives of the Starting Up a Project Process (SU) are to:
- Ensure that there is a Business Case or business justification and this is documented within the Outline Business Case. The Business Case document will not be completed until the Initiation Stage
- Review the Project Approach and examine the best way to deliver the project, this can be obtained using advice from Subject Matter Experts, reviewing previous Lessons Reports and Logs or even using external support from suppliers for example
- Select the resources (People) who will complete the work required to Initiate the project and fill the other roles within the Project Team
- Create the Project Brief which contains the information on the scope of the project and contains the majority of the information collected in relation to the Project
- Create a detailed Stage Plan to plan and complete the work required during the Initiation Stage

The Starting Up a Project Process provides the Project Board with the information to approve the project to proceed to Initiation Stage

The activities undertaken during the Starting Up a Project Process (SU) are:
- The project trigger – is the Project Mandate which is provided by Corporate or Program Management
- The Project Mandate is expanded into the Project Brief and is used by the Project Board to decide whether or not to authorise the initiation of the project
  - If the Project is part of a Program, the Project Brief will be provided by the Program – In essence most of the work required within the Starting Up a Project Process (SU) is completed by the Program
- The Project Brief is assembled and the Outline Business Case is refined with close cooperation from the Project Board, Project Manager and stakeholders
- The completion of the Project Brief and the Business Case is an iterative process and is a constant cycle of meetings\discussions and reviews

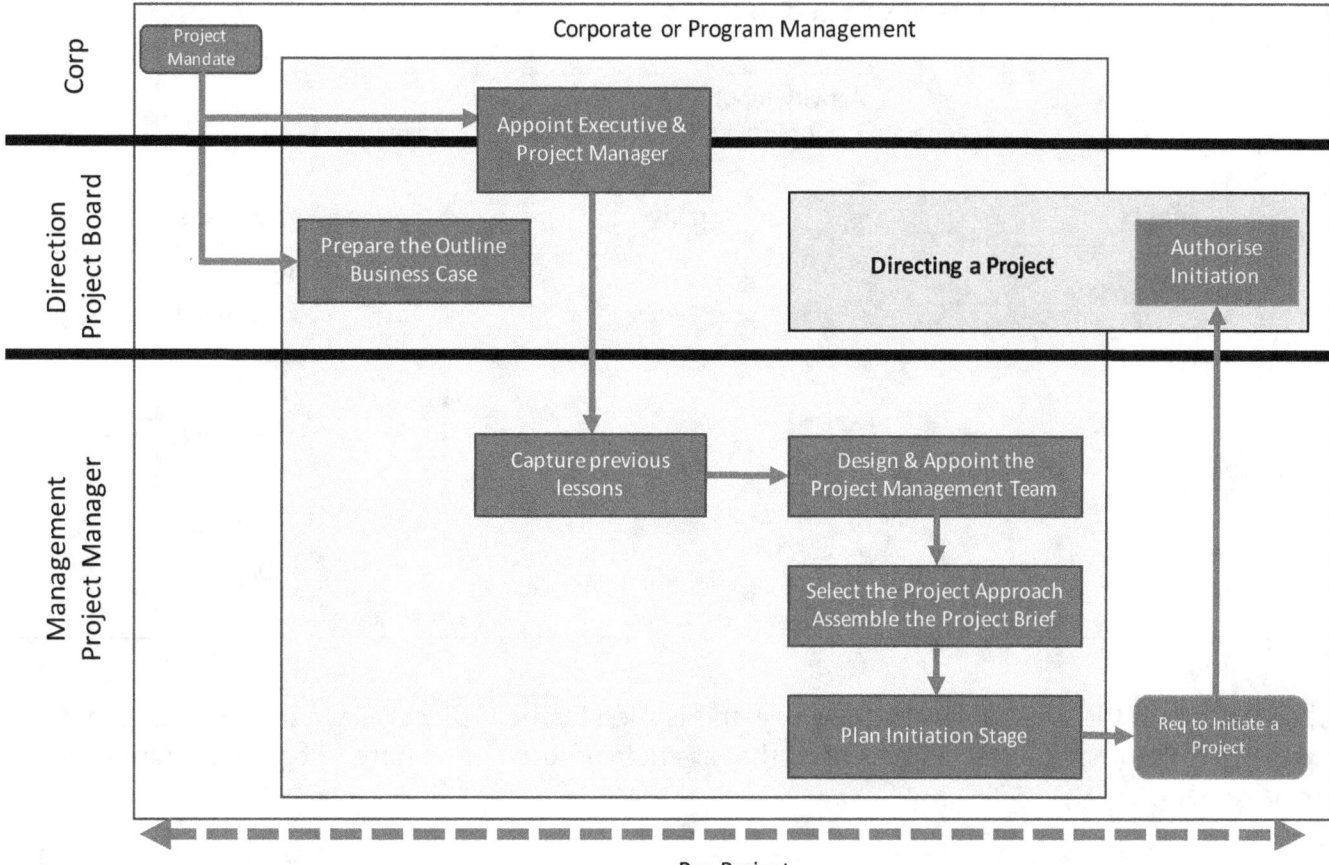

Figure 63 - Starting Up a Project Process (SU)

The activities completed within the Starting Up a Project Process (SU) are:
1. Corporate or Program Management appoints the Executive and the Project Board
2. Capture previous Lessons
3. Designing and appointing the Project Management Team
4. Prepare the Outline Business Case
5. Select the Project Approach and assemble the Project Brief
6. Plan the Initiation Stage

2-6 are completed primarily by the Project Manager with support from the Project Executive

Appoint the Project Executive and Project Manager

The appointment of the Executive is made by Corporate\Program Management and the Project Manager is selected by the Executive. The Executive is the person responsible for the project and is the main decision maker (the Project Board is not a democracy), the Executive represents the interests of the Business whilst the Project Manager will manage the overall project on a day-2-day basis

The appointment of these roles follows the same steps, which are defined below:
- The responsibilities are established and the role descriptions are prepared.
- Identification of candidates and the selection of the most appropriate person
- Estimate the time and effort required and confirmation of the person's availability
- Acceptance of the role and the required commitment

- Assignment of the person selected to the role

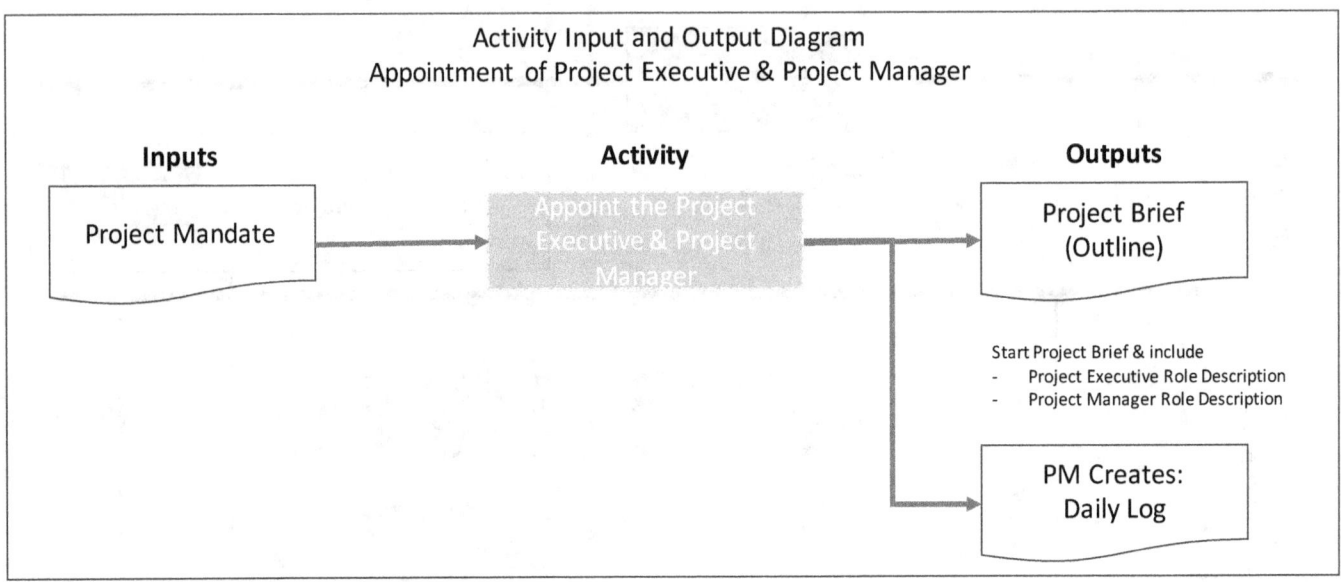

Figure 64 - Appoint Project Executive & Project Manager

The final task is the creation of the Daily Log, this is sued by the Project Manager as a repository to track information, requests, tasks, actions that are not captured elsewhere or do not require formal management

Capture Previous Lessons

Projects can (and should) learn from previous projects, the positives and the negatives, this is the purpose of the Lessons Log and Lessons Report.

The Project Manager will create a new Lessons Log to be used for the duration of the project and will add useful lessons. The Lessons Log will be updated throughout the duration of the project.

Capturing previous lessons is a principle of Prince2 is fundamental to the project's success. The responsibility for producing and maintaining the Lessons Logs is the Project Manager

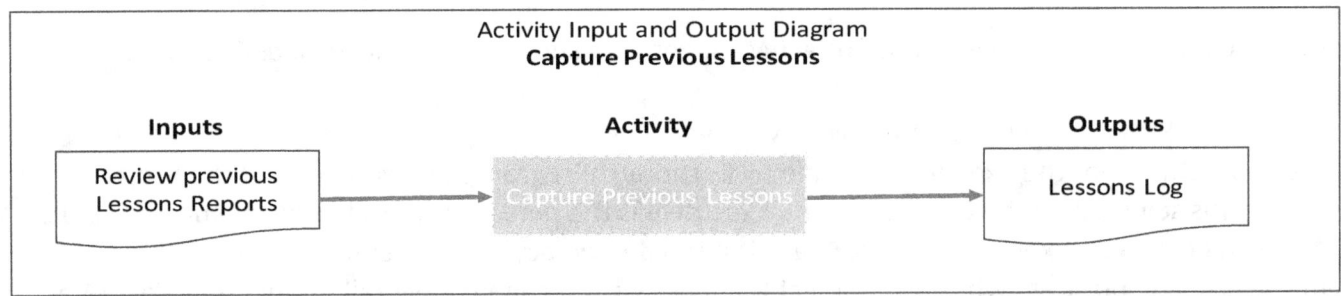

Figure 65 - Capture Previous Lessons

Design & Appoint the Project Management Team
The Project Manager will review previous Project Management Teams and their Role Descriptions, these tasks are:

- Create Role Descriptions for the project and examine the need for Team Managers and Team Members, Project Support and how to communicate between these roles
- Estimate the time and effort required from each of the roles and select the most suitable person. It may be necessary for training or familiarisation to be completed.
- Confirm acceptance of the role

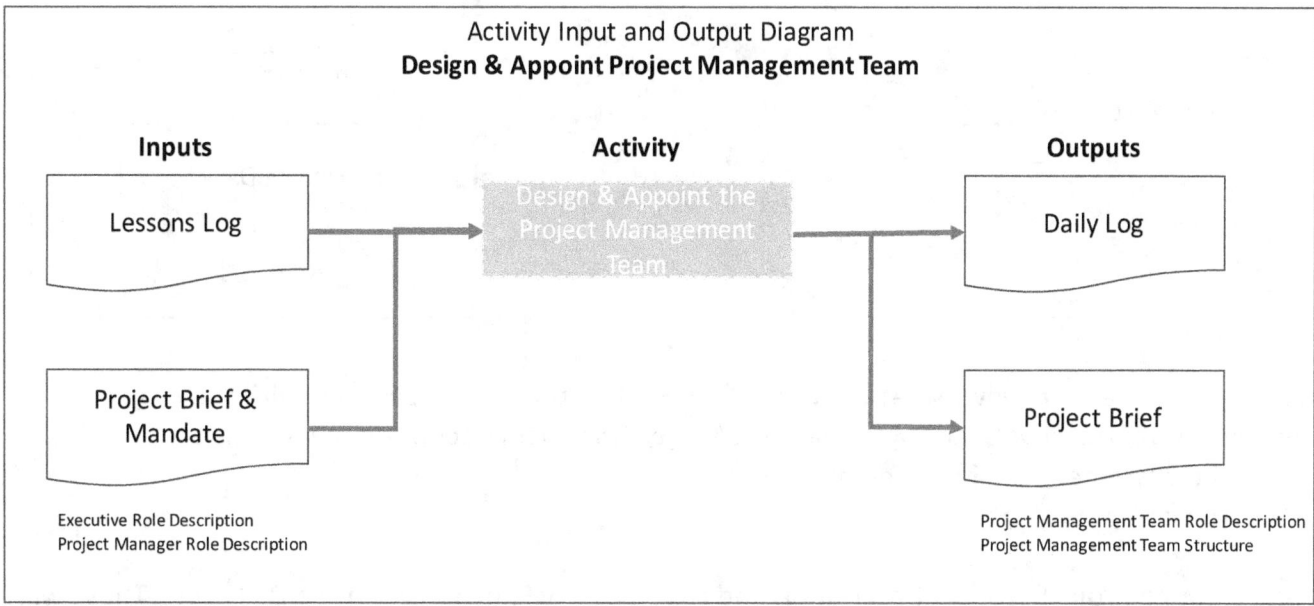

Figure 66 - Design & Appoint the Project Management Team

The Executive is responsible for the appointment of the Project Management Team, whilst the Project Manager is responsible for the Project Team Structure and the Project Role Descriptions. The Project Manager will keep track of the progress of this activity within the Daily Log

Outline Business Case
The preparation of the Outline Business Case includes the creation of the Project Product Description, it is important to ensure that all stakeholders know why the project exists and what the justification and benefits are in relation to the project. This is detailed in the Business Case, the Business Case is the main justification and driver for the project, it is important to ensure the Outline Business Case has sufficient information and is completed as soon as possible

The Outline Business Case is usually a high-level overview of the project and is created by the Executive with the support of the Project Manager. The source of the information is the Project Mandate and the Lessons Log, the Executive and the Project Manager expand this to include the following:

- How the project will support the Corporate or Strategic Objectives
- How the Project will be funded
- The format of the Business Case (How to best present it to the higher-level management)

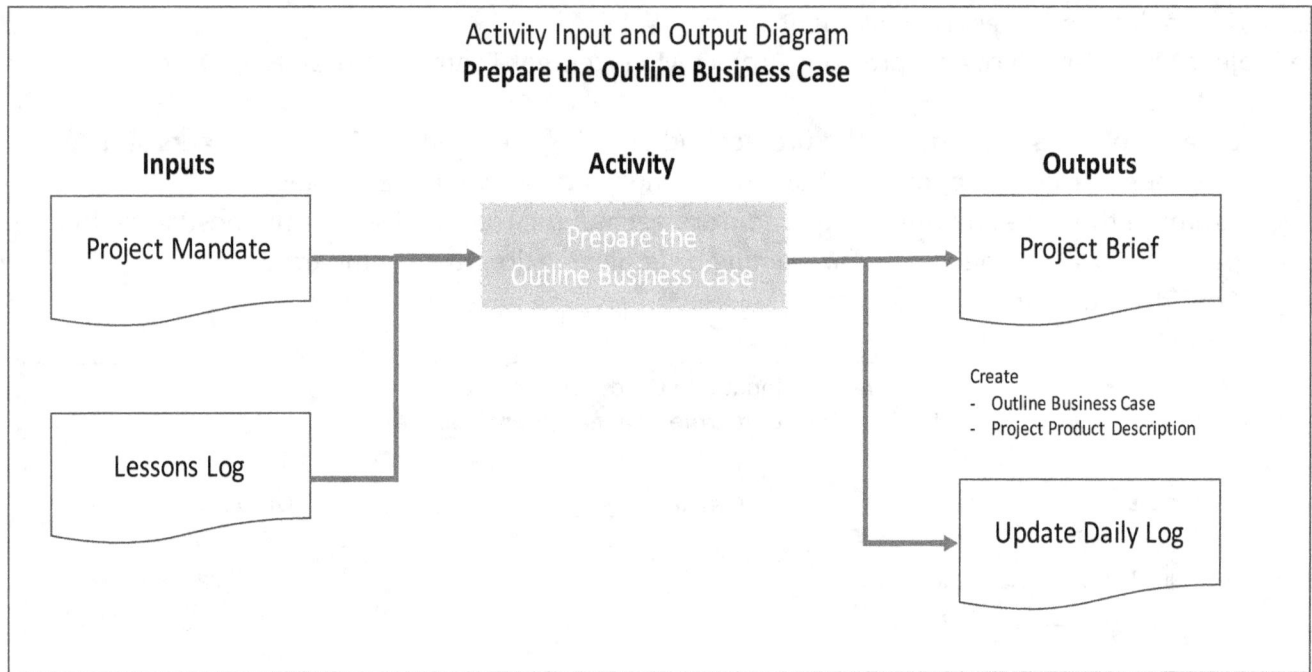

Figure 67 - Prepare the Outline Business Case

The Project Manager reviews what the project will deliver through discussions with the Project Executive and the Senior User, they create the Project Product Description and considers
- The customers quality expectations
- The acceptance criteria

When creating Project Product Description and captures any known risks in the Daily Log. These will be reviewed at a later date and where required be placed in the Outline Business Case

Select the Project Approach and Assembly of the Project Brief
Selecting the Project Approach is the answer to the question

"what is the best way to deliver the Project?

For example, is there an off the shelf solution? can we use internal resources or external resources? what lessons can be learnt? what are the sources of information?"

There should also be consideration in relation to company standards or program standards, skills required, training requirements.

All of the above will form part of the Project Approach which will then form part of the Project Brief. The Project Manager is responsible for the Project Approach Activity

Assembling the Project Brief
Using the information that is used to assemble the Project Approach, is then used to assemble or create the Project Brief. The Project Brief takes the information from:
- The Outline Business Case including a summary of the known risks
- The Project Product Description which includes the Quality Criteria

- The Project Approach which includes an overview of the Project Team Structure and the Roles Descriptions

The assembly of the Project Brief is the responsibility of the Project Manager, supported by the Senior Users who will review it and the Project Executive will approve it.

The Project Brief also contains updates to the Project Objectives and the desired outcomes, it also confirms the Project Scope. This information is obtained from the Project Mandate

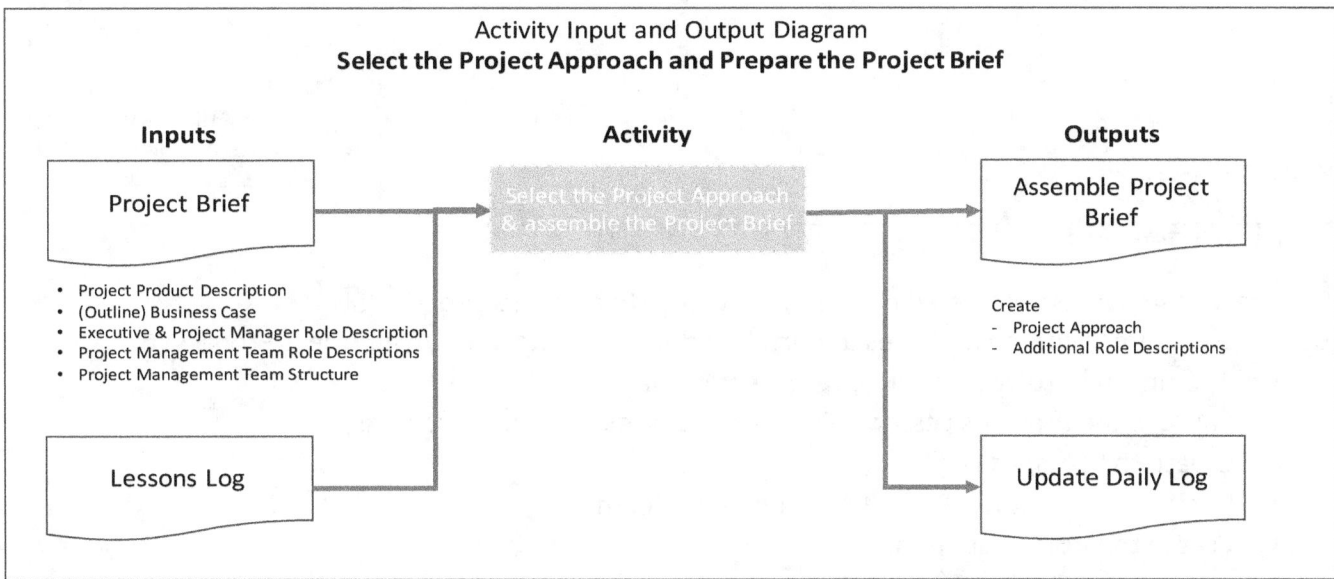

Figure 68 - Select Project Approach, Assemble Project Brief

Initiation Stage Planning

Planning the Initiation Stage, this is the final activity within the Starting Up a Project Process (SU), the Starting Up a Project Process (SU) checks the justification for the project, whilst the Initiation Stage will plan the project, create the Product Descriptions and Sub-Product Descriptions and provide the detailed Business Case, with the final out being the Project Initiation Documentation (PID)

The Starting Up a Project Process (SU) does not need to be a long process, however the Initiation Stage can take time to complete and requires a plan to manage and run the Initiation Stage

Prince2 recommends the following tasks are completed within this activity:
- Defined the Reporting and Control mechanisms or arrangements for the Initiation Stage
- Produce the Initiation Stage Plan, include the time, cost and resource data
- Review the Risks contained in the Daily Log to assess their potential impact upon the Initiation Stage
- Request the Project Board approves Authorisation to Initiate the Project allowing the project to continue

The Next Stage Plan is created by the Project Manager and reviewed by the Senior User, with approval from the Executive

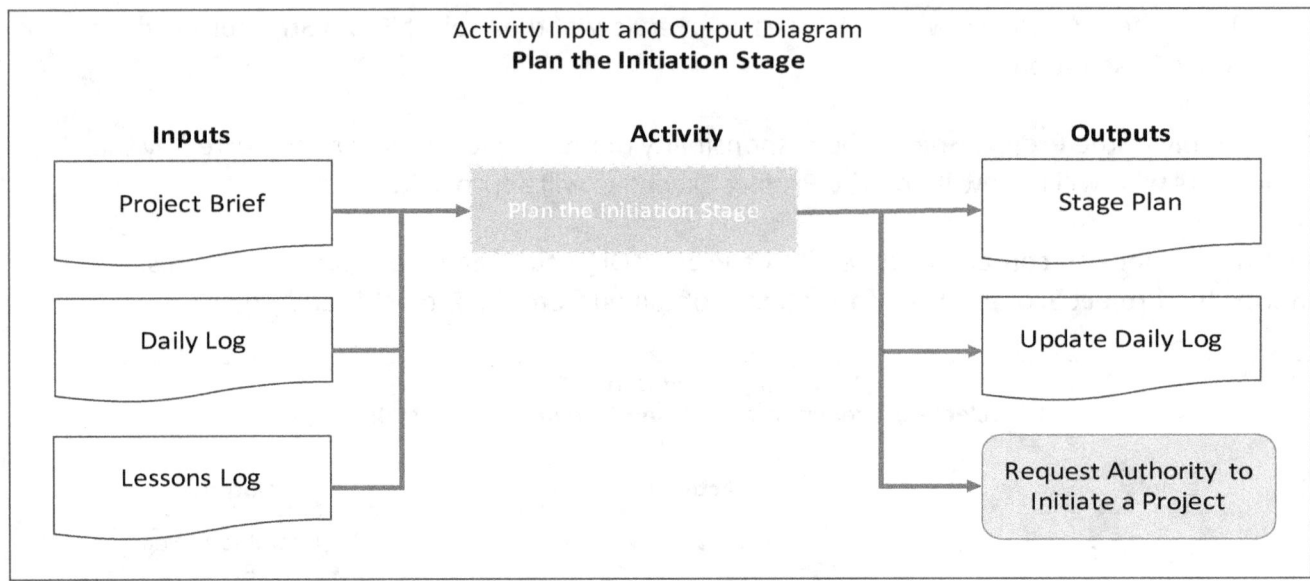

Figure 69 - Plan Initiation Stage

Summary of Activities completed during the Starting Up a Project Process (SU)
Below is a summary of the activities undertaken during the Starting Up a Project Process
- Appoint the Project Executive & Project Manager
- Capture the Previous Lessons (From previous lessons logs & reports)
- Create the Lessons Log
- Design & appoint the Project Management Team
- Create the Role Descriptions
- Prepare the Outline Business Case
- Create the Product Description
- Plan the Initiation Stage

The Executive is responsible for the appointment of the Project Manager, the Project Management Team and the creation of the Outline Business Case

The Project Manager is responsible for the:
- Role Descriptions
- Capturing and reviewing the previous lessons
- The Project Approach
- Assembly of the Project Brief
- Updating and maintaining the Daily Log
- Creating the Initiation Stage Plan

Initiating a Project Process (IP)
The Objective of the Initiating a Project Process (IP) is to understand the work that is required to deliver the required products. This is needed before deciding to proceed with the project. The Project Manager will ask the following questions about the project to support this process:
- What are the reasons for the project?
- What are the Benefits?
- What are the Risks?
- How will we ensure that Quality will be achieved?

- How will risks, issues and changes be managed (Identified, assessed, managed)
- How will Progress be monitored, who needs to be informed and how often will be they be informed?
- How will Prince2 be tailored to fit the Project?

Whilst Starting Up a Project (SU) checks if the Project is viable, initiating a Project is about building a solid foundation for the Project to proceed and ensuring all stakeholders are clear on what will be achieved by the project

Think of the Initiating a Project Process in the same terms as the foundation for a house, the foundation is the solid base that the house is built on, Initiation is the same foundation for the project and provides the solid foundation to enable the project to be successful.

The Project Manager will create a number of management products to provide information on how the project will be managed, the costs, how quality will be checked, planning and communication

The activities within the Initiating a Project Process (IP) are:
- Preparation of the Risk Management Approach – which will answer how risks will be managed during the project
- Preparation of the Change Control Approach – which will give information on how the products will be managed during the project
- Preparation of the Quality Management Approach – Which will give the information on how quality will be ensured
- Communication Management Approach– which will give the information related to project communication with stakeholders
- Setup the Project Controls – provides information on how the Project Board will control the Project
- Create the Project Plan – including costs, timescales, risks, quality
- Refine the Business Case – from Outline Business Case to the Detailed Business Case
- Assemble the Project Initiation Documentation (PID)

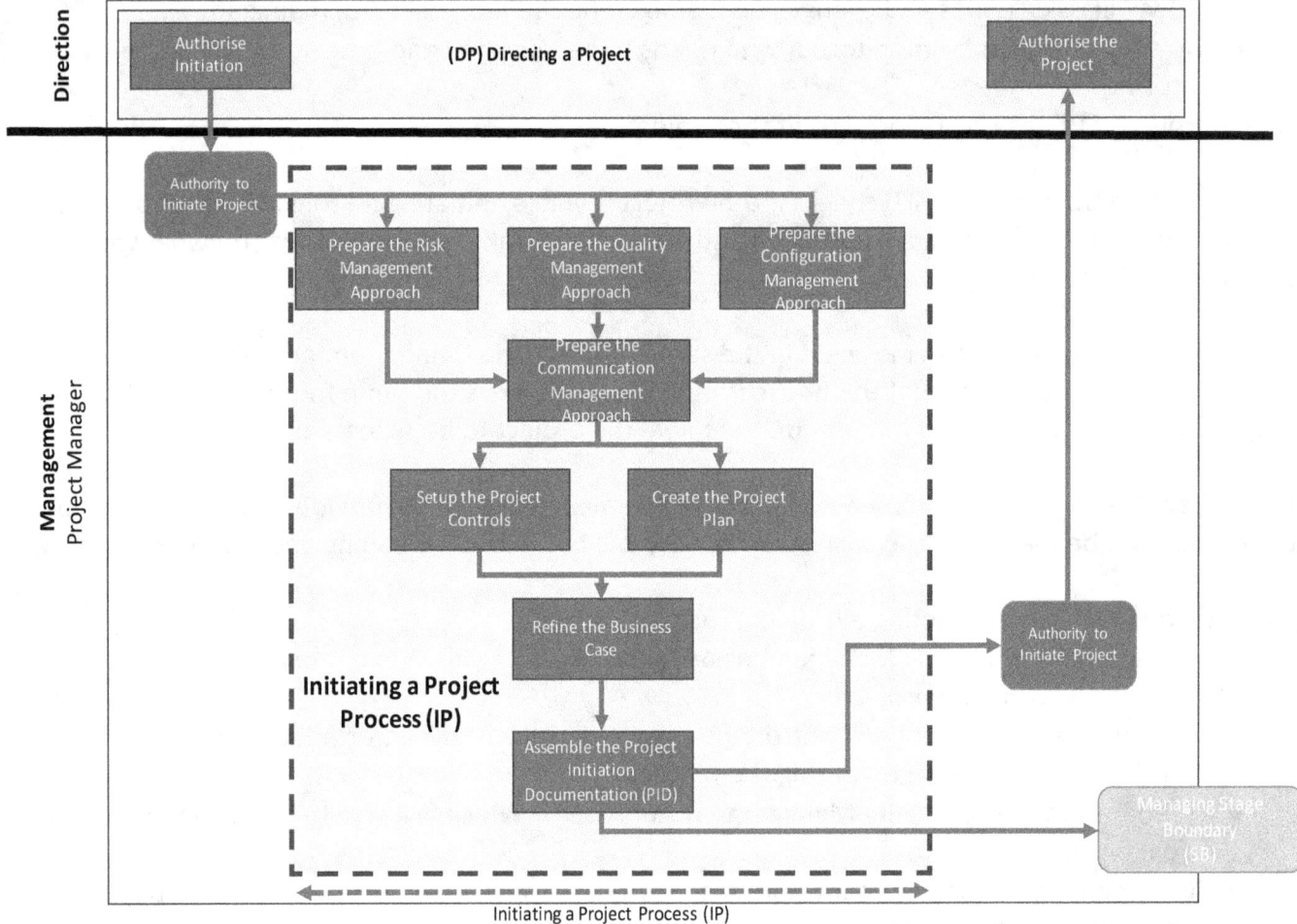

Figure 70 - Initiating a Project Process (IP)

The Project Manager will begin with the 4 Management Approaches and will then create the Project Controls and the Project Plan and Project Controls based upon the information contained within the Management approaches. The Management approaches as with the Business Case are iterative and will continue to be updated during the Initiation Stage.

The Detailed Business Case cannot be completed until after the Project Plan as the Project Plan provides information to support the creation of the Business Case (Time, Cost, Resources etc)

The final activity is to create the Project Initiation Documentation (PID)

The Risk Management Approach
The Risk Management Approach is an explanation about how the Project will manage Risk and it will contain
- Information on how Risks will be documented
- The procedures that will be followed,
- The Roles & Responsibilities in relation to the management of risks
- The Risk Tolerances
- Measurements for Probability & Impact
- Reporting techniques

The Project Manager will normally use the following inputs when preparing the Risk Management Approach:

- Project Brief – Details the standards that should be followed and includes a summary of known risks
- Lessons Log – Will contain risks from previous or similar projects
- Daily Log – Contains Risks that are currently being managed informally, or information about how Risks will be gathered or have been gathered in Starting Up a Project (SU)

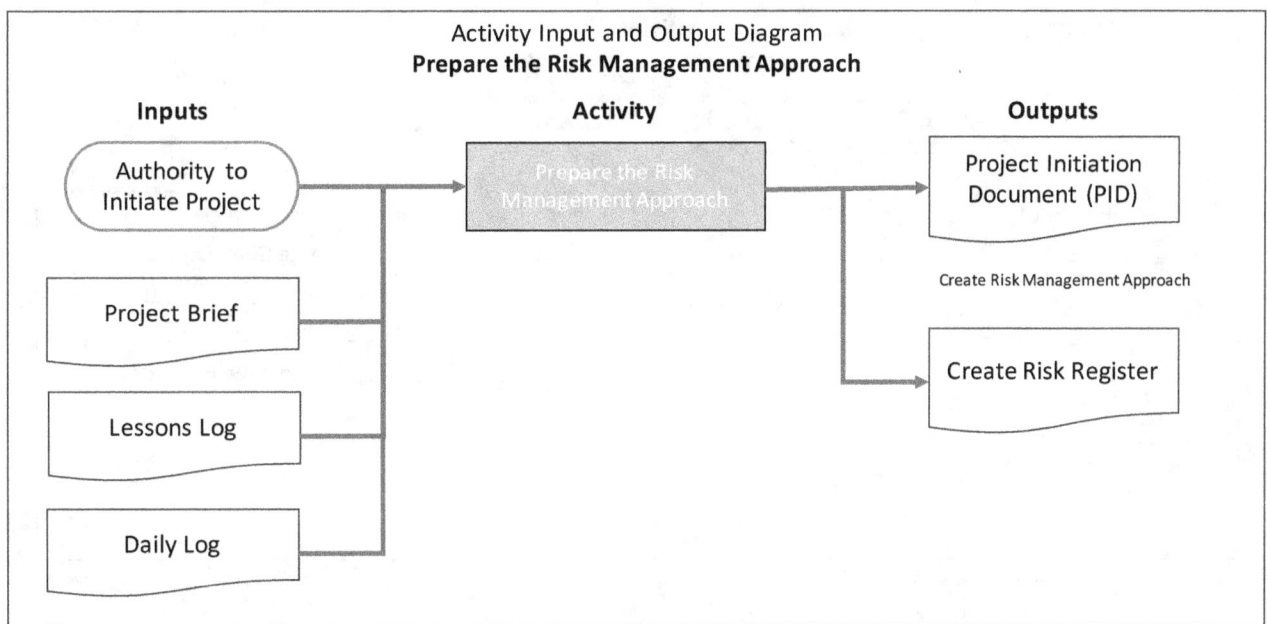

Figure 71 - Prepare the Risk Management Approach

The outputs of this activity are:

- The Risk Register – P260 of the Prince2 2009 Manual and P329 of the Prince 2017 Manual
- The Risk Management Approach – Appx A of the Prince2 2009 Manual and the Prince 2017 Manual

Whilst the Project Manager creates the Risk Management Approach, Project Support (if available) will setup the Risk Register and maintain it.

Change Control Approach

The Change Control Approach defines how the products will be managed during the project.

The Change Control Approach is used to identify how and by whom, the projects products will be controlled and protected and aims to answer the follow;

- How and where the projects products will be stored
- What storage and retrieval security will be used
- How the products and version will be identified
- How changes to products will be controlled
- Where responsibility for configuration management will lie

There are two kinds of Products in Prince2 projects:

- Management Products – For example the Project Brief, Project Plan are produced to help manage the project – these documents are created for each project
- Specialist Products are the products the project will create – these are the products that are wanted\needed by the users – For example a new piece of software for the Finance department, or a new piece of hardware for Engineering

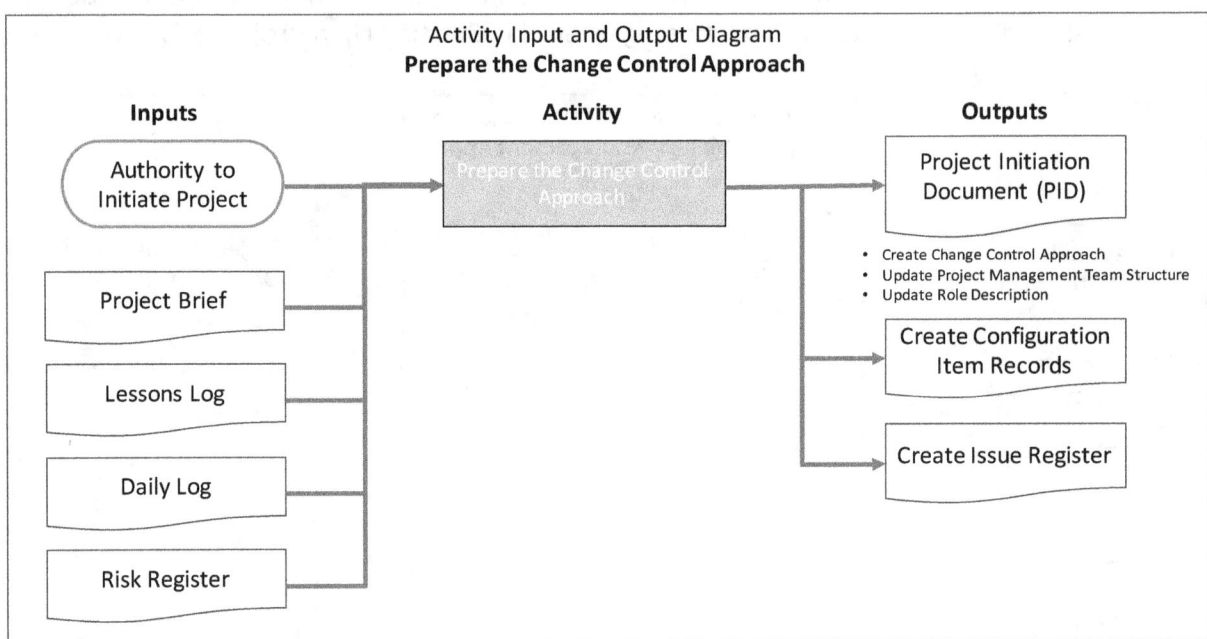

Figure 72 - Prepare the Change Management Approach

The outputs for the activity are:
- The Configuration Item Record – a one page summary for the project products
- The Change Control Approach (Produced by the Project Manager)
- The Issue Register – Used to capture and maintain information on each issue and is monitored by the Project Manager on a regular basis

The Change Control Approach includes the information below:
- The Configuration Management Control Procedure
- The Change Control Procedure
- The Issue Management Procedure
- Roles & Responsibilities

Quality Management Approach

The objective of the Quality Management Approach is to define the quality techniques and standards that will be applied to the project including the responsibilities for achieving the required quality levels

Quality is a Theme of Prince2 and the outputs of this activity are:
- Quality Management Approach– created by the Project Manager
- Quality Register – Which contains a summary of all details relating to planned and completed quality activities

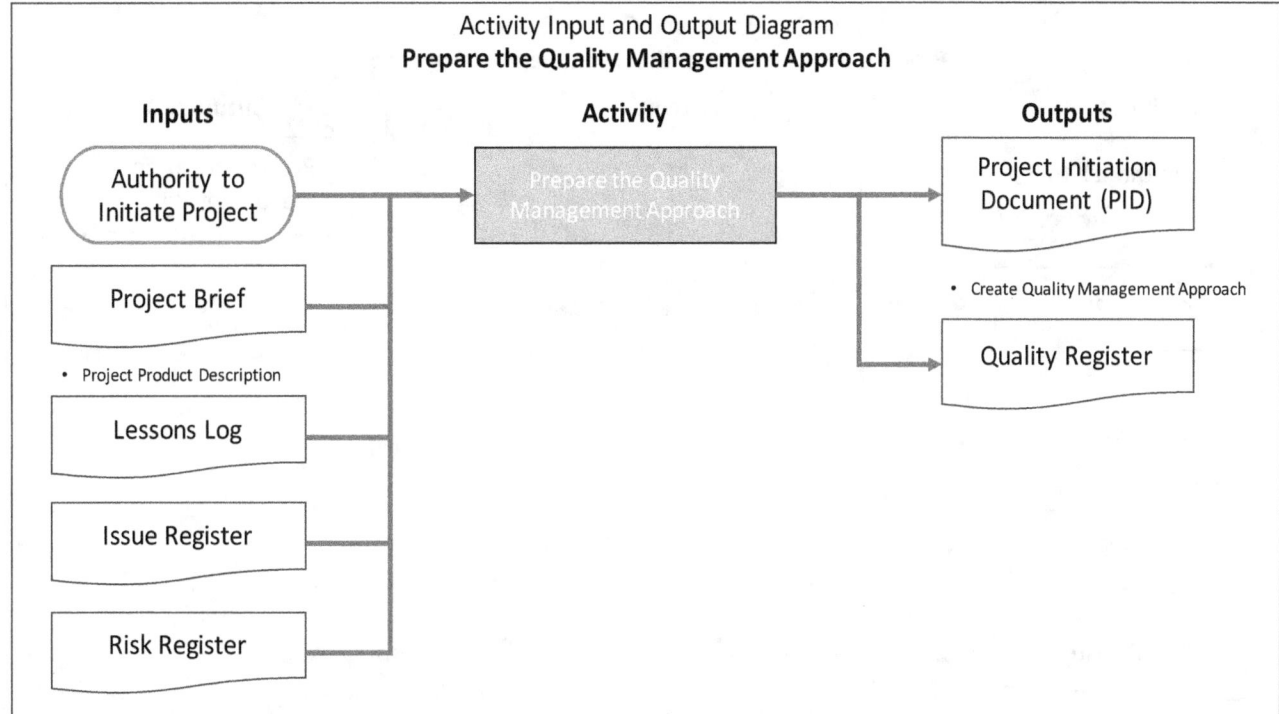

Figure 73 - Prepare the Quality Management Approach

The Quality Management Approach contains the following information:
- Quality Management Procedure – The procedure for planning, quality control, quality assurance, quality approval
- Tools and techniques that will be used
- Timing of quality management activities
- Roles & Responsibilities

The Quality Management Approach is approved by Project Assurance, ensuring it is in line with the Corporate or Program Management Standards

Communication Management Approach

The objective of the Communication Management Approach is to document the procedures for communication during the project, how communication will be done, the frequency, who will communicate and the format of the communication etc

As part of the process in creating the Communication Management Approach, the Project Manager will complete the following:
- Review the project Brief and document any communication requirements it contains
- Review the Lessons Log for any lessons from previous projects
- Identify stakeholders and discuss\confirm their communication requirements

The Project Manager will then define the Communication Management Approach and Project Assurance will review this.

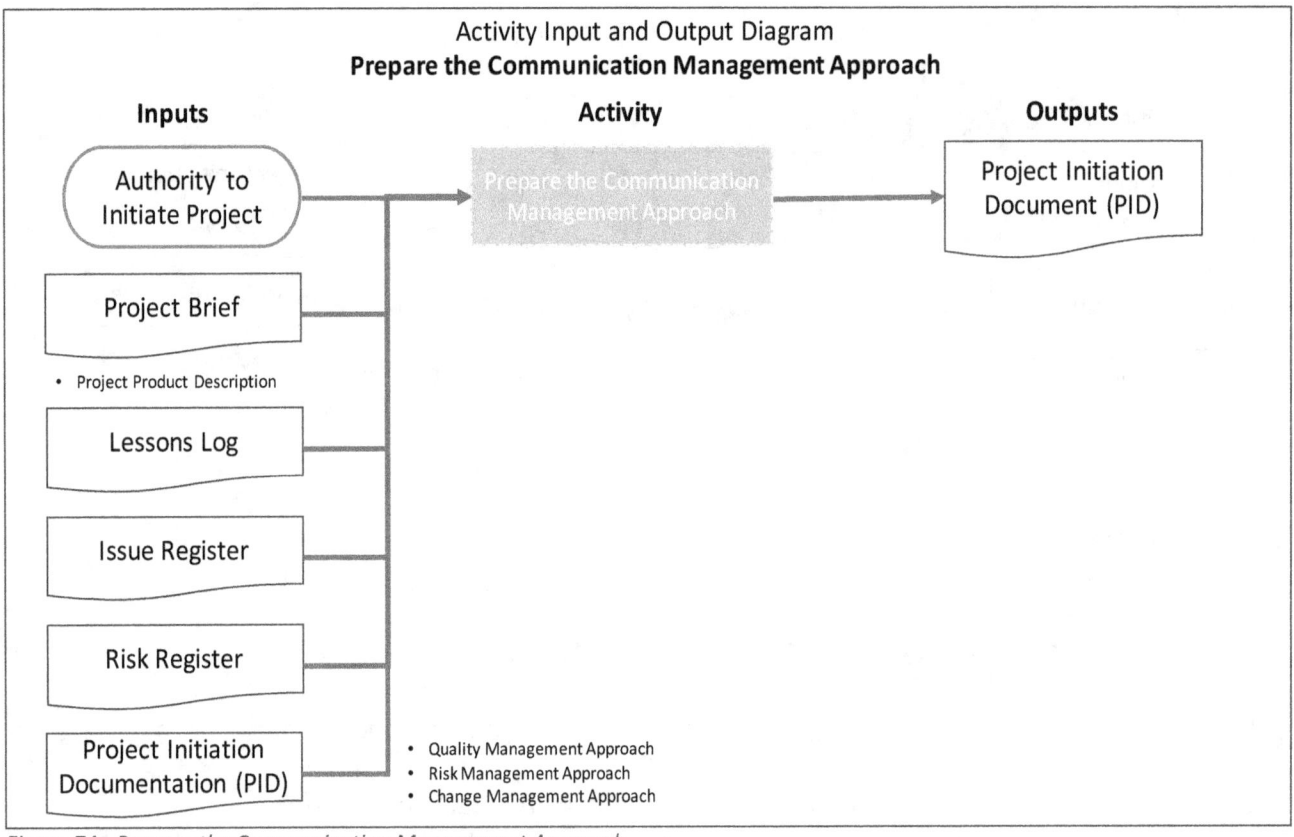

Figure 74 - Prepare the Communication Management Approach

Setting Up the Project Controls

The Project Controls enable the project to be managed more effectively and efficiently, the types on control are:

- Project Board to Project Manager
- Project Manager to the Team Manager controlling the work carried by the Team Manager and their respective teams

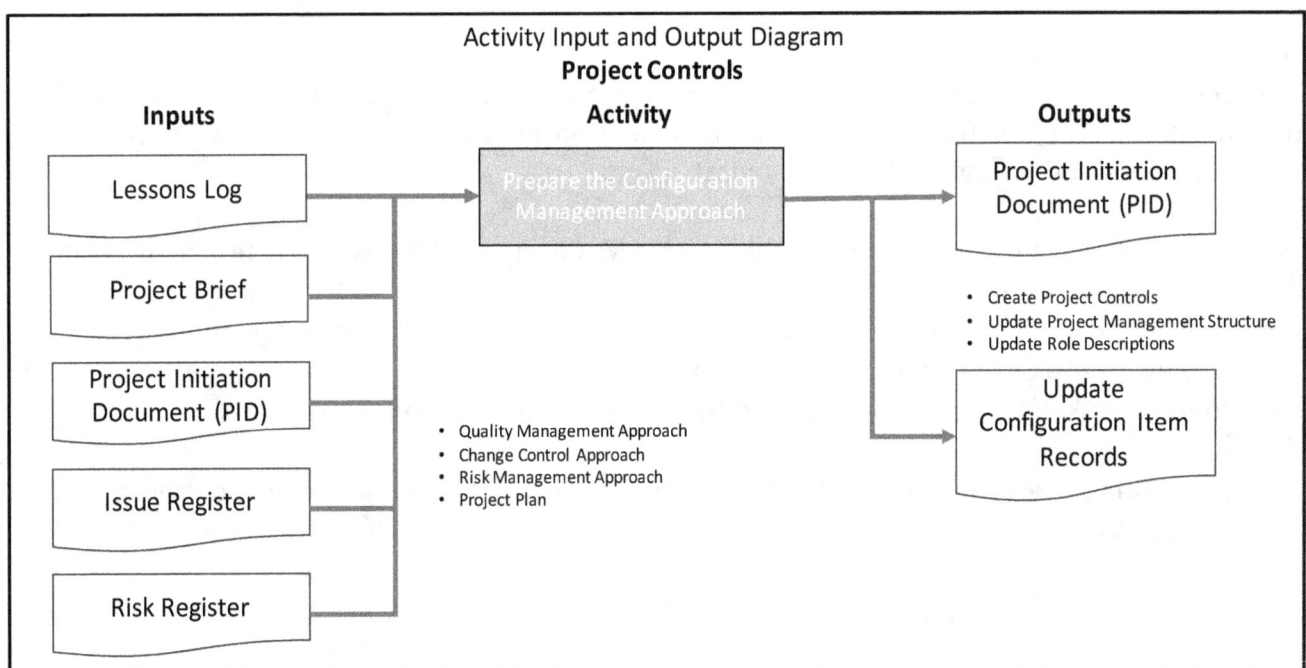

Figure 75 - Setting Up Project Controls

The main outputs derived from the setting up Project Controls is the Project Control Document; the Project Control Document will become a part of the Project Initiation Documentation (PID) and is created by the Project Manager.

At this point the number of stages within the project will be defined and this will include the number of End Stage Assessments that will be required from the Project Board

The Change Theme provides information on how to capture and analyse issues and the Progress Theme provides information on the escalation, tolerances and monitoring progress

Prince2 recommends that the following actions or activities are completed:
- Review the Project Brief, Quality Management Approach, Lessons Learned and Risk Register for key information that may support the creation of the Project Controls
- Define the number of stages and stage boundaries to support the level of control appropriate to the project
- Review Lessons from similar projects
- Define the decision-making process to ensure the direction and decision-making process is defined and the Project Manager knows the correct escalation path and decision path. This should also become part of the Project Team Structure
- Revie and confirm the Tolerances assigned to the Project Manager by the Project Board and the Project Manager and the Team Manager

The Project Controls will be reviewed by the Project Assurance

The Project Plan
As explained previously the Project Plan is not a Gannt chart, but contains the information on Timescales, Costs (both Opex and Capex), Resources required to deliver and support the project, the Products that will be produced by the Project, Risks, Tolerances, Controls and Quality.

More information on the Project Plan is contained in Appendix A of the Prince Manual and the Plans Theme

Prince2 recommends that the following tasks are completed to support this activity:
- Review the Project Brief to ensure you understand
  - The Milestones
  - Standards
  - Constraints
  - Dependencies
  - Assumptions
- Review the Lessons Log
- Review the Risk Register
- Review the Issue Register
- Agree the format for the Project Plan
- Agree the method to be used for the estimating process
- Review the Management approaches and where required incorporate the information into the Project Plan

- Create the following for the major products within the plan:
  - Product Breakdown Structure
  - Product Flow Diagram
  - Product Descriptions
- Review the Project Product Description and if required update this based upon the new information
- Identify and confirm the resources required
- Identify the Project Controls, activities and timings to ensure these can be added to the plan

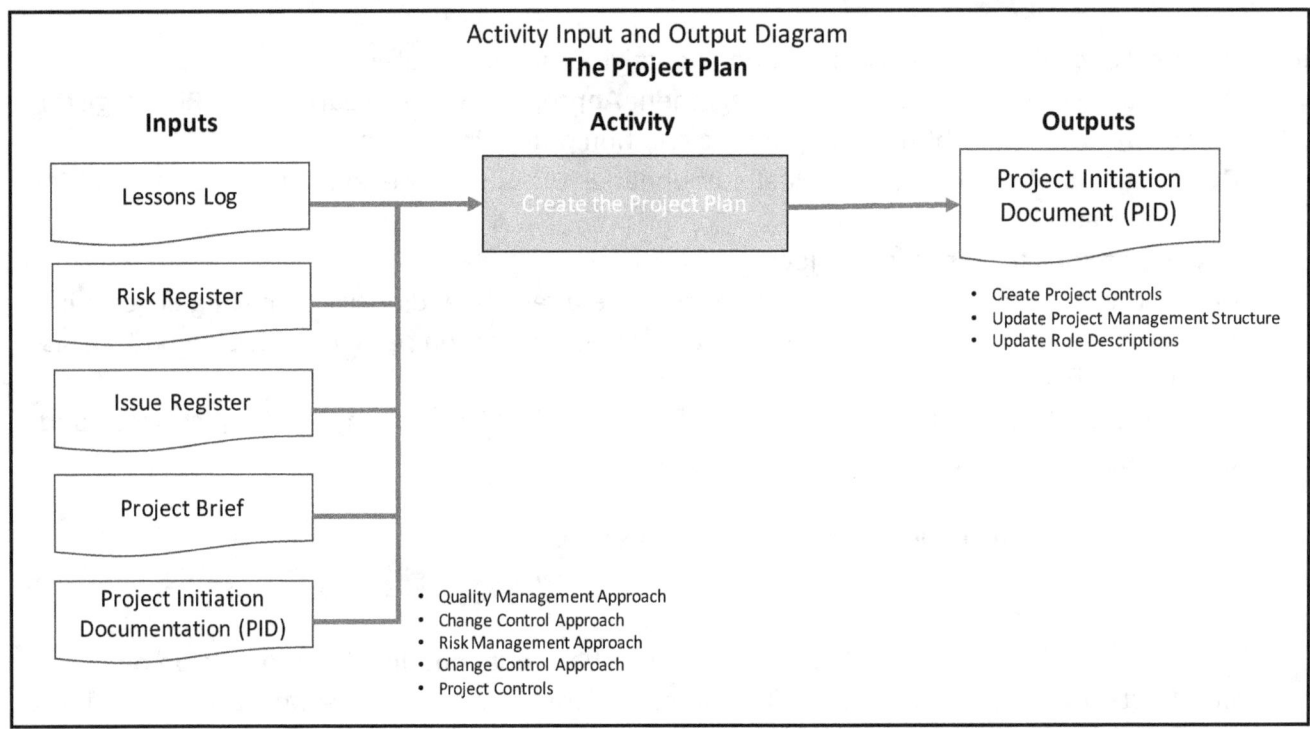

Figure 76 - The Project Plan

The Project Plan is a key element of the Project Initiation Documentation (PID) and also supports the effective foundation to support a successful project and should not be rushed.

The Project Manager creates the Project Initiation Documentation (PID) with support from Subject Matter Experts.

Project Assurance will review the Project Controls and ensure that it meets the needs of the Project Board and associated stakeholders, the Project Board will approve the Project Controls

Detailed Business Case
The Business Case is started as part of the Starting Up a Project Process (SU) and is the Outline Business Case which contains enough information to confirm that it is a viable and achievable project. This document should now be updated by the Executive and the Project Manager using the information gathered during the Initiation Stage.

The main documents to support this are:
  - Project Plan
  - The Outline Business Case

- o Project Brief
- o Risk Register

Prince2 recommends that the following activities are completed:
- o Review the Project Brief for any information that should be included in the Detailed Business Case
- o Review the Lessons Log and Lessons from previous projects
- o Include
  - o Time & Cost from the Project Plan
  - o Risks from the Risk Register
  - o Benefits and tolerances for each identified benefit

The Executive is responsible for the Business Case and the Project Managers role is to assist. The Executive can also be supported from other stakeholders as needed to create the Detailed Business Case

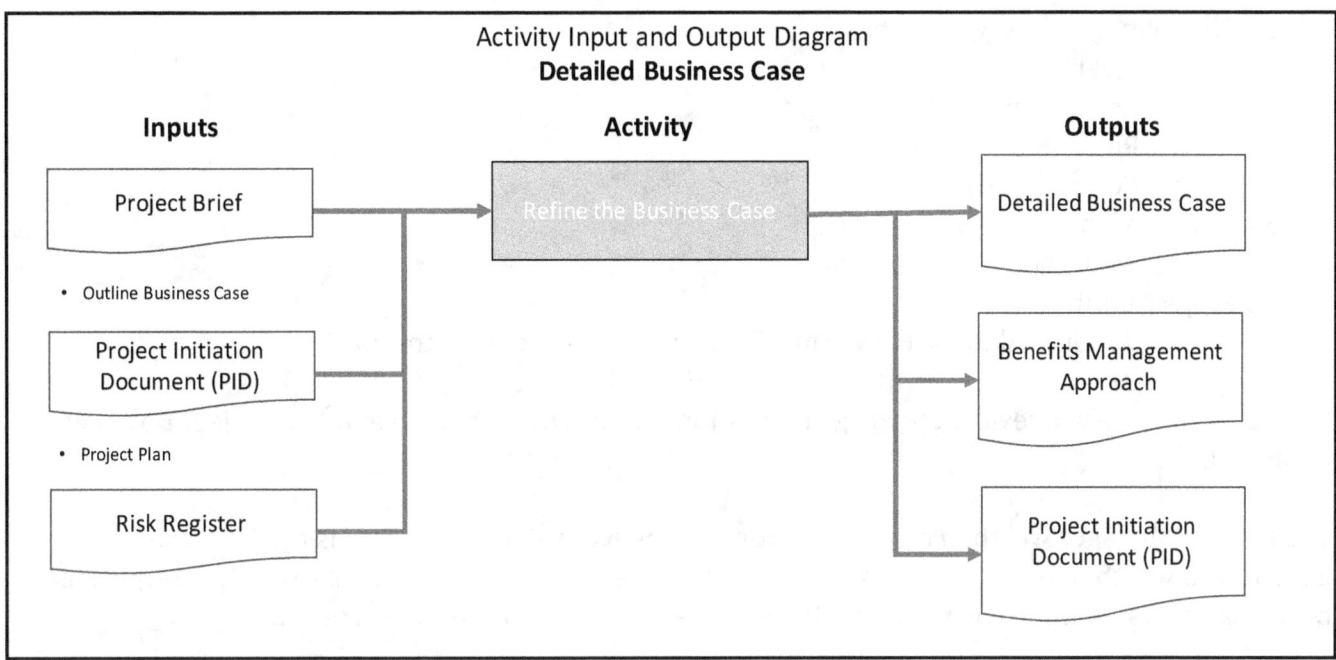

Figure 77 - Detailed Business Case

Benefit Management Approach
The Benefit Management Approach is the final document created during this stage by the Project Manager. This document contains the following information:
- o Describes each of the identified benefits
- o Describes how and when each benefit will be realised
- o Describe how each benefit will be measured and by whom

The Detailed Business Case and the Benefit Management Approach will be reviewed by Project Assurance on behalf of the Project Board prior to their approval

Assemble the Project Initiation Documentation (PID)
The Project Initiation Documentation (PID) is a collection or consolidation of documents that were created in both Starting Up a Project (SU) and Initiating a Project (IP). This provides the key

documentation required to start the project. The Project Initiation Documentation (PID) provides the:
- o The what
- o The Who
- o The Why
- o The How
- o The When
- o The cost

The Project Initiation Documentation (PID) once compiled will be approved and then baselined. It will then be used in future reviews to check against the original forecasts

The Project Manager assembles the Project Initiation Documentation (PID) and includes the following information and documents
- o Project Brief
- o Project Management Team Structure and Roles & Descriptions
- o The Management Approaches
  - o Quality
  - o Configuration Management
  - o Risk
  - o Communication
- o Project Plan
- o Project Approach
- o Project Controls
- o Project Tailoring details (How Prince2 has been tailored to fit this project)

Project Assurance will review the Project Initiation Documentation (PID) and the Project Board will approve it

The Project Manager will then request authority to deliver the project. This is made to the Project Board, who will then make the decision to approve the project to proceed or stop. This request can be either formal or informal, however the approval must be minuted or recorded

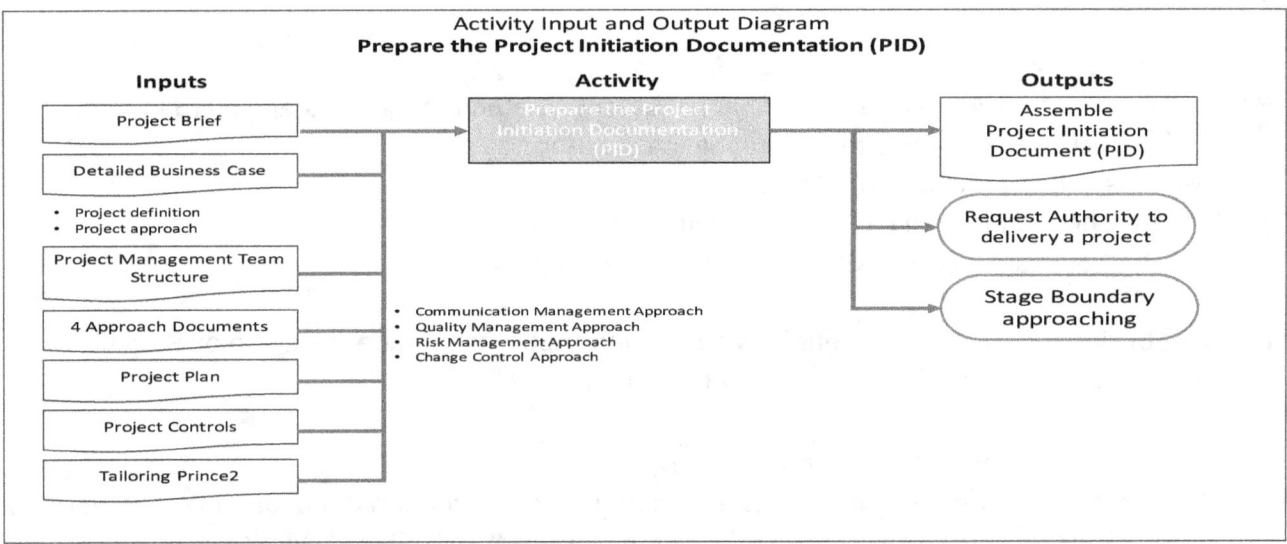

Figure 78 - Prepare the Project Initiation Document (PID)

Directing a Project

The Directing a Project Process enables the Project Board to be accountable for the project by making key decisions and having total control of the project

The objectives of the Directing a Project Process are:
- o Provide authority to initiate the project
- o Provide authority to deliver the project's products
- o Provide direction and control during the project
- o Provide the interface between Corporate or Program Management
- o Provide authority to close the project
- o Ensure the post-project benefits are reviewed

The Directing a Project Process is the process of providing approvals at given points and Ad-Hoc direction as required to the Project Manager

The Trigger for the project to start is the Request to Initiate a Project, this is a request made by the Project Manager at the end of the Starting Up a Project Process (SU). The Project Manager has day2-day control or management of the project whilst the Project Board monitors the project. The Project Board manage by exception, receive regular reports, make decisions and exercise their control.

The communication between the Project Manager and the Project Board is documented within the Communication Management Strategy

The Project Board also act in an advisory role providing guidance to the Project Manager throughout the lifecycle of the project, the Project Manager can seek advice from the Project Board at anytime

The Project Board is also responsible for the ensuring that there is a Continued Business Justification for the project and in the event, this is no longer the case and the project is no longer viable. The Project Board would can decide to close or shut down the project

There are 5 activities within the Directing a Project Process, these are:
- o Authorising Initiation – Allows the Initiation Stage to start
- o Authorising the Project – Allows the project to start and produce products
- o Authorising a stage or an Exception Plan –
    - o Reviewing the existing stage and authorising the next stage to begin
    - o Authorise an Exception Plant to enable the current stage to be completed
- o Giving Ad-Hoc advice or direction – The Project Board acts as an advisor to the Project Manager and provides direction as required, this can be anytime throughout the life of the project
- o Authorising Project Closure – Closure or Shutting the project down

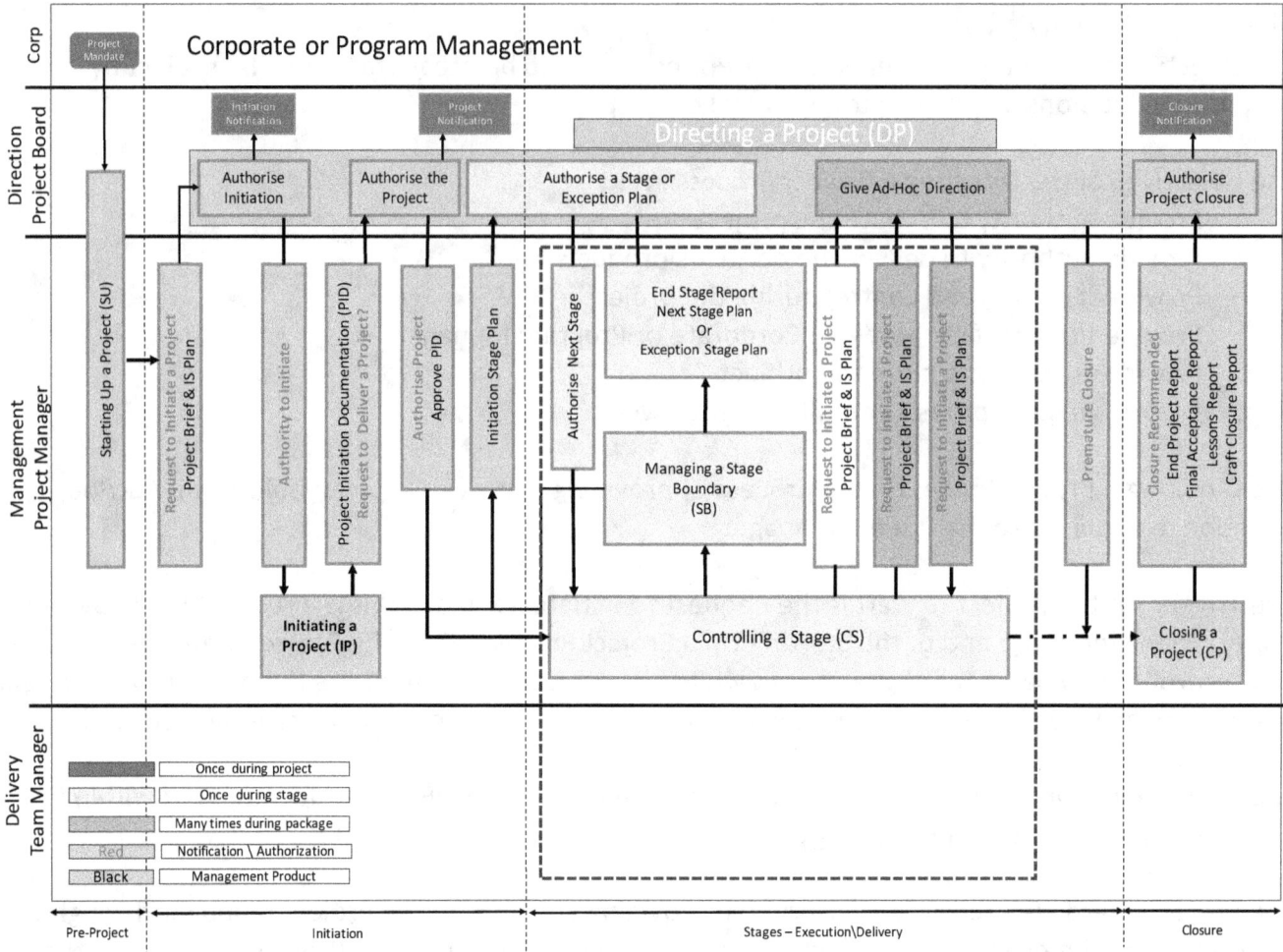

Figure 79 - Directing a Project Process (DP)

Activities — Authorise Initiation

The Authorise Initiation is the first decision the Project Board is required to make and is the first time they officially meet to make a project decision

The Project Board makes the decision to approve or authorise the Initiation Stage to start, this is the approval of the investment on behalf of the business. The funding required for the Initiation Stage is detailed within the Stage Plan, which will also include the deliverables and the plan

The information contained within the Project Brief provides the justification for the overall project and aids the Project Board in making the decision to proceed

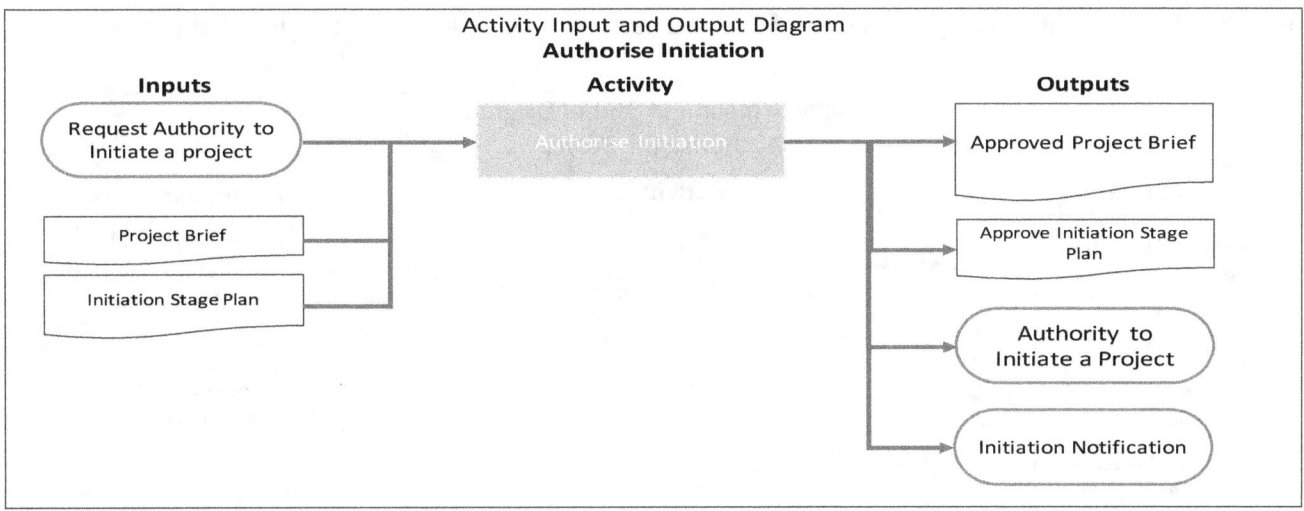
Figure 80 - Authorise Initiation

The following actions should be completed during this activity:
- Review and approve the Project Brief (this contains the project definition, project approach & the project management team) and is prepared by the Project Manager
- Review and approve the Project Product Description (includes the Quality and Acceptance Criteria and verifies the project is viable)
- Review and approve the Initiation Stage Plan
- Communicate with all stakeholder that the project will be initiated if approved by the Project Board
- Authorise the project to proceed to Initiation Stage

Activities – Authorise the Project

The Authorise the Project is triggered upon the receipt of the request to "authorise" from the Project Manager. The terminology within Prince2 is "Authorisation to deliver the project"

This is the 2nd Major decision made by the Project Board and is taken to allow the Initiation Stage to commence.

The following will be confirmed by the Project Board:
- The Business Case is viable and justifiable
- The Project Plan can deliver the products
- That they can monitor and control the project

The Project Board will use the information contained within the Project Initiation Documentation (PID) to confirm the following:
- The Project Definition is accurate and any lessons have been incorporated and risks are understood
- The four management approaches (Quality, Risk, Configuration Management and Communications) are sufficient for the project
- The Roles & Responsibilities are created and have been tailored to suit the project
- The Product Descriptions are created and have been tailored to suit the project
- The Tolerances are agreed and have been tailored to suit the project
- The Project Controls are in place are created and have been tailored to suit the project

The Project Board will review the Benefit Management Approach and approve is satisfactory

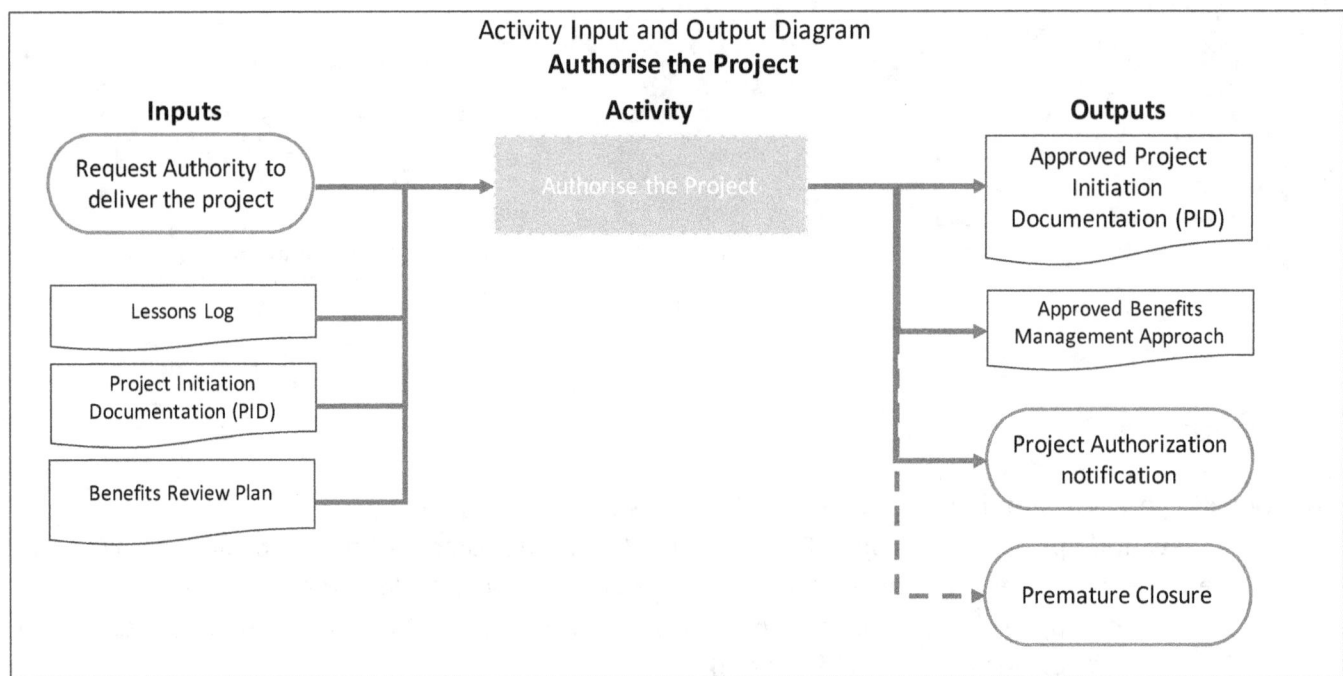

Figure 81 - Authorise the Project

The outputs from this activity are:
- The Approved Project Initiation Documentation (PID)
- Approved Benefit Management Approach
- Project Authorisation Notification (or Premature Closure Notification) to the Project Manager

Activity – Authorise Initiation Stage Plan (or Exception Plan)
Prior to the next stage commencing, The Project Board reviews the work completed and makes the decision to allow the next stage to commence or request further information, or to request premature closure of the project

The Project Board or the Project Manager may request Project Assurance to review the stage by checking that the products have been delivered and ensuring that the quality of products is as described within the End Stage ReportThe Project Board will complete the following actions:
- Review and check the performance of the project against the baselined project plan
- Review and check the Lessons Log to ensure lessons are being documented
- Review the Risks and the Risk Summary Profile
- Confirm that the work has been completed for the current stage
- Review and Approve the Next Stage Plan authorising the next stage to start
  - Or Review and Approve the Exception Plan – to allow the current stage to be completed
- Review the Business Case to confirm the project remains viable and justifiable and that tolerances for the next stage are documented and approved

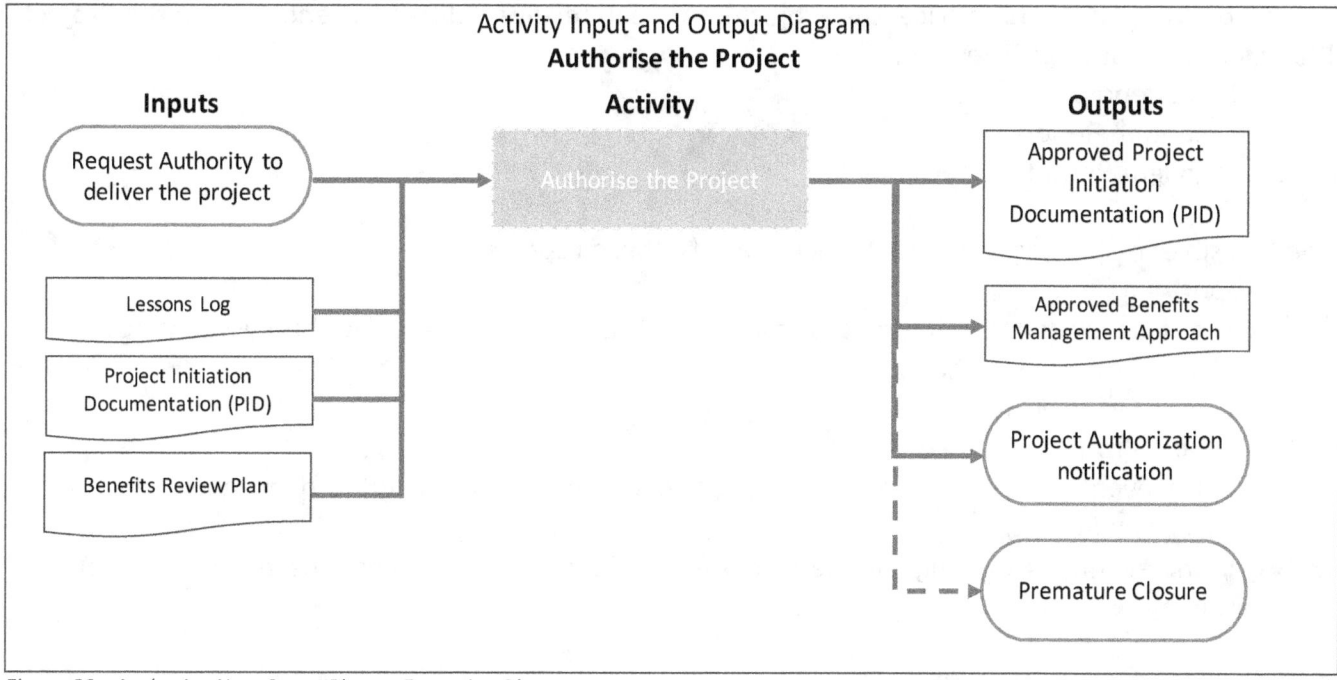

Figure 82 - Authorise Next Stage Plan or Exception Plan

The inputs of this activity are the End Stage Report, Next Stage Plan and Request to Approve the Next Stage Plan. The outputs are the Next Stage Authorisation and the approved documents

In the event there is an Exception, the inputs are the Exception Plan and the Request to Approve the Exception Plan to allow the current stage to be completed

The Project Board can also make the decision to stop the project

Activity – Give Ad-Hoc Direction
The Project Manager can request advice from the Project Board at any point during the project – this is "Requesting Ad-Hoc Direction"

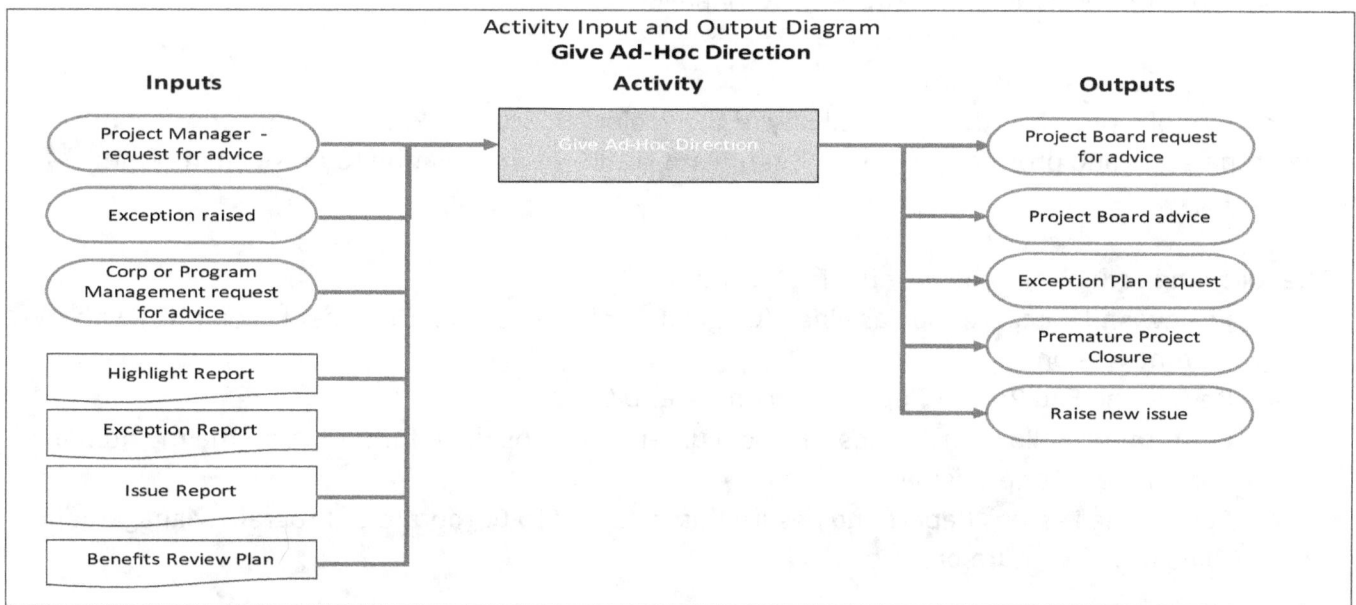

Figure 83 - Give Ad-Hoc Direction

As part of the Give Ad-Hoc advice, the Project Board can receive 3 different reports from the Project Manager during a stage, they are;

1. Issue Report
2. Exception Report
3. Highlight Report

The (Possible) responses from the Project Board to these reports are:

Issue Report

- The issue exceeds the tolerances assigned to the Team Manager, the three issue types are:
    a. Request for Change
    b. Off-Specification
    c. Problem\Concern
- In the event the issue is a large problem or concern – The Project Board could ask for an Exception Report,
- In the event it is a Change Request or Off-Specification – The Project Board can accept or reject

Exception Report

- An Exception Report is used by the Project Manager to advise the Project Board that the stage will go out of or has gone out of tolerance (this is often in relation to Cost or Time)

The Project Board has 3 possible responses:
1. Increase the effected tolerance to enable the stage to be completed
2. Request an Exception Plan to enable the existing stage to be completed
3. Approve the Premature Project Closure

Highlight Report

- The Highlight Report is a regular report delivered to the Board by the Project Manager as part of the Controlling a Stage Process
- The Highlight is reviewed by the Project Board and they may comment if required or request further information from the Project Manager

Activity – Authorise Project Closure

The closure of a project is the responsibility of the Project Board, the Project Manager will complete the preparation and provide the Project Board with sufficient information to make an informed decision

The following actions are taken by the Project Board:
- Review and compare the Baselined (Original) Project Initiation Documentation (PID) with the current version
- Review the End Project Report and compare to the original plan
- Confirm the Follow-on Actions – this document contains the information on the maintenance requirements or processes
- Review the Lessons Report and ensure this is passed to Corporate or Program Management to be used by future projects

- Review and approve the Benefit Management Approach, this continues post project and the reviews will be completed after the project has closed
- Confirm the project has met the Business Case by comparing the Baselined (Original) Business Case to the current Business Case, with a focus upon the Benefits, Risks, Costs

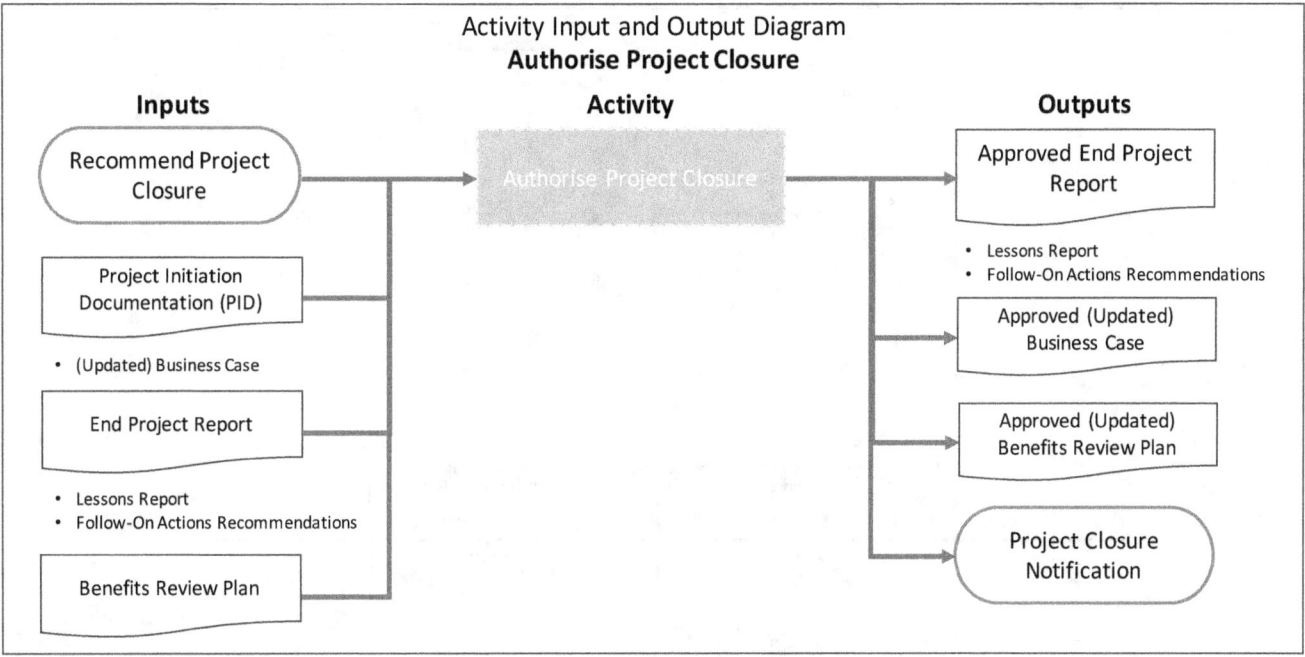

Figure 84 - Authorise Project Closure

The final activity or task of the Project Board is Issue a Project Closure Notification, this notifies all stakeholders that the project will close on a specified date

The outputs of this activity are:
- Approved End Project Report & Benefit Management Approach
- Distribute any Follow-On Actions and Lessons Report documentations
- Issue a formal Project Closure Notification

Controlling a Stage

The purpose of the Controlling a Stage Process (CS) is to allow the Project Manager to assign work to be completed, manage issues, report on progress to the Project Board and take corrective action as required to ensure the stage remains in tolerance

The Objective is to:
- Ensure attention is focused on the delivery of the stage's products
- Monitor and manage Risks and Issues
- Review and Maintain the Business Case
- The agreed products for the stage are delivered to the stated quality standards, costs, effort and agreed timescales
- The Project Management Team is focused upon the delivery within the agreed tolerances

There are 8 activities within the Controlling a Stage Process (CS) and these are divided into 3 parts
- Work Packages

- Monitor and Report
- Manage Issues

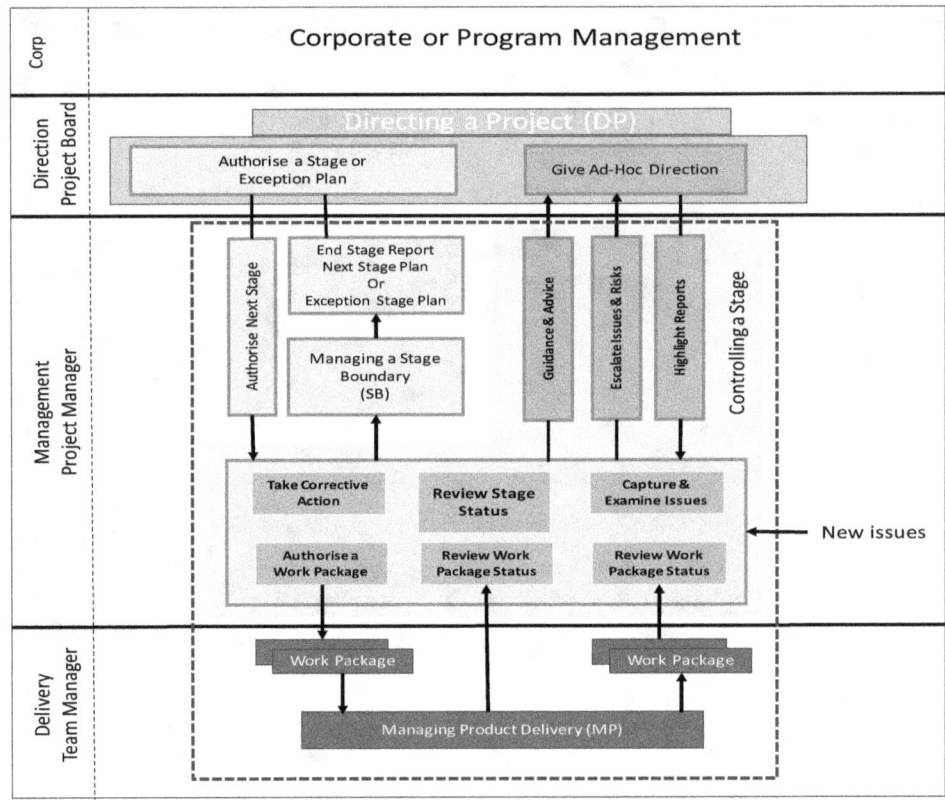

Figure 85 - Controlling a Stage Process (CS)

The activities relating to the Work Package are:
1. Authorise a Work Package – Project Manager assigns Work Packages to Team Manager
2. Review Work Package Status – check on the status of the work package and the product being developed
3. Receive the completed Work Package – Checks Quality & Configuration Management

The Activities relating to Monitoring and Reporting are:
1. Review the stage status against the Stage Plan
2. Provide regular Highlight Reports to the Project Board

The activities relating to Issues are:
1. Capture and examine identified Issues and Risks – categorise and asses probable impact and proximity
2. Escalate Issues and Risks using Exception Reports and send to the Project Board
3. Take corrective action ensuring the stage remains within tolerance

Activity – Authorise a Work Package
Work Packages provide a way to group tasks and control how these are assigned, managed and delivered. The Work Package contains the work required, the quality requirements, timescales required to complete one or more products or sub-products

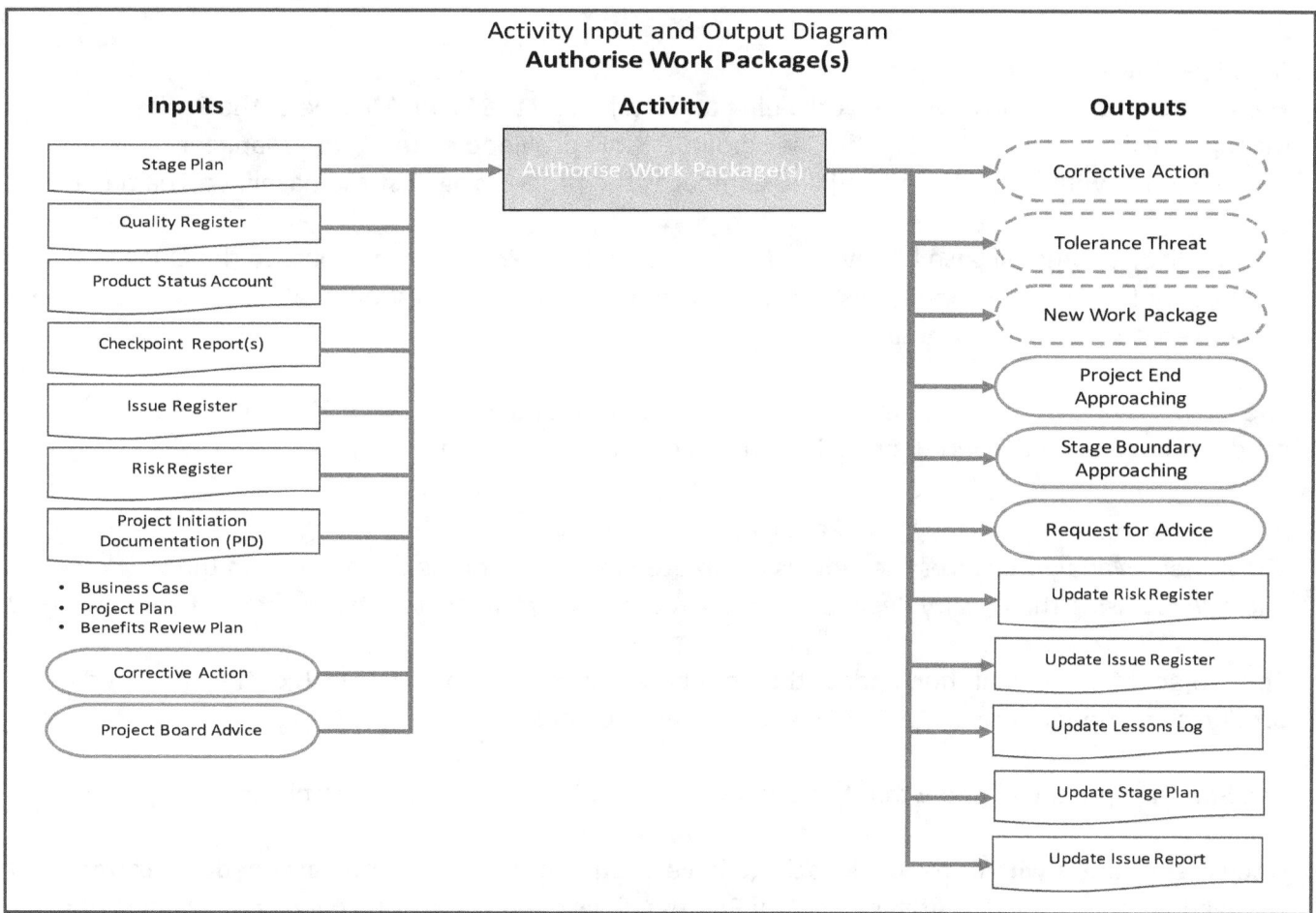

Figure 86 - Authorise a Work Package

The following activities are recommended by Prince2:
- Review the Stage Plan for the next products to be created and the required effort
- The Project Manager will review the quality standards and acceptance process contained with the Project Initiation Documentation (PID)
- The Project Manager will review the associated Product Descriptions for the information to be provided to the Team Manager, such as the techniques to be used, Configuration Management requirements, tolerances, key milestones, reporting requirements and escalation processes\arrangements
- The Project Manager will review the Work Package with the Team Manager ensuring that he fully understands the requirements and acceptance criteria. This will be used to ensure the Work Package is accepted and commences
- The Team Manager will create the Team Plan (which is optional within Prince2) and the Project Manager will review this to ensure the timelines etc have been understood
- The Project Manager will update the Quality Register in relation to any agreed Quality Checks

Future Work Packages can use the Work Package definition and format

The outputs from this activity are:
- An agreed Work Package
- Updated Registers (Quality, Risk, Issue) as required
- Update the Stage Plan with the information on the Work Package start

Activity – Review the Work Package
The Project Manager reviews the work being undertaken by the Team Members, the Project Manager reviews the work using the Checkpoint Report provided by the Team Manager on a regular basis (Defined within the Team Plan) and compares the progress against the baselined Team Plan.

The Quality Register will also be reviewed to ascertain if any Products have passed the Quality Tests and update the Configuration Items Record where required, this is to show that a product has been developed, tested and accepted.

The Project Manager will also review and where required update the Stage Plan to show the products have been delivered, or update the Stage Plan to show any delays

Activity – Receive Completed Work Packages
The Project Manager ensures the work is completed by the Teams as defined within the Work Package, by using the Quality Register to confirm that the products have been checked and approved

The Project Manager will then update the Configuration Item Records for each of the approved products and update the Stage Plan to show them as completed

The Stage is updated to show that the products in the Work Package are complete

Once the products within the Work Package have been approved, they are baselined and cannot be changed without using the Change Control Process. This prevents uncontrolled changes or scope creep within the products

The completed products are stored as described within the Configuration Management Document

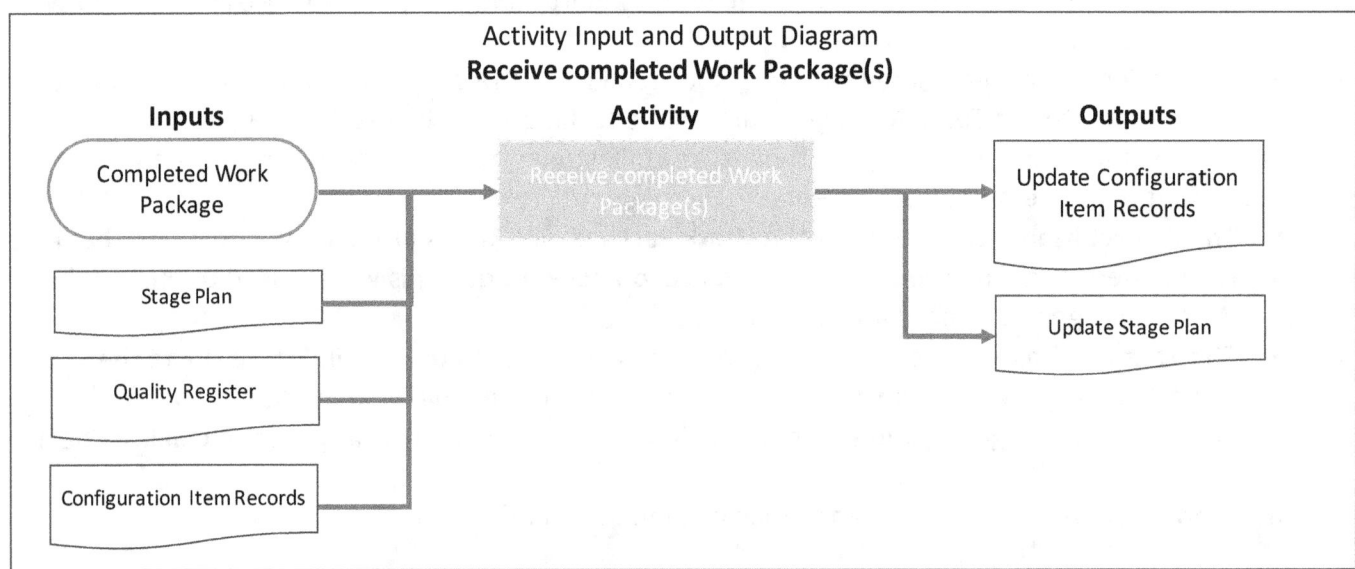

Figure 87 - Receive a Completed Work Package

Activity – Review Stage Status
The Project Manager reviews what has happened to date and compares this with the forecast. This provides the Project Manager with an accurate picture of the current progress within the stage

The best way to describe this is to think of a "dashboard" showing the status for Time, Cost, Risk, Progress, Tolerances and Benefits and this allows the Project Manager to monitor how the stage is progressing

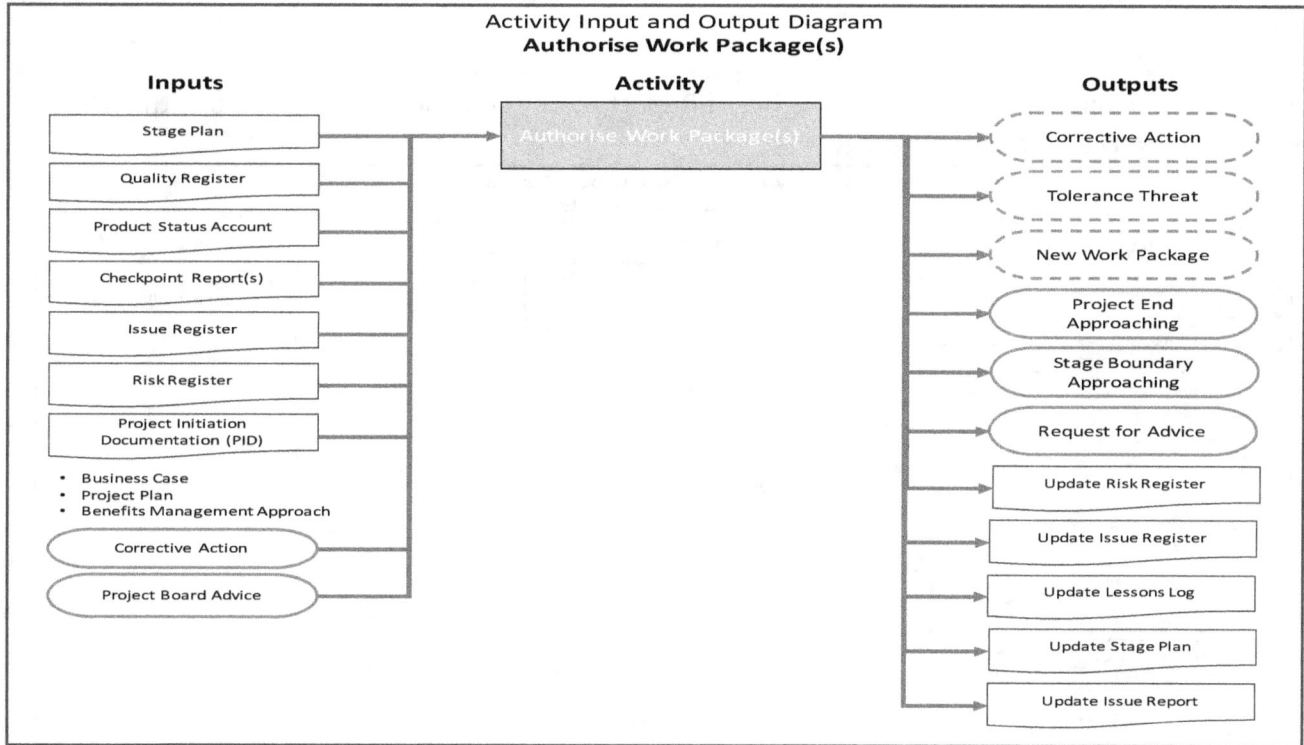

Figure 88 - Authorise Work Package(s)

During the activity, the Project Manager will carry out the following actions:
- Monitor and review the current stage, check Configuration Management Information,
- Capture, Examine, Manage Risks and Issues, check for the progress of corrective actions
- Escalate Issues or Risks that need to be escalated, or corrective action that needs to be undertaken.
- Monitor the Benefit Management Approach to ascertain if it needs to be updated and if the products have been handed over correctly

Activity – Report Highlights
The Project Manager will create the Highlight Report and distribute as defined within the Communication Management Strategy.

The Highlight Report is created by the Project Manager and sent to the Project Board and is used to provide the Project Board with a summary of the stage status and also informs the Project Board of any potential problems that the Project Board can provide advice or assistance.

The Highlight Report is a concise update and is meant to provide the information needed to ensure the Project Board are updated, it will contain the following information:
- Date of the Highlight Report and the period being reported on
- Status Summary providing an overview of the current stage

- Current Reporting Period, Information on – Work Packages, Product Status (Authorised, Completed, Delayed), any corrective action that is in progress
- Next Reporting Period

The Highlight Report will also include any information on Stage Tolerances, information upon risks and issues

The Project Manager will also send the Highlight Report to any stakeholders identified within the Communication Management Strategy

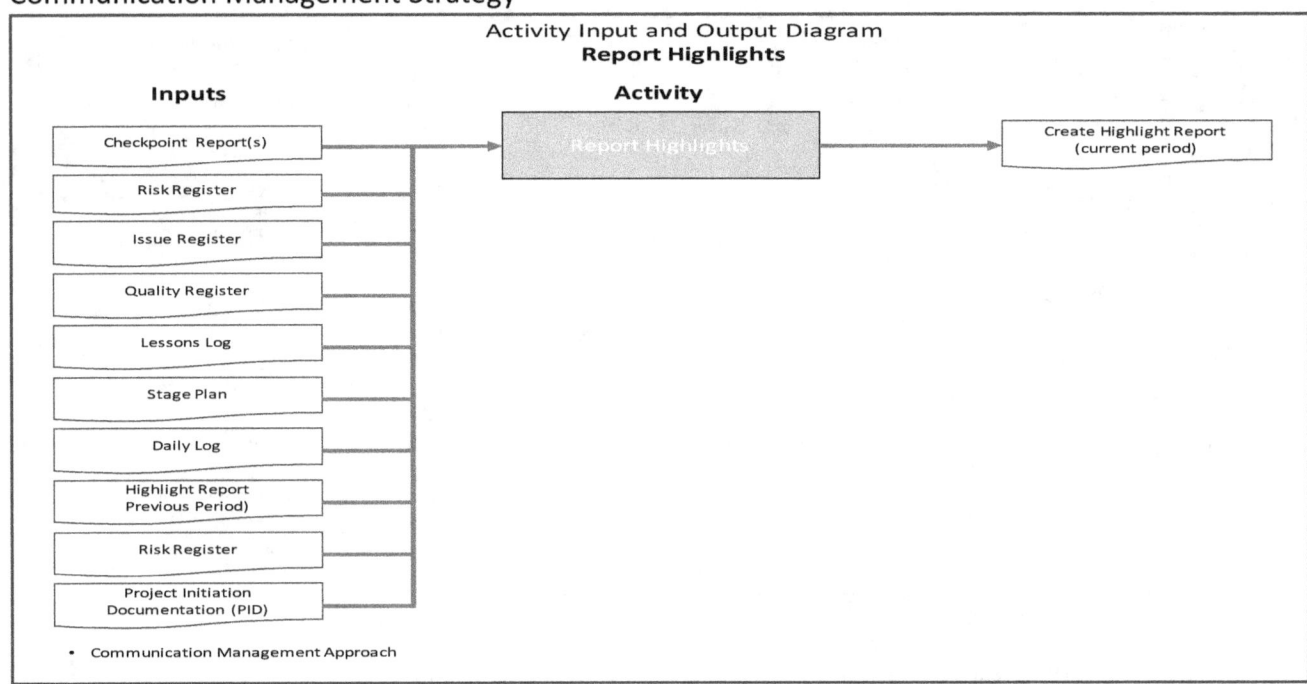

Figure 89 - Report Highlights

Activity – Capture & Examine Risks & Issues

The Project Manager Captures & Examines Issues and Risks, during the lifecycle of the project new risks and issues will be raised, and ca be raised by any stakeholder. If an issue that is raised can be managed by the Project Manager, there is no need to formally manage this within the Issue Register and it can be managed within the Project Managers Tolerances using the Daily Log

For any Issues that require formal management, the steps are as follows:
1. Enter the issue into the Issue Register as soon as it is captured and is deemed to require formal management
2. Categorise the Issue
   a. Request for Change
   b. Off-Specification
   c. Problem\Concern
3. Assess the Severity of the Issues
4. Assess the Priority of the Issue
5. Assess the Impact of the Issue – Stage, Project, Program (Stage Plan, Project Plan, Business Case)
6. Create Issue Report(s)
7. Report the Issue as defined within the Change & control approach and the Communication Management Approach

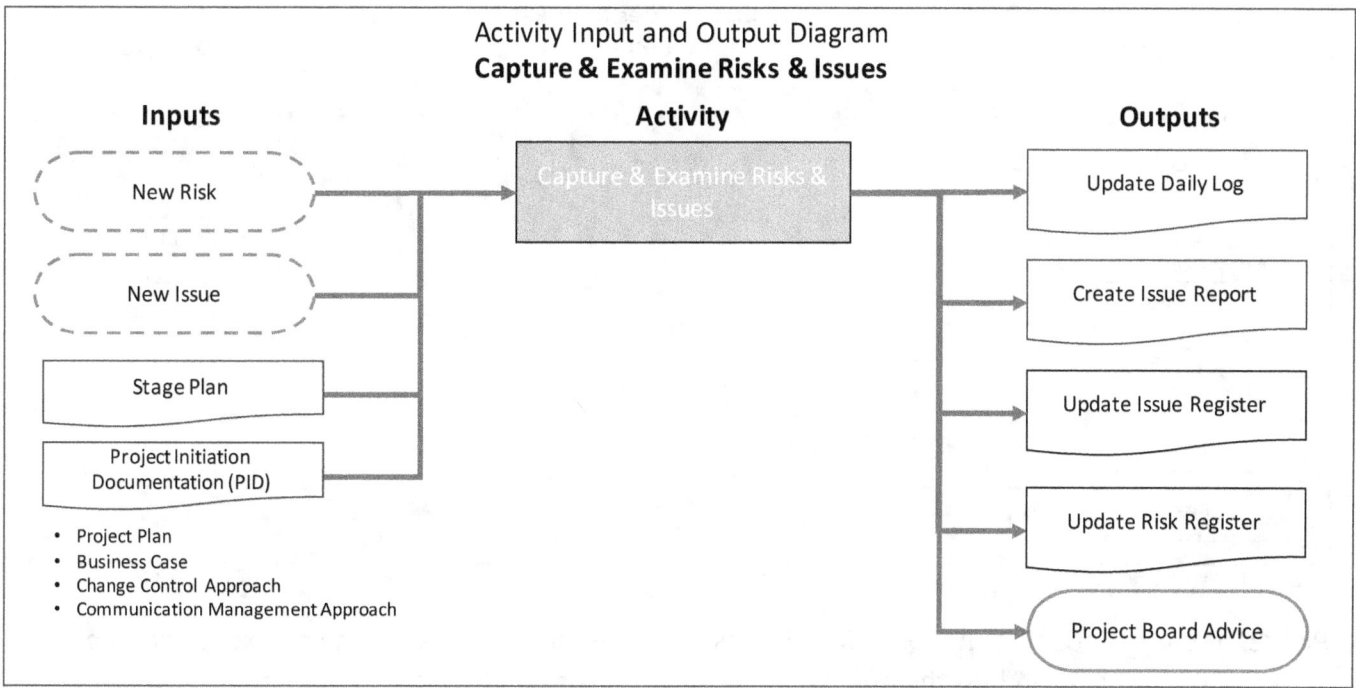

Figure 90 - Capture & Examine Risks

For the management of Risks – See the Risk Theme on P65 and Issue & Change Control on P83

Once the Project Manager has identified the Issues\Risk and this has been documented and assessed, there are 3 options:

- Take Corrective Action – an updated Work Package will be created to implement the identified corrective action and ensures the stage remains in tolerance
- Seeks advice from the Project Board
- Escalates to the Project Board using the "Escalate Issues & Risks"

Activity – Escalate Issues & Risks

The role of the Project Manager is to escalate Issues or Risks if either of these will take the stage out of tolerance

The steps to escalate the are

1. The Project Manager raises an early notification to the Project Board, this can be in the form of the Highlight Report or an informal notification explaining the Risk or Issue
2. The Project Manager then completes the investigation into the identified Risk or Issues and raises an Exception Report
3. If deemed necessary the Project Board will then request an Exception Plan and provide direction on how to proceed

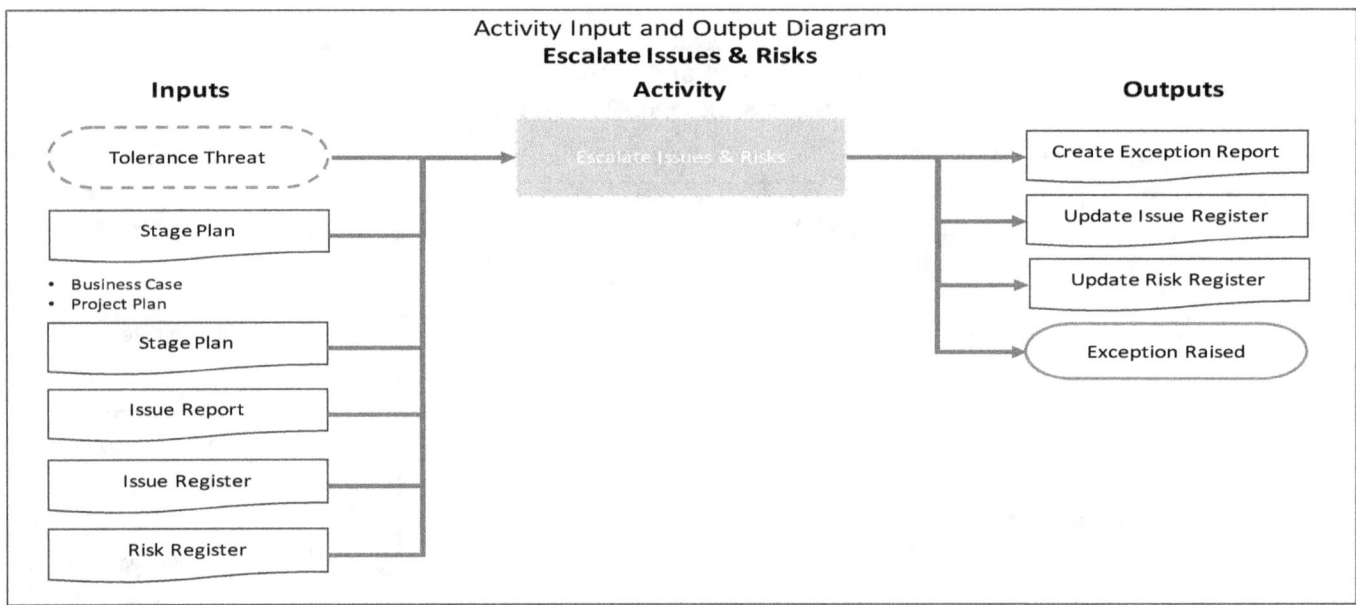

Figure 91 - Escalate Risks & Issues

Prince2 recommends that the following actions are completed when creating an Exception Report:
- The Project examines the effects of the Risk or Issues on the Stage Plan, Project Plan and the Projects Objectives
- Once the Risk or Issue has been assessed, the Project Manager will determine the options to either get the stage back on track or ensure it stays on track and assess these options against the Business Case and the Project Finances
- Assess each options impact on the overall project
- Create the Exception Report and recommend the option(s) to the Project Board

The Project Board will review the Exception Report and make a decision on how to proceed, the response could be any of those identified below
- Request more information from the Project Manager
- Select an option recommended by the Project Manager or an option identified by the Project Board and provide direction
- Increase the tolerances to ensure the stage can be completed
- Request an Exception Plan from the Project Manager
- Advice the Project Manager to close the project prematurely

Activity – Take Corrective Action

The Project Manager has approval to resolve minor issues and risks that do not put the stage out of tolerance

According to Prince2, "taking corrective action is managed by the Project Manager as they implement the advice usually given by the Project Board to correct the issue or risk, while keeping the stage within tolerance"

The Project Manager may be required to update or create a new work package and assign it to the Team Manager

Upon completion of the corrective actions, the Project Manager will review the work and updates using the normal documents:

- Issue Register and Issue Report – if there is an update to the Issues or update the Risk Register if there is an identified Risk
- Update the Stage Plan to include the additional work
- Configuration Item Records to show what has changed within the product

Corrective Action is used when extra work is required and the stage remains in tolerance
An Exception Plan is used when the stage will go out of tolerance – for example the stage will cost more than originally planned or exceed the time allocated

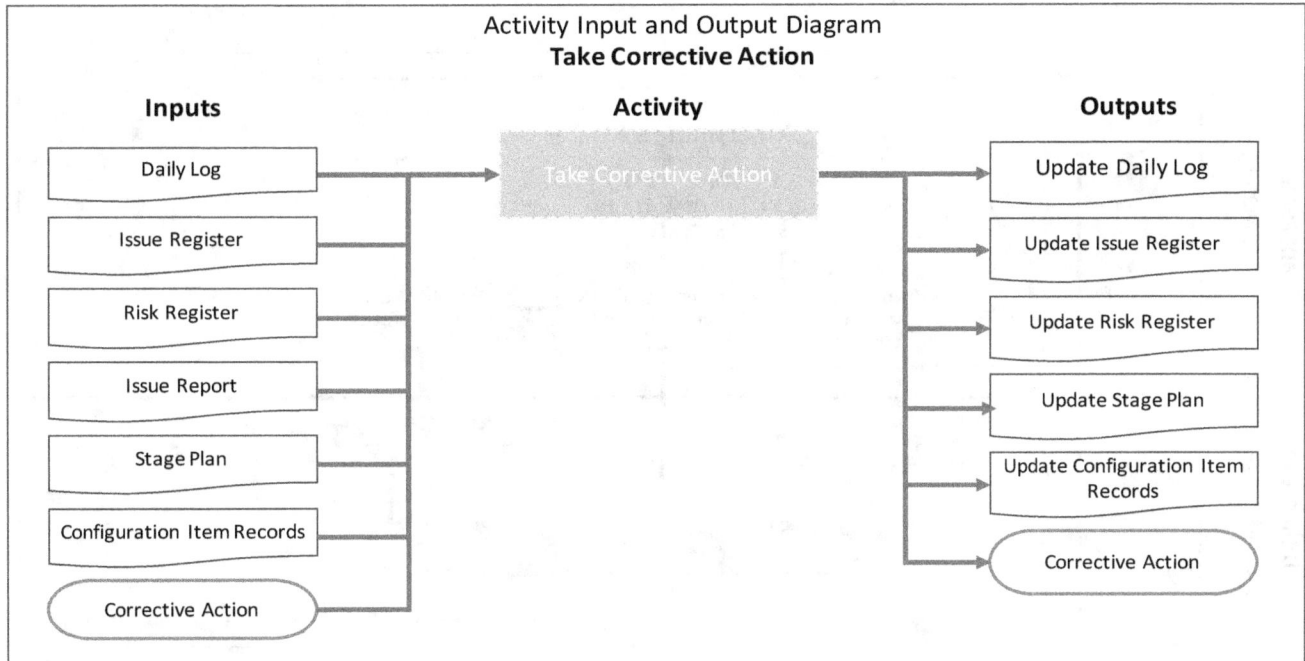

Figure 92 - Take Corrective Action

Managing Product Delivery

Introduction

The objective of the Managing Product Delivery Process is to manage and control the work between the Project Manager and the Team Manager by placing certain formal requirements on the accepting, executing and delivery of the products

The Managing Product Delivery Process Ensures:

- The Products assigned to the team are authorised and agreed
- The Team Manager and Team Members have sufficient details and understanding about what is to be produced
- The Team Manager understands the time, effort and cost associated
- The products within the work package are delivered to the customer expectations and within agreed tolerances
- The Team Manager provides accurate progress information to the Project Manager

The completes the following tasks ensuring the products are delivered:

- Agrees ad accepts the Work Package from the Project Manager

- Create the Team Plan (Optional Plan) to show how the products will be delivered
- Delivers the products
- Demonstrates the products within the Quality Review Meeting
- Obtains the approvals for the developed products
- Delivers the completed products to the Project Manager

Managing Product Delivery

Within the Managing Product Delivery Process there 3 activities
- Accepting the Work Package (the Team Manager accepts this from the Project Manager)
- Executing the Work Package
- Delivering the Work Package

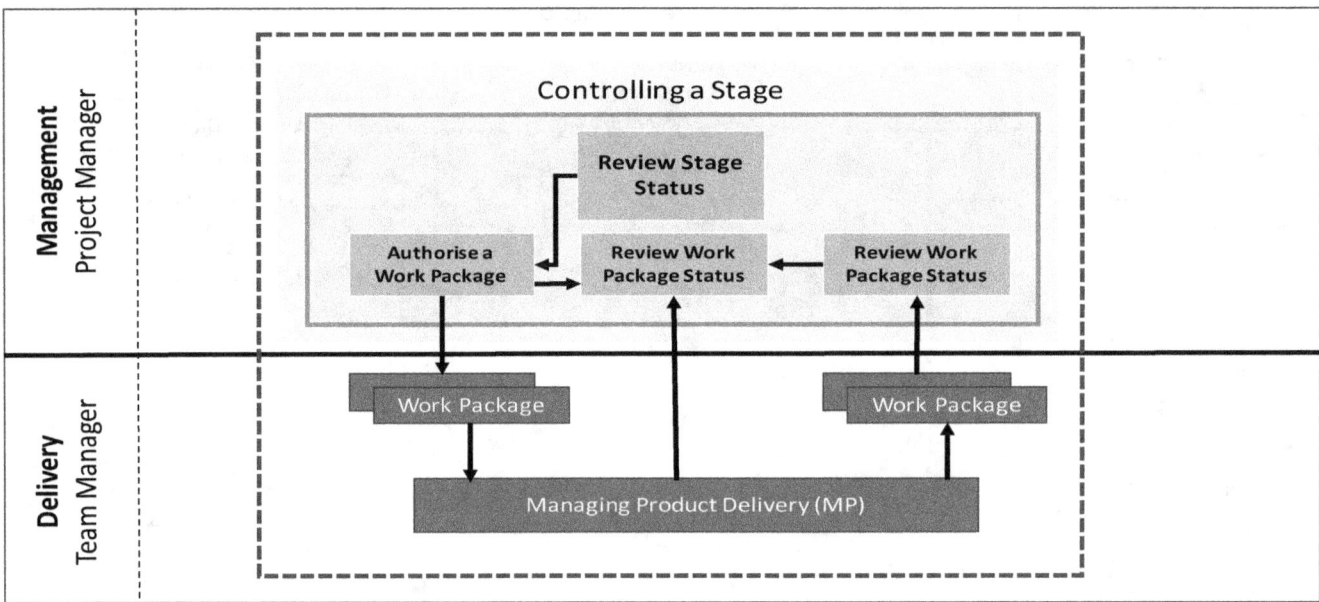

Figure 93 - Managing Product Delivery

Managing a Product Delivery Process is based upon the view of the Team Manager
- Accepting a Work Package
    - The Team Manager accepts the Work Package from the Project Manager and creates the Team Plan (Optional) to manage the delivery of the products
- Executing the Work Package
    - The Team Manager and Team Members produce the products
    - Completes the quality checks
    - Obtains approvals
    - The Team Manager Reports to the Project Manager using the Checkpoint Reports
- Deliver the Work Package – is the delivery of the work package to the Project Manager – which is the list of work and not the actual products
    - The Quality register is updated, the approvals are requested, the products are delivered as documented within the Change & control approach and the Project Manager is notified

Activity – Accepting a Work Package

Accepting a Work Package is the process of obtaining an agreement between the Team Manager and the Project Manager on:

- What is to be delivered
- The reporting requirements
- Interfaces
- Configuration Management requirements
- Problem handling and escalation
- Product Descriptions
- Approval process

The Team Manager will also clarify and constraints with the Project Manager in relation to Time, Cost and effort

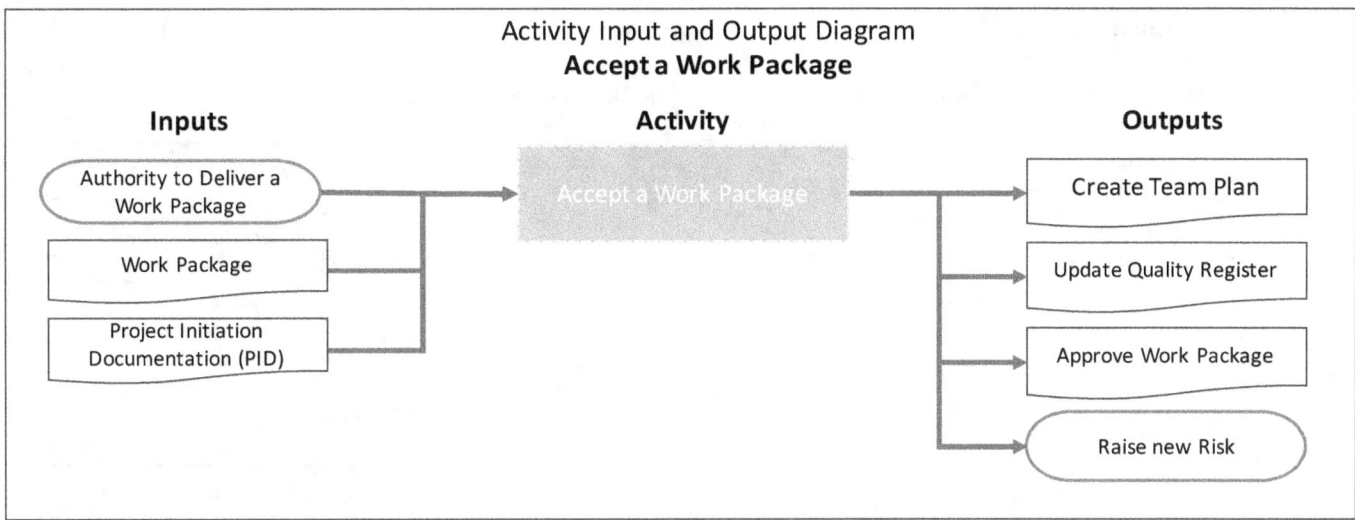

Figure 94 - Accepting a Work Package

The Team Plan is optional and if agreed that it is required, the Team Manager creates the Team Plan that shows how the products will be produced. The Team Plan is reviewed by the Project Manager.

The Team Manager will also:

- Add the planned Quality Reviews into the Quality Register
- Agree with the Project Manager to deliver the Work Package

The documents updated during this activity are:

- Creates the Team Plan
- The Quality Register is updated
- The Configuration Item Records to show the status of any products that have changed

Activity – Execute a Work Package

The Team Manager will manage the production of the products and ensure they remain within the agreed tolerances. If the Team Manager identifies a tolerance will be exceeded, this mi must be escalated to the Project Manager

The Accepting a Work Package and Delivering a Work Package are the "paperwork processes" relating to the Accepting a Work Package. Executing a Work Package is essentially the actual work to deliver the products identified within the Work Package, The Accepting and Delivering a Work Package can be relatively short in terms of time as the main focus is on the Execute a Work Package

Prince2 recommends the following actions should be undertaken by the Team Manager:
- Develops the products to identified and required quality criteria, this is derived from the Product Descriptions for the products
- Ensures the work is completed using the required and correct techniques and processes
- Updates the Quality Register to record any Quality Activities
- Records the effort expended – monitors the resource usage against the Team Plan
- Monitors Risks and Issues

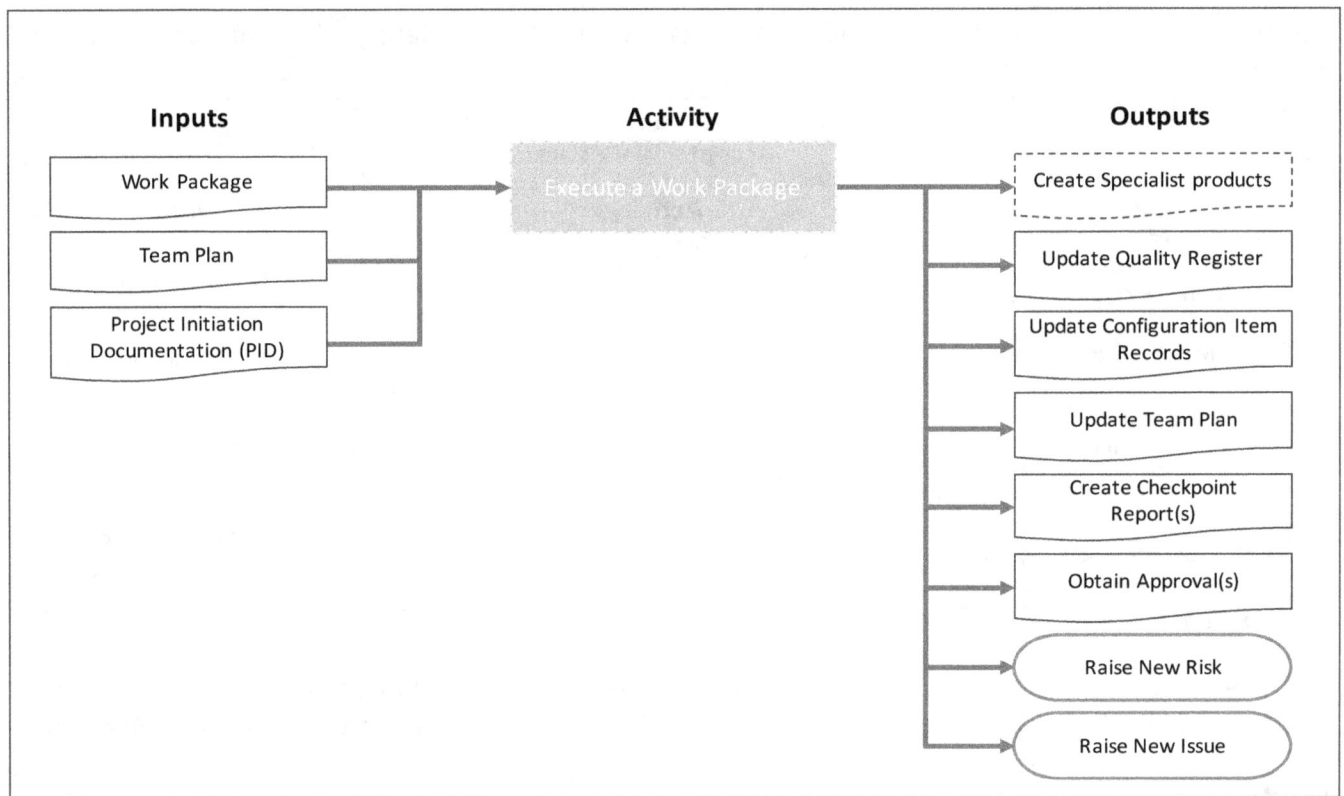

Figure 95 - Execute a Work Package

Other actions that are recommended by Prince2 are:
- The Project Manager is notified of any issues or risks that may require management or escalation
- Approvals are obtained for the completed products and the Configuration Item Records are updated showing the new status of the Product
  - Developed
  - Quality Checked
  - Approved
- The progress of the work is reviewed, the Team Plan is updated and the Checkpoint Report is created and sent to the Project Manager

Activity – Deliver a Work Package

The Deliver a Work Package is the delivery of the approval or acceptance paperwork to the Project Manager and not necessarily the products derived from the Work Package, the products are delivered to the persons or persons agreed within the Work Package

Prince2 recommends that the following actions are undertaken by the Team Manager:
- Reviews the Quality Register to confirm that the Quality Activities associated with the Work Package are complete
- Checks that all products are approved correctly and by the identified person or persons in the Work Package
- Updates the Team Plan to show that the work has been completed
- The handover procedure identified within the Work Package are followed and the products are handed over in line with these procedures

The final step is to notify the Project Manager that the Work Package is completed. This does not need to be a formal process or meeting, but can be informal – however it should be recorded and the Project Manager should verify that all products have been handed over correctly

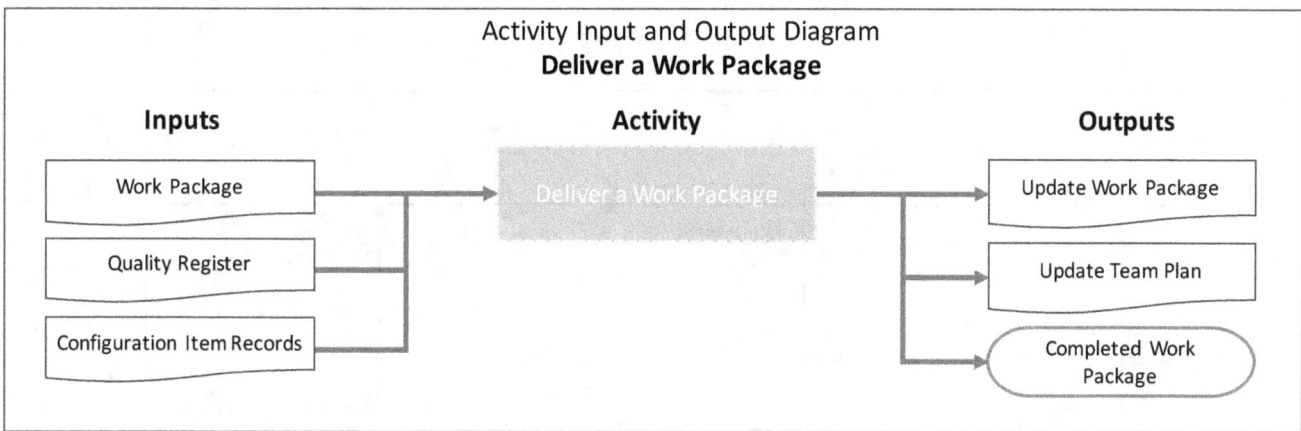

Figure 96 - Deliver a Work Package

Managing a Stage Boundary

Introduction

The objective of the Managing Stage Boundary Process (SB) is to give an overview of the work that must be completed by the Project Manager, which is as follows:
- Assure the Project Board that all products in the current stage are produced and have been approved
- Reviews and updates (if necessary) the Project Initiation Documentation (PID), the Business Case, the Project Plan and the Risk Register
- Records any lessons in the Lessons Log
- Prepares the Next Stage Plan and Request Authorisation to start the next stage

The Managing Stage Boundary Process (SB) is started close to or near the end of the current stage and before the next stage begins.

If the current stage is forecasted to go out of tolerance, the Project Manager will create an Exception Report and a subsequent Exception Plan if requested asking to continue with the Next Stage.

The Project Board is in control of the Project, the Stage Boundary process provides the Project Board with the information to enable them to maintain control

The Project Board will consider the following:
- They will consider the Continued Business Justification for the project
- They will confirm that the current stage has delivered all of its planned products and any identified benefits
- They will review the Next Stage Plan
- Using this information, they will consider whether to allow the project to continue of be shut down

There are 5 activities within the Managing a Stage Boundary Process, these are:
- Plan the Next Stage
- Update the Project Plan
- Update the Business Case
- Report the Stage End
  - Or "Produce and Exception Plan"

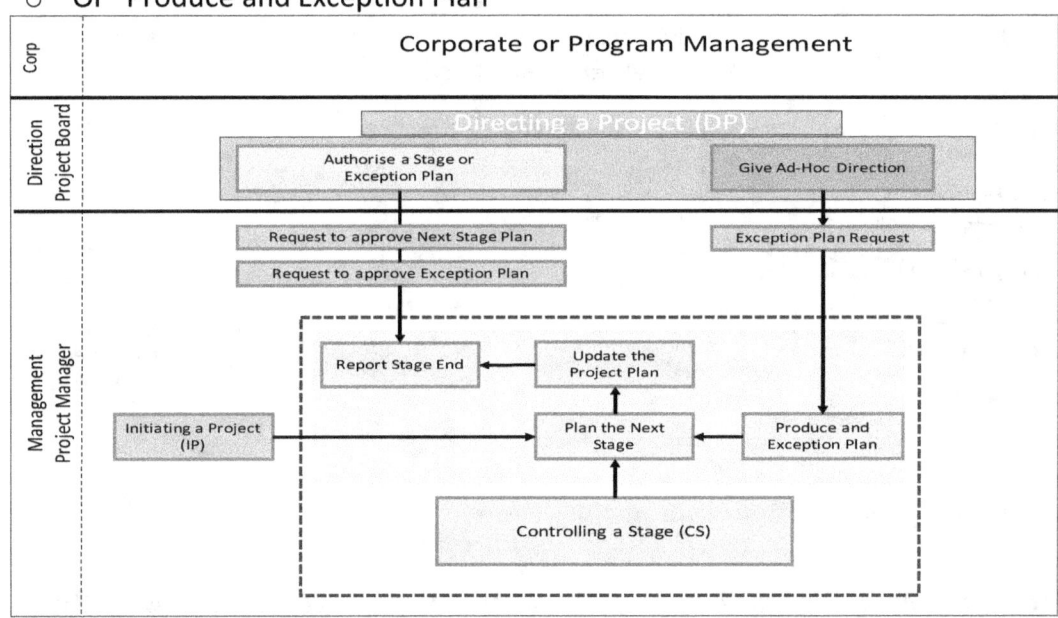

Figure 97 - Managing a Stage Boundary Process

An outline of the activities:

Plan the Stage - involves creating a stage plan for the next stage and using the lessons learned from previous stages

Update the Project Plan – is done to confirm what has been achieved and forecast the next stage, the Project Plan is a document that is updated throughout the lifecycle of the project and is updated with the actuals during each stage

Update the Business Case – This is crucial, the Business Case is reviewed at the end of each stage by the Project Board to ensure continued viability. The performance of the current stage could impact the Business Case in either a positive or negative way and this information should be incorporated

Report Stage End – The End Stage Report is created by the Project Manager to show what has been completed within the current stage compared to the Approved Stage Plan

Produce an Exception Report – This plan will replace the current Stage Plan if approved by the Project Board. If approved the Project Manager continues Controlling a Stage (CS) until it is completed

Managing a Stage Boundary is completed at the end each management stage, however there are two exceptions to this,
- Initiation Stage – The Stage Boundary Process is optional and often depends on the size, complexity or risk associated with the project
- The Last Stage never contains the Managing Stage Boundary, this is replaced by the "Closing a Project Process (CP)" which becomes the last stage within the Project

Activity – Plan the Next Stage
The Stage Plan for the Next Stage is as stated about created at or near the end of the current stage. The Next Stage Plan is created by the Project Manager and as with the Project Plan will involve support from other stakeholders within the project to ensure the plan is sufficiently detailed

Prince2 recommends the Project Manager complete the following actions when creating the Next Stage Plan:
- The Project Initiation Documentation (PID) is reviewed for any changes in
  - Quality Expectations
  - Acceptance Criteria
  - Project Approach
  - Team Roles
  - 4 Management Approaches
- Review the Lessons Log to ascertain which lessons can be incorporated into the Next Stage Plan
- Review the Project Initiation Documentation (PID) to understand the Products required from the next stage
- Create or Update the Configuration Item Records for the products that will be created in the next stage
- Update the Quality Register with the planned Quality Activities

The Next Stage Plan should contain enough detail to allow the Project Manager to manage the stage on a day-2-day basis

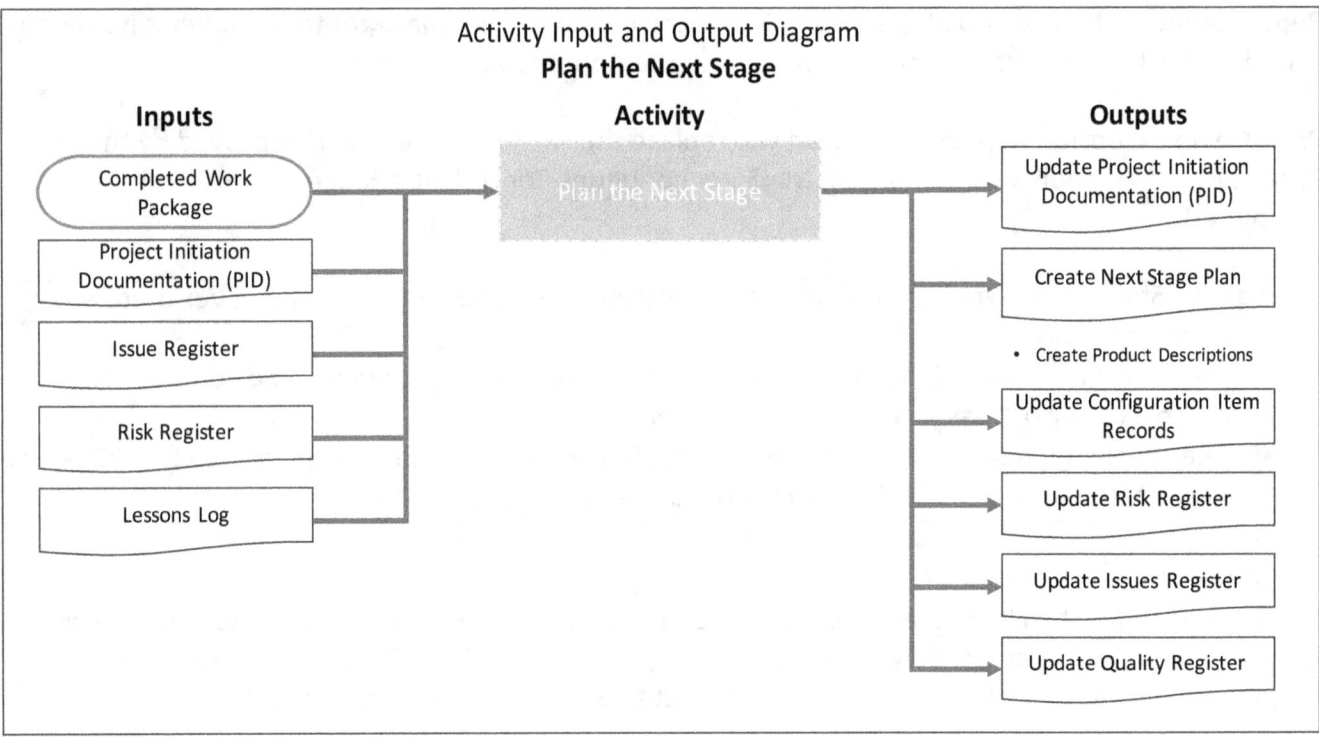

Figure 98 - Create Next Stage Plan

Activity – Update the Project Plan

The Project Manager updates the Project Plan to include the actual progress from the current stage and should include the forecast for the next stage, including the information on the time and cost. The Project Board then uses this information to make a comparison with the original plan that was baselined as part of the Project Initiation Documentation (PID)

Changes to the plan could have an effect on the Business Case and in this scenario the Business Case is updated based upon the new information (See the next activity)

Prince2 recommends the Project Manager completes the following actions as part of this activity:

- The Project Manager revises the Project Plan with the actuals from the current stage to show what has been completed
- The Project Manager includes the new forecast information in the Project Plan for the Next Stage
- Ascertain if any further changes are required for the Project Plan

The documents that are updated in this activity are the Project Plan and where required, the Issue and Risk Register

The Project Board uses the Project Plan during the lifecycle of the project to measure progress.

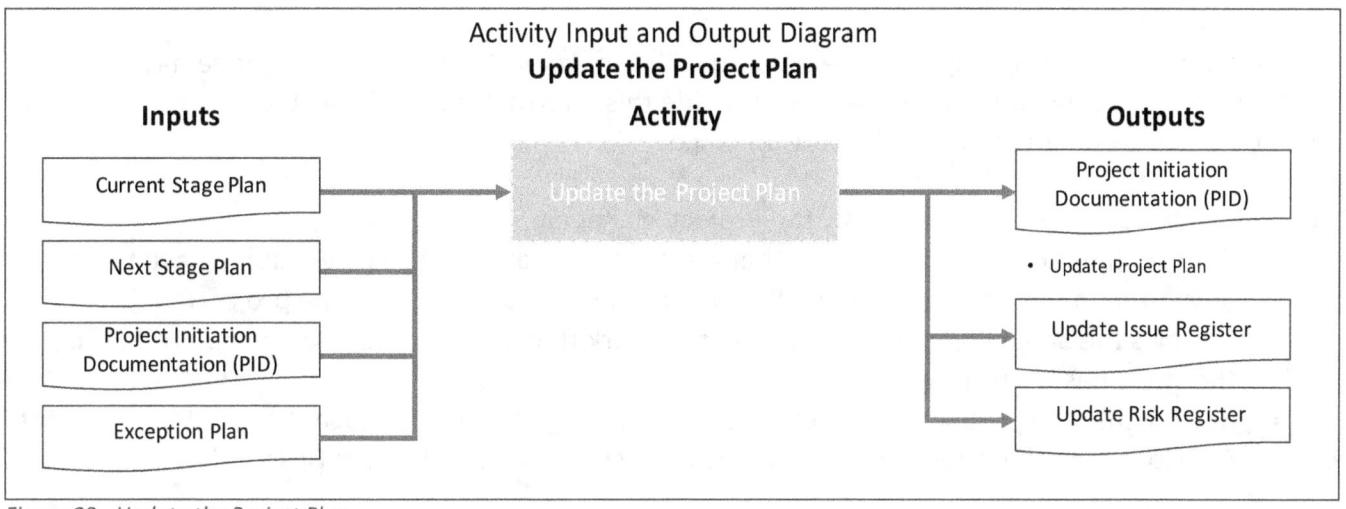

Figure 99 - Update the Project Plan

Activity – Update the Business Case

As part of the Managing Stage Boundary Process (SB) the Business Case is updated to confirm the project is continues to be viable. The Project Board also needs to reconfirm that the benefits can still be achieved within the identified aspect of Time, Cost, Quality, Risk and Scope. The Business Case is updated by the Project Manager and the Executive and is presented to the Project Board for review.

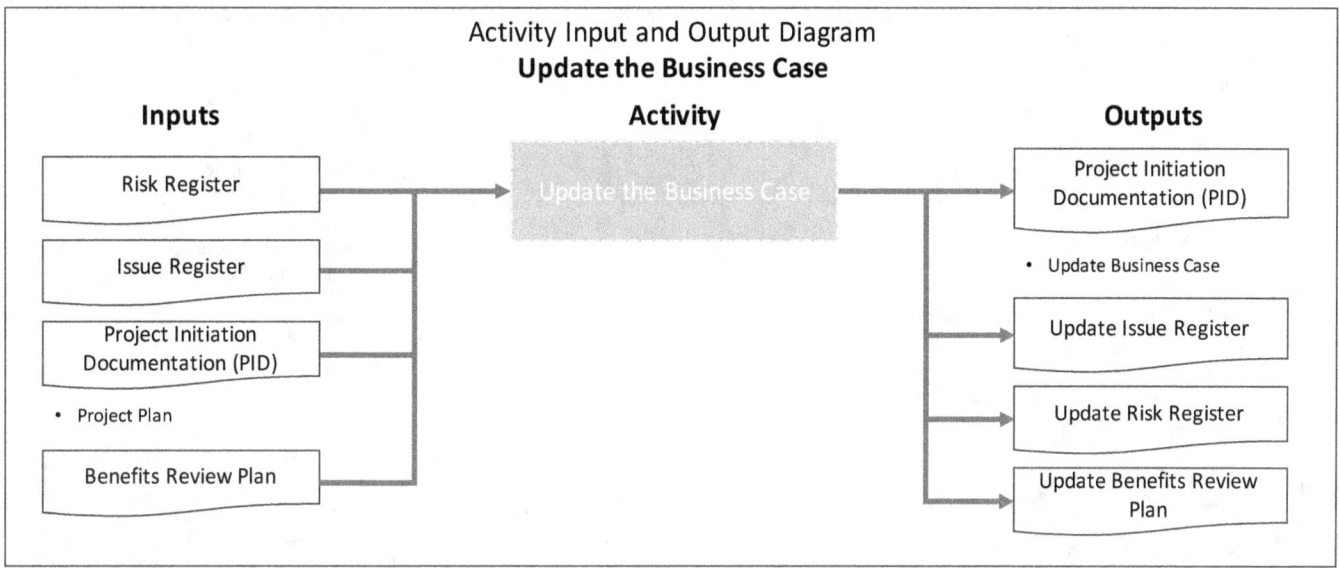

Figure 100 - Update the Business Case

Prince2 recommends the Project Manager completes the following when reviewing and revising the Business Case:

- Review if any changes have been made in relation to the Risks or the appetite for Risks within the Project, Corporate or Program Management
- Assess the Risk Register and any Risks that are active
- Update the Benefit Management Approach in the event any benefits have materialised or are no longer valid
- Review the Issue Register to ascertain if any issues will have any impact on the Business Case
- Review the Project Plan in the event any changes in relation to cost, time, quality, benefits or any other area that could impact the Business Case

Activity – Report Stage End
The End of the Stage is where the Project Board will want to understand how the stage has performed against the original forecast. To provide this information the Project Manager creates the End Stage Report near the end of the current stage.

The following actions are completed by the Project Manager:
- Confirm that any planned benefits that were planned during the current stage have been delivered (In most project the benefits do not materialise until after the project)
- Reviews the Stage Plan and confirms that all work that should have been completed during the stage has been completed
- Review that the products that were produced during the current stage (Quality Management Activities) and that they have been approved in line with the Product Description

The End Stage Report is given to the Project Board as part of the Managing Stage Boundary Process and is the main output of this activity

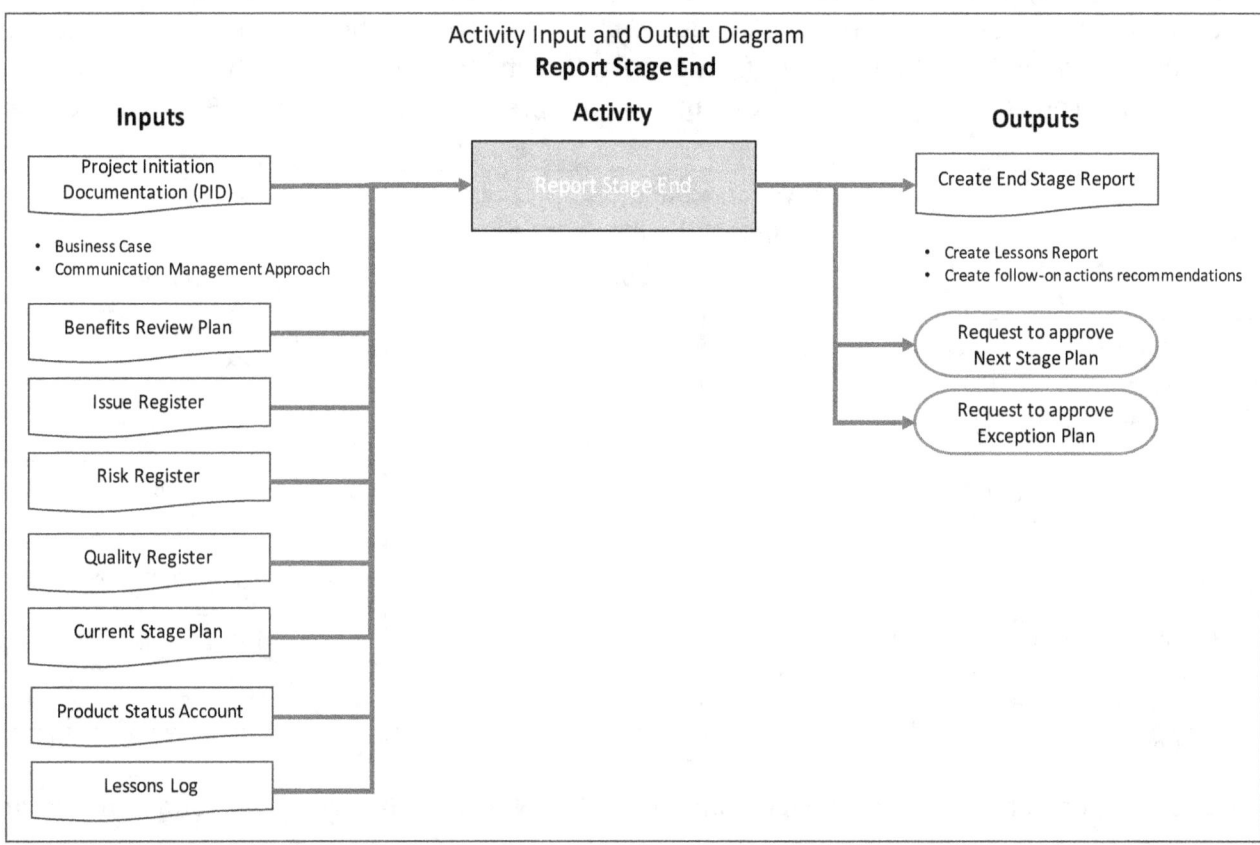

Figure 101 - Report Stage End

Activity – Produce an Exception Plan
This activity is only required when a stage is out of tolerance and an Exception Plan has been requested by the Project Board and is needed to complete the current stage.

The Exception Plan is requested by the Project Board after they have received and reviewed the Exception Report that provides an overview of the stage tolerance that is forecasted or has been exceeded and provides the information on how to get the project back on track and complete the current stage

The creation of the Exception Plan is the same process as creating the Next Stage Plan

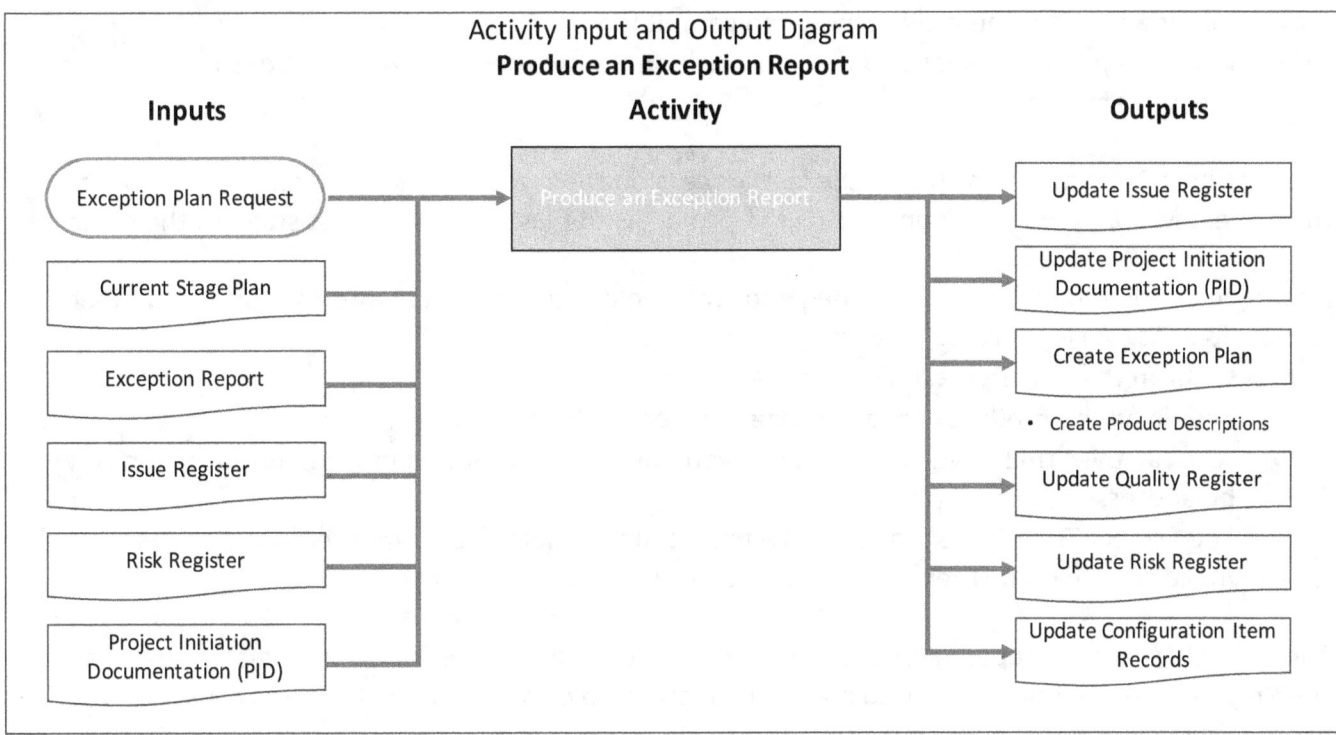

Figure 102 - Produce an Exception Report

To create the Exception Plan the inputs are:
- The Exception Report containing the recommended actions as presented to the Project Board
- The Current Stage Plan to confirm what is needed or has been produced
- Project Initiation Documentation (PID) which contains the Project Plan as this is needs to include any additional activities that are contained within the Exception Plan

Additional tasks\actions that may be required are:
- If you need to create any additional or new products, the product based planning technique should be used
- Update the Quality Register to include any additional Quality Management Activities that are contained within the Exception Plan
- Create or update the Configuration Item Records for the products that will be produced by the exception plan

The outputs of this activity are the Exception Plan and the updated Project Initiation Documentation (PID). The Project Board will give approval to the Project Manager to complete the current stage using the Exception Plan, however they can decide to close the project

Closing a Project Process
Introduction
The objective of the Closing a Project Process (CP) is to:
- Verify that the project products have been accepted by the users
- Ensure that all products can be supported post project
    - The relevant support model or process is in place and has been tested

- Review the performance of the project by comparing the project to the baselined documents
- Assess any benefits that have been realised and plan the review of any benefits that will materialise after the project has been completed
- Address any open issues and risks and include them in the Follow-On Actions and recommendations

The Closing a Project Process (CP) is the last process on the management level and the last process the Project Manager will work on, closing the project is the last part of the last stage of the project

All projects should have a clearly defined end with the correct handover information and defined responsibilities. A clear project end is:
- Confirm that all original objectives have been met
- The delivered products have been transferred to the customer
- All objectives that have not been achieved have been identified in the event they can or will be addressed in the future
- The Project Team is disbanded and all associated costs are documented and the ability to make certain no further costs can be attributed to the project.

The Project Manager prepares for the project to be closed and provides the information necessary to the Project Board to enable them to make the decision to close the project. This is called "Authorise Project Closure"

The 5 Activities within the Closing a Project Process (CP) are:
- Preparing the planned closure of the Project confirming that all products have been delivered and accepted
- Preparing Premature Close – this is completed instead of the planned closure if requested by the Project Board
- The Hand-Over of the products to the customer as documented within the Configuration Management Approach
- Evaluation of the project comparing the project against the original objectives against the actuals to support the creation of the End Project Report
- The recommendation of Project Closure – this can be a simple notification to the Project Board to close the Project (The Project Manager does not close the project; the Project Board makes the decision to close the project)

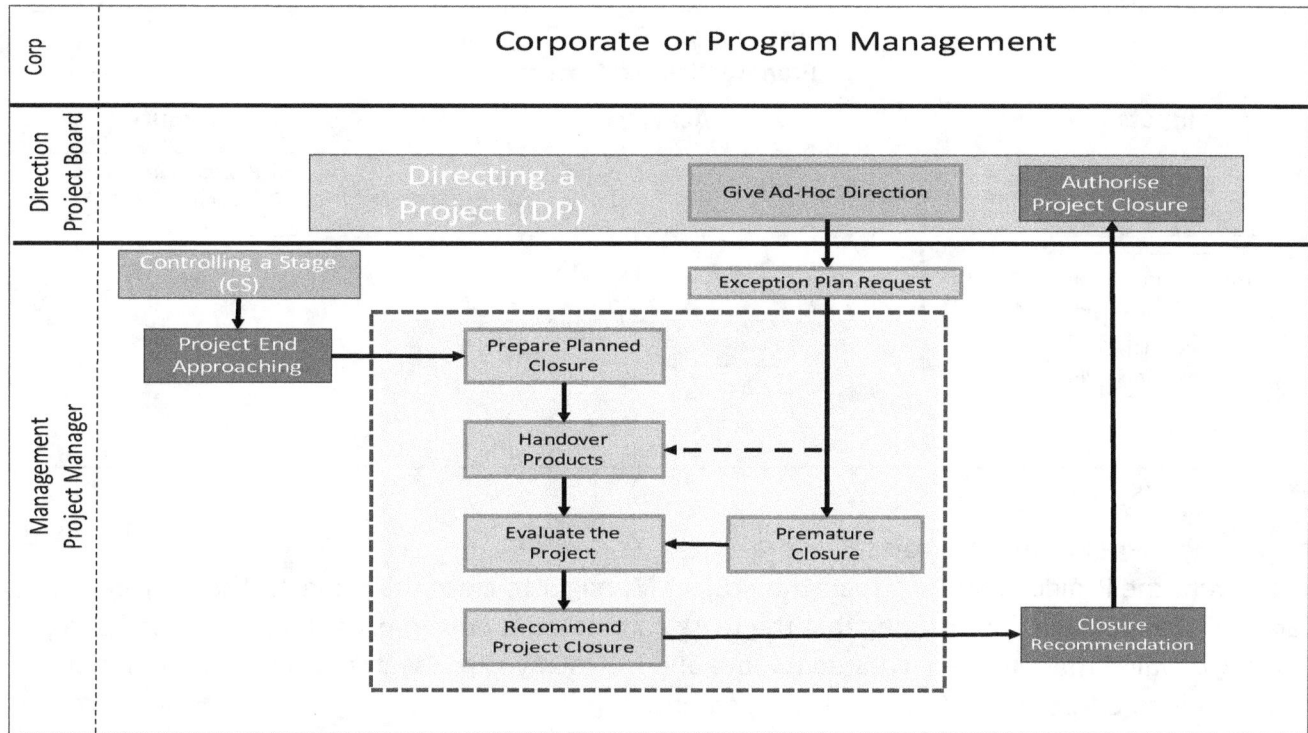

Figure 103 - Closing a Project Process (CP)

Activity – Planned Closure

The Prepare Planned Closure is the process of confirming that all products have been produced & accepted

The Project Manager will complete the following:

- The Project Manager will update the Project Plan to show the products that have been delivered
- The Product Status Account is requested from the Project Support (The Product Status Account is a report on the status of all products being produced by the project)
- The Project Manager will confirm that all products have been delivered according to the quality criteria and the acceptance criteria as defined within the Project Product Description. This will also be checked by the Project Board who will confirm that all products have been accepted and the acceptance criteria have been met
- The Project Manager will confirm that all resources assigned to the project can be released, this includes any equipment and is not just concerned with people, ensuring no further charges can be attributed to the project

Upon completion of these tasks, the Project Manager can complete the handover of the products, update the End Project Report and recommend the Project Closure to the Project Board

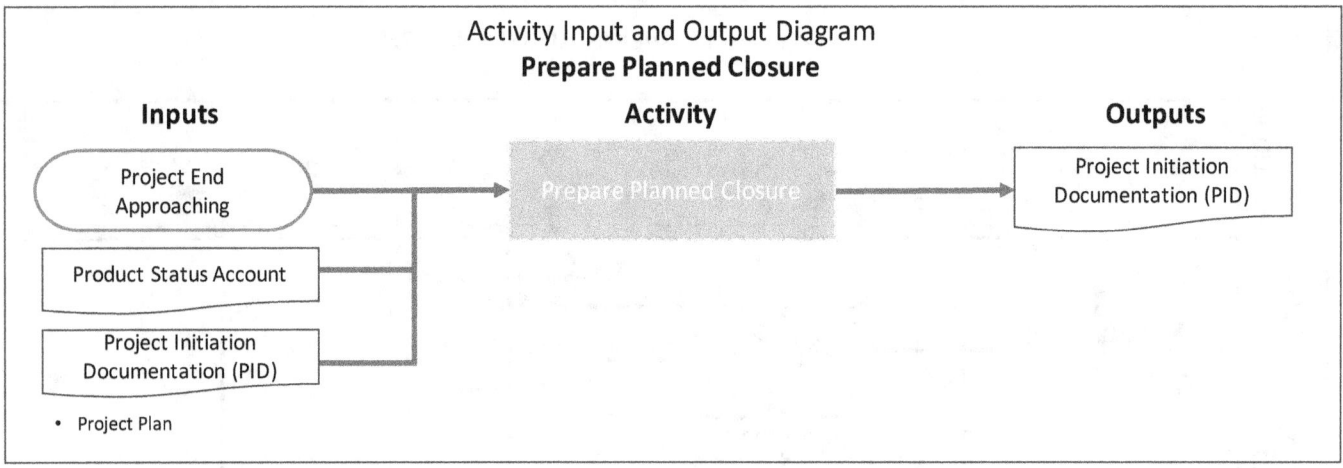

Figure 104 - Prepare Planned Closure

Activity – Prepare Premature Project Closure

In the event the Project Board instructs the Project Manager to close the project. The Project Manager is responsible for ensuring that the work completed is not simply abandoned, and salvages anything of value that has been created to date and raises any gaps created by closing the project prematurely to Corporate or Program Management

The Prepare Premature Project Closure Process is done instead of Prepare Planned Closure if requested by the Project Board and can happen at any point within a project

The following actions are completed by the Project Manager:
- The Project Manager will record the Premature Closure within the Issue Register
- The Project Plan will be updated with the actual information from the current stage and will document what was completed when the project was closed and importantly will list what has not been completed
- Request the Product Status Account from Project Support to ensure that the following is identified:
  - The products that have been developed, under development, yet to be started etc
  - Products that may be useful to other projects
- Agree what will be done with the completed products, and also agree what will happen with the products that are under development – these may be finished as part of the closure criteria
- Request approval from the Project Board to release the resources (this is the same process as within the activities of the Planned Closure)

Upon completion of these tasks, the Project Manager can complete the handover of the products, update the End Project Report and recommend the Project Closure to the Project Board

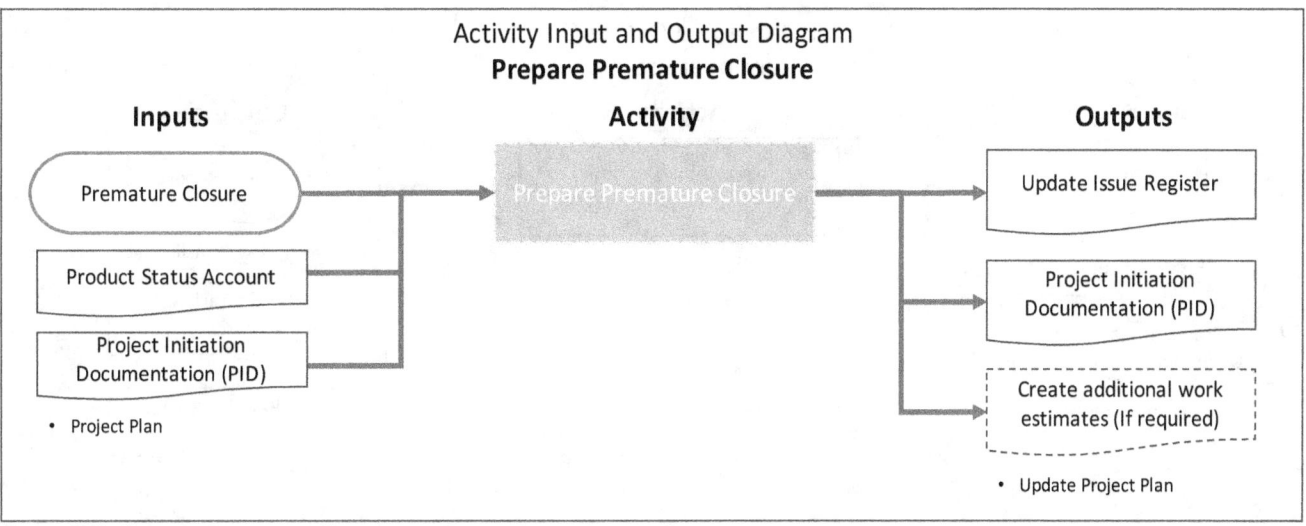

Figure 105 - Prepare Premature Closure

Activity – Handover Project Products

All products produced by the project must be passed onto the correct person, team or area as defined in the Project Product Description before the project is closed.

The Benefit Management Approach should be reviewed and if needed updated to include any post-project benefit reviews relating to the products and include the details of who will perform these reviews (this will not be the Project Manager as this is post-project)

The following actions are recommended to be completed within this activity:

- Create or prepare the Follow-On Actions Recommendations for the products from the information contained within the Risk and Issue Registers
- Confirm the Benefit Management Approach includes the post-project activities to confirm the benefits have been realised
- The Configuration Management Approach will include the handover requirements for the products, this should include:
    - Confirm the maintenance or support processes are in place
    - Confirm if any "warranty Period" is required and how this will be provided
    - Confirm if any support contract is required or in place
    - Document the Acceptance Process for Operations

The products are handed over to operations or the agreed user area and this is documented in the Configuration Management Approach

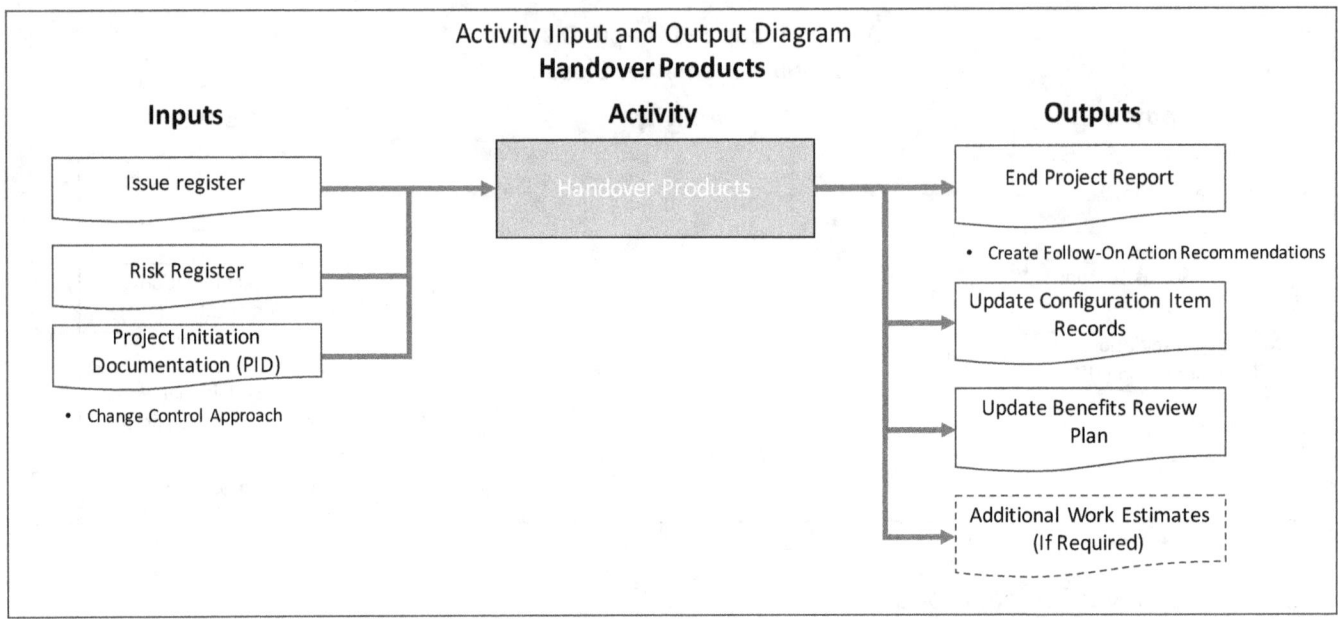

Figure 106 - Handover Products

Activity – Evaluate the Project

Evaluate the Project is the assessment of how successful (or unsuccessful) the project was and to ensure the lessons are learnt from this project

The following actions are recommended within this activity:
- Review all baselined documents from the project start. These include:
  - The Project Initiation Documentation (PID)
  - The Project Plan
  - The Business Case

The Project Manager will create the End Project Report, this will include the following actions:
- The Project Manager will review the baselined document with the final or current versions
  - Project Plan
  - Business Case
  - Project Initiation Documentation (PID)
  - Etc
- Prepare an Executive Summary of the projects performance
- Provide an update on the benefits (if any have materialised)
- Provide an update on how the project performed against its original objectives or targets
- Review the project team performance
- Review the project products

The Project Manager will also create the Lessons Learned Report; however, this is created with the support of the Project Management Team and should include at a minimum the following information:
- An overview of the project and its performance
  - What went well
  - What went badly
  - What could be improved
- The effectiveness of the Quality Management System

- Any useful information or recommendations in relation to the tailoring of Prince2

The Lessons Learned Report is crucial to supporting future projects and also the ongoing Project Management Processes within an organisation

The Lessons Learned Report is reviewed by the Project Board before they approve the project closure

The outputs from this activity are:
- End Project Report
- Lessons Learned Report

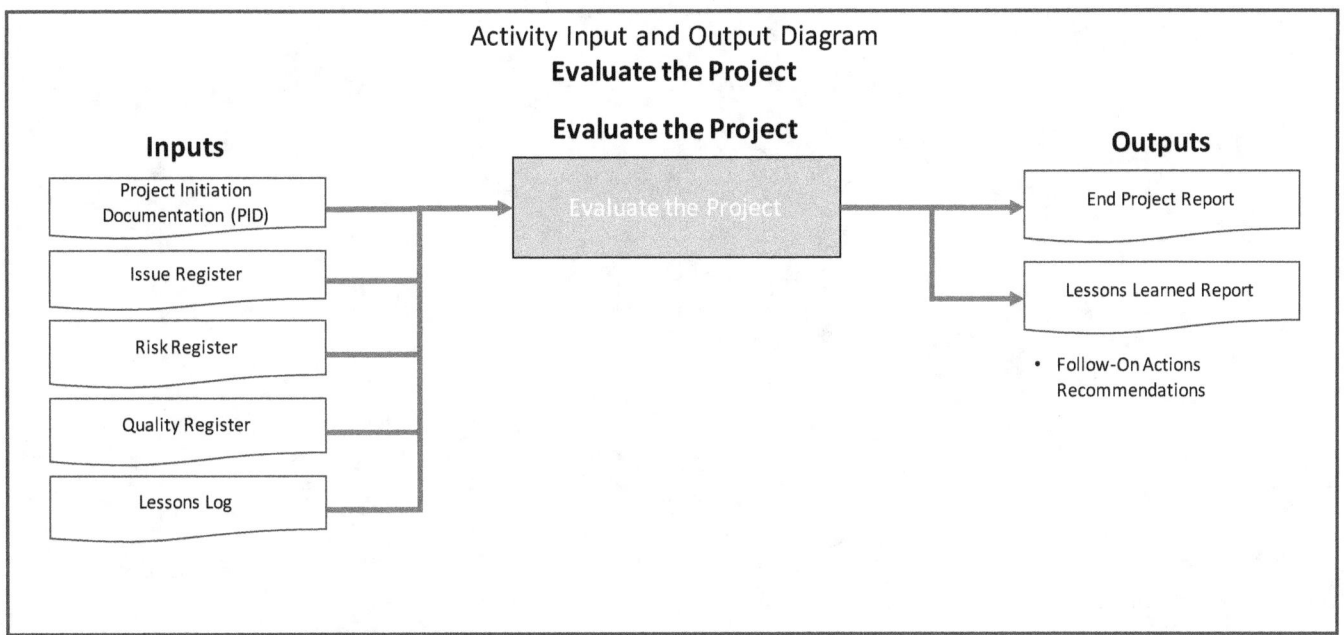

Figure 107 - Evaluate Project

Activity – Recommend Project Closure

Once the Closing a Project Process work has been completed by the Project Manager and it has been confirmed that the project can be closed.

The Project Manager raises the "Recommend Project Closure" to the Project Board

Remember the Project Manager does not close the project, but recommends the closure to the Project Board who then make their final decision in relation to the active project which "Authorise Project Closure"

The following actions are completed within this activity:
- The Project Manager confirms who should be notified by reviewing the Communication Management Strategy
- Close the project documents
  - o Issue Register
  - o Risk Register
  - o Lessons Log

- Confirm that all project related information has been archived and is accessible if required, again this should be documented within the Change & control approach
- Preparation of the Project Closure Notification for the Project Board. This will notify the Project Board that the project has been closed and a summary on the project products produced

The last activity is a Directing a Project Process and is the Project Boards decision to "Authorise Project Closure" this is taken once they have reviewed the Project Closure Notification

Acceptance Criteria
A list of criteria that the product(s) must meet before the customer will accept them, these should be measurable definitions of the attributes required for the products to be acceptable to the key stakeholders

Activity
A process, function or task that occurs over time and has recognizable results and is managed. Is usually part of a process or plan

Approval
The formal confirmation that a product is complete and meets its requirements as defined within its Product Description

Approver
A person or group (For example, Project Board, Working Group) who is identified as qualified and authorized to approve a (management or specialist) product as being complete and fit for purpose.

Assumption
A statement that is taken as being true for the purposes of planning, but which could change later. An assumption is made where some facts are not yet known or decided, and is usually reserved for matters of such significance that, if they change or turn out not to be true, there will need to be considerable replanning.

Assurance
All the systematic actions necessary to provide confidence that the target (system, process, organization, programme, project, outcome, benefit, capability, product output, deliverable) is appropriate. Appropriateness might be defined subjectively or objectively in different circumstances. The implication is that assurance will have a level of independence from that which is being assured. See also 'Project Assurance' and 'quality assurance'.

Authority
The right to allocate resources and make decisions (applies to project, stage and team levels).

Authorization
The point at which an authority is granted.

Avoid (risk response)
A risk response to a threat where the threat either can no longer have an impact or can no longer happen.

Baseline
Reference levels against which an entity is monitored and controlled.

Baselined management product
A type of management product that defines aspects of the project and, once approved, is subject to change control.

Benefit
The measurable improvement resulting from an outcome perceived as an advantage by one or more stakeholders.

Benefit Management Approach
A plan that defines how and when a measurement of the achievement of the project's benefits can be made. If the project is being managed within a programme, this information may be created and maintained at the programme level.

Benefits tolerance
The permissible deviation in the expected benefit that is allowed before the deviation needs to be escalated to the next level of management. Benefits tolerance is documented in the Business Case. See also 'tolerance'.

Business Case
The justification for an organizational activity (project), which typically contains costs, benefits, risks and timescales, and against which continuing viability is tested.

Change Authority
A person or group to which the Project Board may delegate responsibility for the consideration of requests for change or off-specifications. The Change Authority may be given a change budget and can approve changes within that budget.

Change budget
The money allocated to the Change Authority available to be spent on authorized requests for change.

Change Control Approach
A Change Control Approach is a description of how and by whom the project's products will be controlled and protected

Change control
The procedure that ensures that all changes that may affect the project's agreed objectives are identified, assessed and either approved, rejected or deferred.

Checkpoint
A team-level, time-driven review of progress.

Checkpoint Report
A progress report of the information gathered at a checkpoint, which is given by a team to the Project Manager and which provides reporting data as defined in the Work Package.

Closure notification

Advice from the Project Board to inform all stakeholders and the host sites that the project resources canbe disbanded and support services, such as space, equipment and access, demobilized. It should indicate a closure date for costs to be charged to the project.

Closure recommendation

A recommendation prepared by the Project Manager for the Project Board to send as a project closure notification when the board is satisfied that the project can be closed.

Communication Management Approach

A description of the means and frequency of communication between the project and the project's stakeholders.

Configuration item

An entity that is subject to configuration management. The entity may be a component of a product, a product, or a set of products in a release.

Configuration Item Record

A record that describes the status, version and variant of a configuration item, and any details of important relationships between them.

Configuration management

Technical and administrative activities concerned with the creation, maintenance and controlled change of configuration throughout the life of a product.

Configuration management system

The set of processes, tools and databases that are used to manage configuration data. Typically, a project will use the configuration management system of either the customer or supplier organization.

Constraints

The restrictions or limitations that the project is bound by.

Contingency

Something that is held in reserve typically to handle time and cost variances, or risks. PRINCE2 does not advocate the use of contingency because estimating variancesare managed by setting tolerances, and risks are managed through appropriate risk responses (including the fallback response that is contingent on the risk occurring).

Corporate or programme standards

These are over-arching standards that the project must adhere to. They will influence the four project strategies (Communication Management Strategy, Change & control approach, Quality Management Strategy and Risk Management Strategy) and the project controls.

Corrective action

A set of actions to resolve a threat to a plan's tolerances or a defect in a product.

Cost tolerance

The permissible deviation in a plan's cost that is allowed before the deviation needs to be escalated to the next level of management. Cost tolerance is documented in the respective plan. See also 'tolerance'.

Customer

The person or group who commissioned the work and will benefit from the end results.

Customer's quality expectations

A statement about the quality expected from the project product, captured in the Project Product Description.

Daily Log

Used to record problems/concerns that can be handled by the Project Manager informally.

Deliverable (Output)

A specialist product that is handed over to a user(s). Note that management products are not outputs but are created solely for the purpose of managing the project.

Dependencies (plan)

The relationship between products or activities. For example, the development of Product C cannot start until Products A and B have been completed. Dependencies can be internal or external. Internal dependencies are those under the controlof the Project Manager. External dependencies are those outside the control of the Project Manager – for example, the delivery of a product required by this project from another project.

Dis-benefit

An outcome that is perceived as negative by one or more stakeholders. It is an actual consequence of an activity whereas, by definition, a risk has some uncertainty about whether it will materialize.

End Project Report

A report given by the Project Manager to the Project Board, that confirms the handover of all products and provides an updated Business Case and an assessment of how well the project has done against the original Project Initiation Documentation.

End Stage assessment

The review by the Project Board and Project Manager of the End Stage Report to decide whether to approve the next Stage Plan. According to the size and criticality of the project, the review may be formal or informal. The authority to proceed should be documented as a formal record.

End Stage Report

A report given by the Project Manager to the Project Board at the end of each management stage of the project. This provides information about the project performance during the stage and the project status at stage end.

Enhance (risk response)

A risk response to an opportunity where proactive actions are taken to enhance both the probability of the event occurring and the impact of the event should it occur.

Event-driven control

A control that takes place when a specific event occurs. This could be, for example, the end of a stage, the completion of the Project Initiation Documentation, or the creation of an Exception Report. It could also include organizational events that may affect the project, such as the end of the financial year.

Exception

A situation where it can be forecast that there will be a deviation beyond the tolerance levels agreed between Project Manager and Project Board (or between Project Board and corporate or programme management).

Exception assessment

This is a review by the Project Board to approve (or reject) an Exception Plan.

Exception Plan

This is a plan that often follows an Exception Report. For a Stage Plan exception, it covers the period from the present to the end of the current stage. If the exception were at project level, the Project Plan would be replaced.

Exception Report

A description of the exception situation, its impact, options, recommendation and impact of the recommendation. This report is prepared by the Project Manager for the Project Board.

Executive

The single individual with overall responsibility for ensuring that a project meets its objectives and delivers the projected benefits. This individual should ensure that the project maintains its business focus, that ithas clear authority, and that the work, including risks, is actively managed. The Executive is the chair of the Project Board. He or she represents the customer and is responsible for the Business Case.

Exploit (risk response)

A risk response to an opportunity by seizing the opportunity to ensure that it will happen and that the impact will be realized.

Fallback (risk response)

A risk response to a threat by putting in place a fallback plan for the actions that will be taken to reduce the impact of the threat should the risk occur.

Follow-on action recommendations

Recommended actions related to unfinished work, ongoing issues and risks, and any other activities needed to take a product to the next phase of its life. These are summarized and included in the End Stage Report (for phased handover) and End Project Report.

Governance (Corporate)

The ongoing activity of maintaining a sound system of internal control by which the directors and officers of an organization ensure that effective management systems, including financial monitoring and control systems, have been put in place to protect assets, earning capacity and the reputation of the organization.

Governance (project)

Those areas of corporate governance that are specifically related to project activities. Effective governance of project management ensures that an organization's project portfolio is aligned to the organization's objectives, is delivered efficiently and is sustainable.

Handover

The transfer of ownership of a set of products to the respective user(s). The set of products is known as a release. There may be more than one handover in the life of a project (phased delivery). The final handover takes place in the Closing a Project process.

Highlight Report

A time-driven report from the Project Manager to the Project Board on stage progress.

Impact (of risk)

The result of a particular threat or opportunity actually occurring, or the anticipation of such a result.

Inherent risk

The exposure arising from a specific risk before any action has been taken to manage it.

Initiation stage

The period from when the Project Board authorizes initiation to when they authorize the project (ordecide not to go ahead with the project). The detailed planning and establishment of the project management infrastructure is covered by the Initiating a Project process.

Issue

A relevant event that has happened, was not planned, and requires management action. It can be any concern, query, request for change, suggestion or off- specification raised during a project. Project issues can be about anything to do with the project.

Issue Register

A register used to capture and maintain information on all of the issues that are being managed formally. The Issue Register should be monitored by the Project Manager on a regular basis.

Issue Report

A report containing the description, impact assessment and recommendations for a request for change, off- specification or a problem/concern. It is only created for those issues that need to be handled formally.

Lessons Log

An informal repository for lessons that apply to this project or future projects.

Lessons Report

A report that documents any lessons that can be usefully applied to other projects. The purpose of the report is to provoke action so that the positive lessons from a project become embedded in the organization's way of working and that the organization is able to avoid the negative lessons on future projects.

Logs

Informal repositories managed by the Project Manager that do not require any agreement by the Project Board on their format and composition. PRINCE2 has two logs: the Daily Log and the Lessons Log.

Management product

A product that will be required as part of managing the project, and establishing and maintaining quality (for example, Highlight Report, End Stage Report etc.). The management products stay constant, whatever the type of project, and can be used as described, or with any relevant modifications, for all projects. There are three types of management product: baselines, records and reports.

Management stage

The section of a project that the Project Manager is managing on behalf of the Project Board at any one time, at the end of which the Project Board will wish to review progress to date, the state of the Project Plan, the Business Case and risks, and the next Stage Plan in order to decide whether to continue with the project.

Milestone

A significant event in a plan's schedule, such as completion of key Work Packages, a technical stage, or a management stage.

Off-specification

Something that should be provided by the project, but currently is not (or is forecast not to be) provided. This might be a missing product or a product not meeting its specifications. It is one type of issue.

Operational and maintenance acceptance

A specific type of acceptance by the person or group who will support the product once it is handed over into the operational environment.

Outcome

The result of change, normally affecting real-world behaviour and/or circumstances. Outcomes are desired when a change is conceived. They are achieved as a result of the activities undertaken to effect the change.

Output

A specialist product that is handed over to a user(s). Note that management products are not outputs but are created solely for the purpose of managing the project.

Performance targets
A plan's goals for time, cost, quality, scope, benefits and risk.

Plan
A detailed proposal for doing or achieving something which specifies the what, when, how and by whom. In PRINCE2 there are only the following types of plan: Project Plan, Stage Plan, Team Plan, Exception Plan and Benefit Management Approach.

Planned closure
The PRINCE2 activity to close a project.

Planning horizon
The period of time for which it is possible to accurately plan.

Portfolio
All the programmes and stand-alone projects being undertaken by an organization, a group of organizations, or an organizational unit.

Premature closure
The PRINCE2 activity to close a project before its planned closure. The Project Manager must ensure that work in progress is not simply abandoned, but that the project salvages any value created to date, and checks that any gaps left by the cancellation of the project are raised to corporate or programme management.

Prerequisites (plan)
Any fundamental aspects that must be in place, and remain in place, for a plan to succeed.

PRINCE2
A method that supports some selected aspects of project management. The acronym stands for Projects in a Controlled Environment.

PRINCE2 principles
The guiding obligations for good project management practice that form the basis of a project being managed using PRINCE2.

PRINCE2 project
A project that applies the PRINCE2 principles.

Probability
This is the evaluated likelihood of a particular threat or opportunity actually happening, including a consideration of the frequency with which this may arise.

Problem/Concern
A type of issue (other than a request for change or off- specification) that the Project Manager needs to resolve or escalate.

Procedure
A series of actions for a particular aspect of project management established specifically for the project – for example, a risk management procedure.

Process
A structured set of activities designed to accomplish a specific objective. A process takes one or more defined inputs and turns them into defined outputs.

Producer
The person or group responsible for developing a product.

Product
An input or output, whether tangible or intangible, that can be described in advance, created and tested. PRINCE2 has two types of products – management products and specialist products.

Product breakdown structure
A hierarchy of all the products to be produced during a plan.

Product checklist
A list of the major products of a plan, plus key dates in their delivery.

Product Description
A description of a product's purpose, composition, derivation and quality criteria. It is produced at planning time, as soon as possible after the need for the product is identified.

Product flow diagram
A diagram showing the sequence of production and interdependencies of the products listed in a product breakdown structure.

Product Status Account
A report on the status of products. The required products can be specified by identifier or the part of the project in which they were developed.

Product-based planning
A technique leading to a comprehensive plan basedon the creation and delivery of required outputs. The technique considers prerequisite products, quality requirements and the dependencies between products.

Programme
A temporary flexible organization structure created to coordinate, direct and oversee the implementation of a set of related projects and activities in order to deliver outcomes and benefits related to the organization's strategic objectives. A programme is likely to have a life that spans several years.

Project
A temporary organization that is created for the purpose of delivering one or more business products according to an agreed Business Case.

Project approach
A description of the way in which the work of the project is to be approached. For example, are we building a product from scratch or buying in a product that already exists?

Project Assurance
The Project Board's responsibilities to assure itself that the project is being conducted correctly. The Project Board members each have a specific area of focus for Project Assurance, namely business assurance for the Executive, user assurance for the Senior User(s), and supplier assurance for the Senior Supplier(s).

Project authorization notification
Advice from the Project Board to inform all stakeholders and the host sites that the project has been authorized and to request any necessary logistical support (e.g. communication facilities, equipment and any project support) sufficient for the duration of the project.

Project Brief
Statement that describes the purpose, cost, timeand performance requirements, and constraints for a project. It is created pre-project during the Starting up a Project process and is used during the Initiating a Project process to create the Project Initiation Documentation and its components. It is superseded by the
Project Initiation Documentation and not maintained.

Project Initiation Documentation
A logical set of documents that brings together the key information needed to start the project on a sound basis and that conveys the information to all concerned with the project.

Project initiation notification
Advice from the Project Board to inform all stakeholders and the host sites that the project is being initiatedand to request any necessary logistical support (e.g. communication facilities, equipment and any project support) sufficient for the initiation stage.

Project lifecycle
The period from the start-up of a project to the acceptance of the project product.

Project management
The planning, delegating, monitoring and control of all aspects of the project, and the motivation of those involved, to achieve the project objectives within the expected performance targets for time, cost, quality, scope, benefits and risks.

Project management team
The entire management structure of the Project Board, and Project Manager, plus any Team Manager, Project Assurance and Project Support roles.

Project Management Team structure
An organization chart showing the people assigned to the project management team roles to be used, and their delegation and reporting relationships.

Project Manager
The person given the authority and responsibility to manage the project on a day-to-day basis to deliver the required products within the constraints agreed with the Project Board.

Project mandate
An external product generated by the authority commissioning the project that forms the trigger for Starting up a Project.

Project office
A temporary office set up to support the delivery of a specific change initiative being delivered as a project. If used, the project office undertakes the responsibility of the Project Support role.

Project Plan
A high-level plan showing the major products of the project, when they will be delivered and at what cost. An initial Project Plan is presented as part of the Project Initiation Documentation. This is revised as information on actual progress appears. It is a major control document for the Project Board to measure actual progress against expectations.

Project product
What the project must deliver in order to gain acceptance.

Project Product Description
A special type of Product Description used to gain agreement from the user on the project's scopeand requirements, to define the customer's quality expectations, and to define the acceptance criteria for the project.

Project Support
An administrative role in the project management team. Project Support can be in the form of advice and help with project management tools, guidance, administrative services such as filing, and the collection of actual data.

Proximity (of risk)
The time factor of risk, i.e. when the risk may occur. The impact of a risk may vary in severity depending on when the risk occurs.

Quality
The totality of features and inherent or assigned characteristics of a product, person, process, service and/or system that bears on its ability to show that it meets expectations or satisfies stated needs, requirements or specifications.

Quality assurance
An independent check that products will be fit for purpose or meet requirements.

Quality control
The process of monitoring specific project resultsto determine whether they comply with relevant standards and of identifying ways to eliminate causes of unsatisfactory performance.

Quality inspection
A systematic, structured assessment of a product carried out by two or more carefully selected people (the review team) in a planned, documented and organized fashion.

Quality management
The coordinated activities to direct and control an organization with regard to quality.

Quality Management Approach
An approach defining the quality techniques and standards to be applied, and the various responsibilities for achieving the required quality levels, during a project.

Quality management system
The complete set of quality standards, procedures and responsibilities for a site or organization. In the project context, 'sites' and 'organizations' should be interpreted as the permanent or semi-permanent organization(s) sponsoring the project work, i.e. they are 'external' to the project's temporary organization. A programme, for instance, can be regarded as a semi-permanent organization that sponsors projects – and it may have a documented quality management system.

Quality records
Evidence kept demonstrating that the required quality assurance and quality control activities have been carried out.

Quality Register
A register containing summary details of all planned and completed quality activities. The Quality Register is used by the Project Manager and Project Assurance as part of reviewing progress.

Quality review technique
A quality inspection technique with defined roles anda specific structure. It is designed to assess whether a product that takes the form of a document (or similar, e.g. a presentation) is complete, adheres to standards and meets the quality criteria agreed for it in the relevant Product Description. The participants are drawn from those with the necessary competence to evaluate its fitness for purpose.

Quality tolerance
The tolerance identified for a product for a quality criterion defining an acceptable range of values. Quality tolerance is documented in the Project Product Description (for the project-level quality tolerance)
and in the Product Description for each product to be delivered.

Records
Dynamic management products that maintain information regarding project progress.

Reduce (risk response)
A response to a risk where proactive actions are taken to reduce the probability of the event occurring by performing some form of control, and/or to reduce the impact of the event should it occur.

Registers
Formal repositories managed by the Project Manager that require agreement by the Project Board on their format, composition and use. PRINCE2 has three registers: Issue Register, Risk Register and Quality Register.

Reject (risk response)
A response to a risk (opportunity) where a conscious and deliberate decision is taken not to exploit or enhance an opportunity, having discerned that itis more economical to do so than to attempt a risk response action. The opportunity should continue to be monitored.

Release
The set of products in a handover. The contents of a release are managed, tested and deployed as a single entity. See also 'handover'.

Reports
Management products providing a snapshot of the status of certain aspects of the project.

Request for change
A proposal for a change to a baseline. It is a type of issue.

Residual risk
The risk remaining after the risk response has been applied.

Responsible authority
The person or group commissioning the project (typically corporate or programme management) who has the authority to commit resources and funds on behalf of the commissioning organization.

Reviewer
A person or group independent of the producer who assesses whether a product meets its requirements as defined in its Product Description.

Risk
An uncertain event or set of events that, should it occur, will have an effect on the achievement of objectives.A risk is measured by a combination of the probability of a perceived threat or opportunity occurring, and the magnitude of its impact on objectives.

Risk actionee
A nominated owner of an action to address a risk. Some actions may not be within the remit of the risk ownerto control explicitly; in that situation, there should be a nominated owner of the action to address the risk. He or she will need to keep the risk owner apprised of the situation.

Risk appetite
An organization's unique attitude towards risk taking that in turn dictates the amount of risk that it considers is acceptable.

Risk estimation
The estimation of probability and impact of an individual risk, taking into account predetermined standards, target risk levels, interdependencies and other relevant factors.

Risk evaluation
The process of understanding the net effect of the identified threats and opportunities on an activity when aggregated together.

Risk management
The systematic application of principles, approaches and processes to the tasks of identifying and assessing risks, and then planning and implementing risk responses.

Risk Management Strategy
A strategy describing the goals of applying risk management, as well as the procedure that will be adopted, roles and responsibilities, risk tolerances, the timing of risk management interventions, the tools and techniques that will be used, and the reporting requirements

Risk Owner
A named individual who is responsible for the management, monitoring and control of all aspectsof a particular risk assigned to them, including the implementation of the selected responses to address the threats or to maximize the opportunities.

Risk profile
A description of the types of risk that are faced by an organization and its exposure to those risks.

Risk Register
A record of identified risks relating to an initiative, including their status and history.

Risk response
Actions that may be taken to bring a situation to a level where exposure to risk is acceptable to the organization. These responses fall into a number of risk response categories.

Risk response category
A category of risk response. For threats, the individual risk response category can be avoid, reduce, transfer, accept or share. For opportunities, the individual risk response category can be exploit, enhance, reject or share.

Risk tolerance
The threshold levels of risk exposure which, when exceeded, will trigger an Exception Report to bring the situation to the attention of the Project Board. Risk tolerances could include limits on the plan's aggregated risks (e.g. cost of aggregated threats to remain less than 10% of the plan's budget), or limits on any individual threat (e.g. any threat to operational service). Risk tolerance is documented in the Risk
Management Strategy.

Risk tolerance line
A line drawn on the summary risk profile. Risks that appear above this line cannot be accepted (lived with) without referring them to a higher authority. For a project, the Project Manager would refer these risks to the Project Board.

Role description
A description of the set of responsibilities specific to a role.

Schedule
Graphical representation of a plan (for example, a Gantt chart), typically describing a sequence of tasks, together with resource allocations, which collectively deliver the plan. In PRINCE2, project activities should only be documented in the schedules associated with a Project Plan, Stage Plan or Team Plan. Actions that are allocated from day-to-day management may be documented in the relevant project log (i.e. Risk Register, Daily Log, Issue Register, Quality Register) if they do not require significant activity.

Scope
For a plan, the sum total of its products and the extent of their requirements. It is described by the product breakdown structure for the plan and associated Product Descriptions.

Scope tolerance
The permissible deviation in a plan's scope that is allowed before the deviation needs to be escalated to the next level of management. Scope tolerance is documented in the respective plan in the form of a note or reference to the product breakdown structure for that plan. See 'tolerance'.

Senior Supplier
The Project Board role that provides knowledge and experience of the main discipline(s) involved in the production of the project's deliverable(s). The Senior Supplier represents the supplier interests within the project and provides supplier resources.

Share (risk response)
A risk response to either a threat or an opportunity through the application of a pain/gain formula: both parties share the gain (within pre-agreed limits) if the cost is less than the cost plan; and both share the pain (again within pre-agreed limits) if the cost plan is exceeded.

Specialist Product
A product whose development is the subject of the plan. The specialist products are specific to an individual project (for example, an advertising campaign, a car park ticketing system, foundations for a building, a new business process etc.) Also known as a deliverable or output.

Sponsor
The main driving force behind a programme or project. PRINCE2 does not define a role for the sponsor, but the sponsor is most likely to be the Executive on the Project Board, or the person who has appointed the Executive.

Stage
See 'management stage' or 'technical stage'.

Stage Plan
A detailed plan used as the basis for project management control throughout a stage.

Stakeholder
Any individual, group or organization that can affect, be affected by, or perceive itself to be affected by, an initiative (programme, project, activity, risk).

Start-up
The pre-project activities undertaken by the Executive and the Project Manager to produce the outline Business Case, Project Brief and Initiation Stage Plan.

Strategy
An approach or line to take, designed to achieve a long- term aim. Strategies can exist at different levels – at the corporate, programme and project level. At the project level, PRINCE2 defines four strategies: Communication Management Strategy, Change & control approach, Quality Management Strategy and Risk Management Strategy.

Supplier
The person, group or groups responsible for the supply of the project's specialist products. tailoring

Tailoring
The appropriate use of PRINCE2 on any given project, ensuring that there is the correct amount of planning, control, governance and use of the processes and themes (whereas the adoption of PRINCE2 across an organization is known as 'embedding').

Team Manager
The person responsible for the production of those products allocated by the Project Manager (as defined in a Work Package) to an appropriate quality, timescale and at a cost acceptable to the Project Board. Thisrole reports to, and takes direction from, the Project Manager. If a Team Manager is not assigned, then the Project Manager undertakes the responsibilities of the Team Manager role.

Team Plan
An optional level of plan used as the basis for team management control when executing Work Packages.

Technical stage
A method of grouping work together by the set of techniques used, or the products created. This results in stages covering elements such as design, build and implementation. Such stages are technical stages and are a separate concept from management stages.

Theme
An aspect of project management that needs tobe continually addressed, and that requires specific treatment for the PRINCE2 processes to be effective.

Time tolerance

The permissible deviation in a plan's time that is allowed before the deviation needs to be escalated to the next level of management. Time tolerance is documented in the respective plan. See also 'tolerance'.

Time-driven control

A management control that is periodic in nature, to enable the next higher authority to monitor progress – e.g. a control that takes place every two weeks. PRINCE2 offers two key time-driven progress reports: Checkpoint Report and Highlight Report.

Tolerance

The permissible deviation above and below a plan's target for time and cost without escalating the deviation to the next level of management. There may also be tolerance levels for quality, scope, benefit and risk. Tolerance is applied at project, stage and team levels.

Tranche

A programme management term describing a group of projects structured around distinct step changes in capability and benefit delivery.

Transfer (risk response)

A response to a threat where a third party takes on responsibility for some of the financial impact of the threat (for example, through insurance or by means of appropriate clauses in a contract).

Trigger

An event or decision that triggers a PRINCE2 process.

User acceptance

A specific type of acceptance by the person or group who will use the product once it is handed over into the operational environment.

User

The person or group who will use one or more of the project's products.

Variant

A variation on a baselined product. For example, an operations manual may have an English variant and a Spanish variant.

Version

A specific baseline of a product. Versions typicallyuse naming conventions that enable the sequenceor date of the baseline to be identified. For example, Project Plan version 2 is the baseline after Project Plan version 1.

Work Package

The set of information relevant to the creation of one or more products. It will contain a description of the work, the Product Description(s), details of any constraintson production, and confirmation of the agreement between the Project Manager and the person or Team Manager who is to implement the Work Package that the work can be done within the constraints.

Appendix B – Project Lifecycle Example

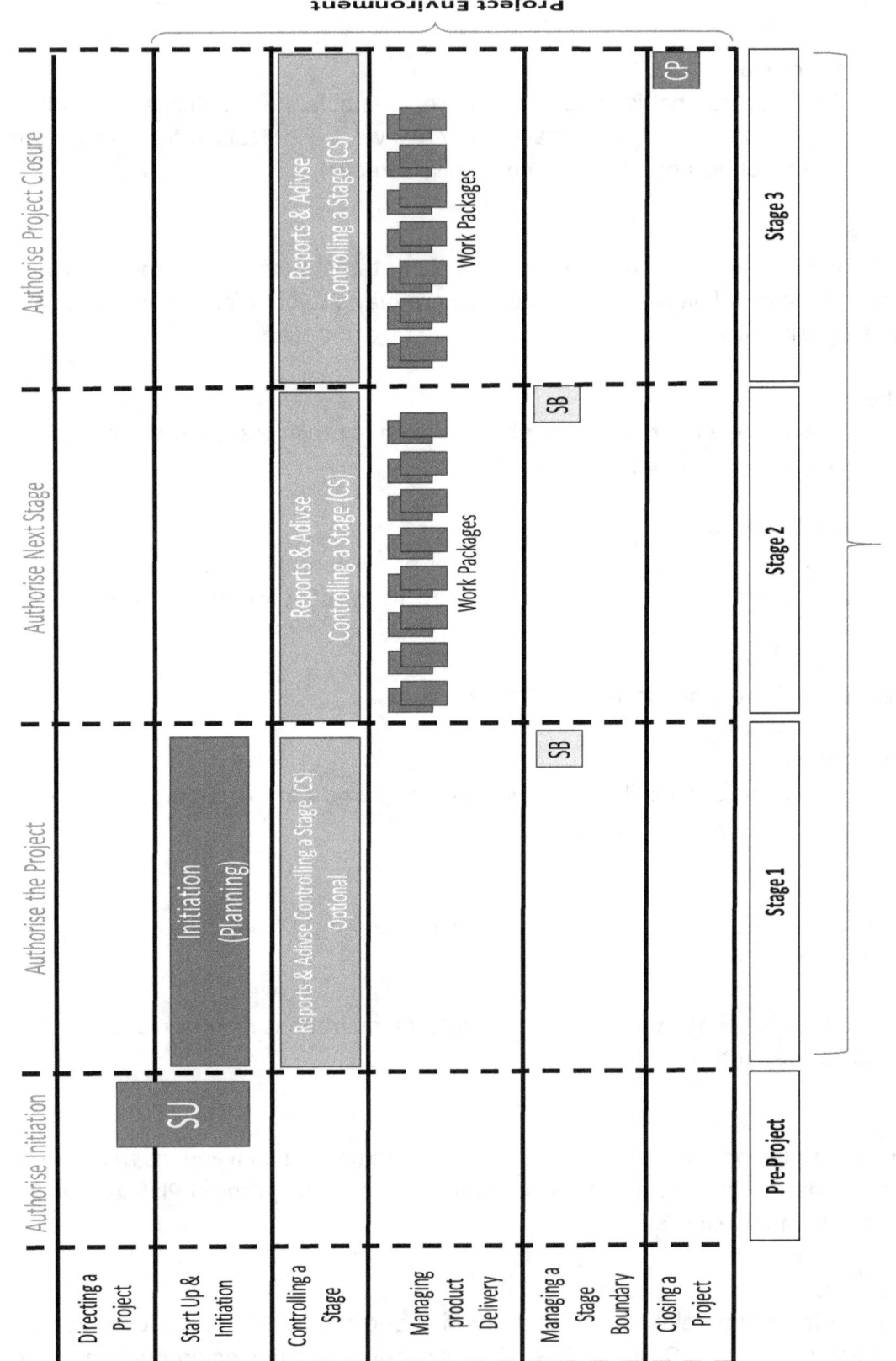

Project Lifecycle Example

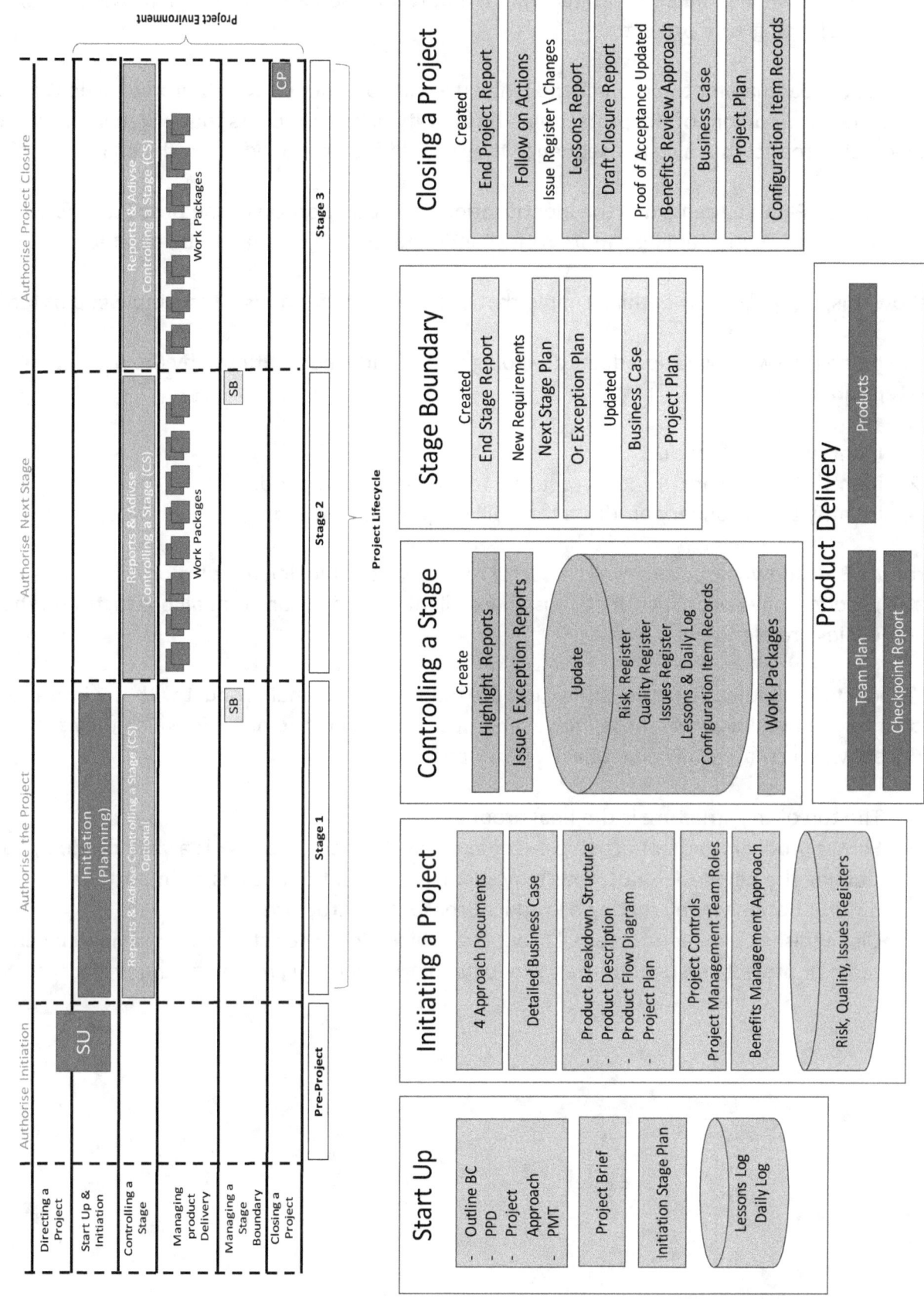

Appendix C – Product Based Planning

Product based planning is a powerful technique that when used effectively can provide a starting point when planning your project

It produces a roadmap for the project and when used in conjunction with a Product Floe Diagram can support the development of the project plan by identifying the products that will make up your Project main product, but also the sequence they should be developed or produced in

Product Based Planning can aid in the identification of a good portion of the products you will deliver as part of your project, enabling a more robust and detailed project plan to be created

To show this, we will use something simple that everyone understands – the simple cup of tea

The first step is to work what products are going to be produced or utilised by the project.
The steps are

1. Identify the end product
2. Identify the primary products required to create the end product
3. Identify the secondary products that will support the creation

A Product Breakdown Structure may be useful to help when thinking about processes and ensure that all products have been identified, it is an excellent tool to ensure that all products and the dependencies are identified

The Product Breakdown Structure shows the breakdown of the final product with the intermediate products and a breakdown of these, however it does not define the order in which they are produced, when creating a Product Based Description:

- The top of the structure is the final product
- Shows products and not activities – for example Trained Helpdesk is a valid product, but training the helpdesk is not. This may seem like semantics but it is an important differentiation when creating a Product Breakdown Structure
- Distinguishes between "External Products" which already exist and are provided by another team or project versus "Internal" products that need to be created by the project

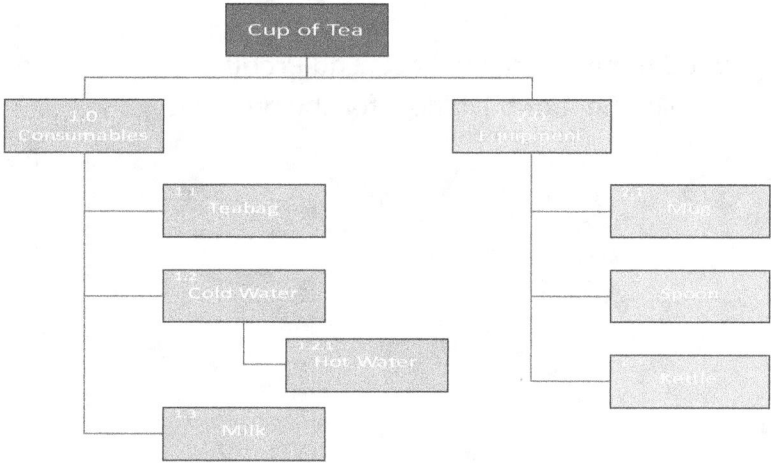

Figure 108 - Product Based Structure - Cup of Tea

So, the Product Breakdown Structure for my "brew" or cup of tea is detailed above.

The final product is the "Cup of Tea"

The assumptions are that:

- The consumables are already provided and available
- The equipment is available

These are all dependencies for the end product

If you follow the full methodology, each of the items listed above would require a Product Description

The next step in the Product Based Planning technique is to use the information contained within the Product Based Structure and convert this into a Product Flow Diagram

The Product Flow Diagram shows the sequence of production or use for the various products identified

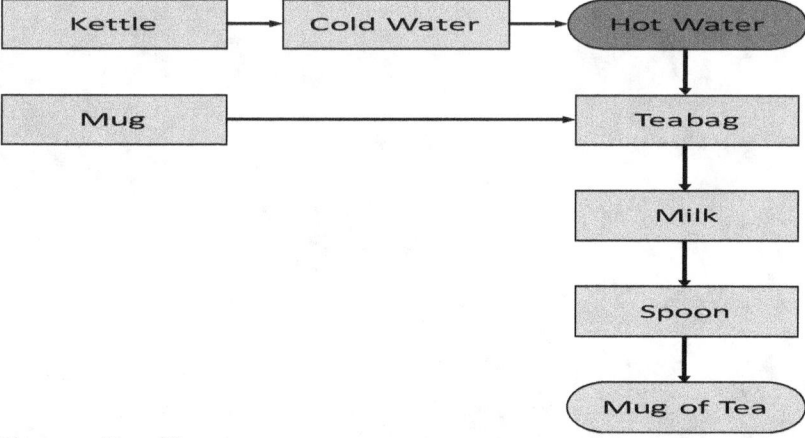

Figure 109 - Product Flow Diagram - Cup of Tea

The results of the Product Based Planning can now assist in the creation of your plan, you now have the information in relation to:

- The products required to make your projects End Product
- The sequence of development or build flow for the products